SO-BEH-425

VP-EXPERT™

Rule-Based Expert System Development Tool

PAPERBACK
SOFTWARE

System Requirements

VP-Expert runs on IBM Personal Computers with:

- 256K or more RAM*
- At least one double-sided diskette drive
- DOS version 2.xx or 3.xx

We have tested *VP-Expert* and have found that it works correctly on the IBM PC, PC-XT, PC-AT, and most compatible systems, many of which are listed in the Customer Information section of this book.

In order to view a graphic trace of a *VP-Expert* consultation, an IBM CGA or EGA, a Hercules monochrome graphics adapter, or a compatible video adapter is required.

*The amount of available RAM limits the size of the knowledge base being used.

Using an Information Base

The exchange of data with compatible database, worksheet, and text files is one of *VP-Expert*'s most significant capabilities. Using such files as an "information base," you can incorporate large quantities of externally stored data into a knowledge base without requiring a significantly more complex rule structure. In fact, using an information base typically allows you to create a drastically reduced and simplified "rule base"—with the additional advantage that data stored externally can be more easily updated and modified. With *VP-Expert*, you can create "friendly" front ends that make modification of those files even easier.

When Is an Expert System Useful?

The fields of medicine, engineering, business, geology, tax analysis, and law—to name a few—are already making substantial use of expert systems. Such systems are being successfully utilized to diagnose illness, analyze structures, train personnel, and recommend strategies.

Knowledge from countless fields can be used in an expert system. The main criterion for determining whether or not a subject is suitable is the answer to this question: Can knowledge on the subject be translated into IF/THEN rules?

```
RULE 1
IF      knowledge = translatable
THEN   subject = suitable;
```

It's almost that simple.

And although *VP-Expert* has serious professional and scientific applications, it can also be used at home. For example, *Paperback Software* used *VP-Expert* to create *Anthony Dias Blue Wines on Disk*, an expert system that recommends wines. *VP-Expert* could also be used to create systems that give advice on gardening, cooking, child-care, car repair. You name it; the possibilities are endless.

How This Manual is Organized

This manual is divided into four major sections:

PART I: The Beginner's Guide

This section of the manual is essential for beginners, and recommended for everyone who will be involved in building expert systems.

Chapter 1 is a tutorial introducing the *VP-Expert* consultation. To perform the tutorial, you'll use two sample knowledge base files that are provided on the program disk. One lets you run end-user or "runtime" consultations; the other lets you perform "development" consultations. The exercises in this chapter give you hands-on experience using a simple knowledge base, and an introduction to important development and end-user menu commands.

Chapter 2, "The VP-Expert Inference Engine" introduces the basic components of a knowledge base, and shows how the inference engine uses a strategy called "backward chaining" to solve problems during a consultation.

Chapter 3, "Using Induction to Create a Knowledge Base," introduces *VP-Expert*'s Induce command, which automatically creates a knowledge base from an "induction table." The rudiments of induction are explained, and a tutorial guides you through an exercise in which you create a simple knowledge base using this capability.

Chapter 4, "Developing the Knowledge Base," contains exercises in which the simple knowledge base in Chapter 3 is expanded and refined. This chapter gives important information about many of *VP-Expert's* most fundamental features.

PART II: Expanding the Knowledge Base: Database and Worksheet Access

Part II covers *VP-Expert's* ability to incorporate data from compatible database and worksheet files into a knowledge base. (When such files are used in this way, we refer to them as an "information base.") Using induction with such files is also covered in this section.

Chapter 5, "Database Access," shows you how to integrate data stored in *VP-Info* or dBASE database files into a knowledge base. In addition, this chapter discusses how to use induction to create a knowledge base from a database induction table. The advantages of such an approach are also explored.

Chapter 6, "Worksheet Access," discusses how *VP-Expert* integrates data stored in *VP-Planner* or Lotus 1-2-3 worksheets into a *VP-Expert* knowledge base. Details about using induction with worksheet tables are also provided.

PART III: The VP-Expert Reference Section

Part III, the reference section of the manual, contains 4 chapters:

Chapter 7, the "Topical Reference" covers numerous subjects under the following seven broad topics:

The Topical Keyword Reference in Chapter 7 groups VP-Expert keywords by function. This treatment is intended to help you navigate the Alphabetical Keyword Reference in Chapter 9.

- Topical Keyword Reference

- Anatomy of a Knowledge Base

- External Program Calls: Using DOS COM, EXE, and BAT Files

- VP-Expert Variables

- VP-Expert Confidence Factors

- How VP-Expert Can Learn

- Creating an Effective Knowledge Base

Chapter 8, the "Menu Command Reference," details all of *VP-Expert's* built-in menu commands, in alphabetical order.

Chapter 9, the "Alphabetical Keyword Reference," documents each and every "keyword" that can be used in the construction of a *VP-Expert* knowledge base. These include the words that begin every clause and statement, special words used in rule construction, and other words reserved for special use in the knowledge base. Keywords are listed alphabetically. (For a functional treatment of keywords, see Chapter 7.)

Chapter 10, the "Math Function Reference," documents the use of *VP-Expert*'s ten available math functions.

APPENDICES

The Appendices contain five sections:

Appendix A documents *VP-Expert*'s built-in Editor.

Appendix B lists each of *VP-Expert*'s keywords.

Appendix C is a menu tree, showing the hierarchical structure of the *VP-Expert* menu system.

Appendix D briefly describes each of *VP-Expert*'s error messages.

Appendix E is a bibliography.

Starting the Program

VP-Expert requires no special installation procedures. To start the program, type the following at the system prompt:

VPX (and press *ENTER*)

This displays the *VP-Expert* opening screen and Main Menu.

Information about *VP-Expert* menu commands is provided in Chapter 8, the Menu Command Reference. For a quick introduction to using *VP-Expert*, see Chapter 1.

The file README.TXT on the program disk contains the latest information on recent changes to *VP-Expert*. To view the contents of this file, type the following at the system prompt:

README (and press *ENTER*)

Copy Protection

The *VP-Expert* program disk is copy-protected. You can still copy the program files onto your hard disk, but the original *VP-Expert* program disk must be in drive A whenever you start the program. For information about obtaining a non-copy-protected program disk (for a nominal fee), see the Software Registration Form in the disk pack in the back of this book.

CHAPTER ONE

The VP-Expert Consultation

This chapter introduces *VP-Expert* by guiding you through several simple consultations. Two knowledge base files will be used: FROMAGE1.KBS and FROMAGE2.KBS. Both are found on the *VP-Expert* program disk.

FROMAGE1.KBS and FROMAGE2.KBS are "cheese advisors," designed to recommend cheeses based on menu information and personal preferences supplied by the user during a consultation. They were not created by a cheese expert, however, so do not plan your next dinner party based on their recommendations. The exercises in this chapter are meant only to introduce you to the *VP-Expert* consultation.

> *Note: Examples are presented through this manual to illustrate different aspects of VP-Expert. Rules contained in these examples were devised solely to document the program, and should not be construed as "expert knowledge."*

1

Running a Consultation

1. To load the program from the system prompt, type **VPX** and press the *ENTER* key.

This opening screen appears:

```
                        V P - E X P E R T

                        Copyright ©1987
                         Brian Sawyer
                       All Rights Reserved

          Editor portion Copyright ©1984, 1985, 1987, Idea Ware Inc.

              Published by Paperback Software International



                     Licensed for the exclusive use of
                      Registered Single-User Licensee




1Help      2Induce   3Edit     4Consult 5Tree      6FileName 7Path     8Quit
Help the user
```

Note that the lightbar stands on the first command, Help (causing the phrase "Help the user" to appear below). Choosing Help at this or any other *VP-Expert* command menu provides on-screen help information.

Giving VP-Expert Commands

You can select a command option from any *VP-Expert* command menu in one of four ways:

- Type the first letter of the command.
- Type the command number.
- Type the function key number.
- Use the arrow keys to scroll the cursor to the command and press the *ENTER* key.

2. Type **C** to select Consult from the Main Menu.

Scrolling the lightbar past the right margin displays additional knowledge base files.

This screen asks you which knowledge base you want to use and presents you with a list of existing knowledge base files. To choose from this list, move the lightbar to a filename (using the arrow keys) and press the *ENTER* key.

3. Choose FROMAGE1.

Now the message "File loaded" and another menu, the Consult Menu, appear:

```
1Help     2Go       3WhatIf   4Variable 5Rule     6Set      7Quit
Help the user
```

4. Using one of the selection methods described in the box above, choose Go to begin the consultation.

The screen that appears next is called the *consultation window*. It displays the message.

```
Welcome to the charming world of cheese!
Press any key to begin the consultation.
```

5. Following the instructions shown on screen, press any key. This displays a question accompanied by a menu of choices:

```
With what course will you be serving cheese?
Appetizer              Salad                  Dessert
```

At this menu as well as all menus that accompany questions:

- The right and left arrow keys move the lightbar between menu choices.

- Pressing the *ENTER* key chooses the highlighted option (placing a triangle next to the chosen item).
- Pressing the *END* key finalizes the selection.

Note: To cancel a selection before pressing END, press the DEL key while the lightbar is over the item you wish to "unchoose."

6. Choose **Salad** from the menu.

Next, this prompt appears:

```
What is your preference in cheese?
Mild              Flavorful              Pungent
```

7. Choose **Pungent.**

Finally, one more question is displayed:

```
What consistency of cheese would you prefer?
Soft              Firm
```

8. Select **Firm.**

The consultation now concludes with the recommendation, "The most appropriate cheese for this course is Kasseri served with crackers and bread."

```
Welcome to the charming world of cheese!
Press any key to begin the consultation.
With what course will you be serving cheese?
Appetizer                Salad ◄              Dessert

What is your preference in cheese?
Mild                     Flavorful            Pungent ◄

What consistency of cheese would you prefer?
Soft             Firm ◄


The most appropriate cheese for this course is Kasseri
served with crackers and bread.




1Help     2Go      3WhatIf   4Variable 5Rule     6Set      7Quit
Help the user                                               /
```

Choosing Quit from the Main Menu quits the program and returns you to the system prompt.

9. Type **Q** (for Quit) to return to the *VP-Expert* Main Menu.

? for Unknown

When a question is asked during a consultation, several instructions appear at the bottom of the screen to remind you how to move the cursor, select from a menu of choices, and so forth.

? for Unknown, at the end of this line, reminds you to type a question mark if you do not know the answer to a question.

In order for this option to work, the knowledge base must be specifically written to accommodate an ''unknown'' value. The knowledge base example in this chapter is not; therefore, a **?** response to a question results in an unsuccessful consultation (i.e., no conclusion is drawn).

For more information about ''unknown'' values, see UNKNOWN in Chapter 9.

The Rules and Results Windows

The consultation just performed used a single consultation window, which is typical of an ''end user,'' or ''runtime,'' consultation. However, when developing an expert system, there are two more windows you can add: the *rules window* and the *results window*.

The Rules Window

For a complete explanation of how the inference engine uses the knowledge base to solve problems, see Chapter 2.

The *rules window*, in the lower left portion of the screen, provides a window to the knowledge base. It allows you to observe the activity of the *VP-Expert* ''inference engine'' (in effect, the intelligence of the expert system) as it interacts with the knowledge base during a consultation. At the end of this chapter, you will learn how to slow normal scrolling in this window so you can follow the inference engine in its path through the knowledge base.

The Results Window

The *results window*, in the lower right corner of the screen, notes conclusions—both intermediate and final—derived during the course of the consultation. These are expressed as equations like *variable = value CNF n.*

As you'll see in the next exercise, the FROMAGE2 knowledge base uses variable names whose meanings are self-explanatory, e.g., *Course, Preference, Consistency,* and so on. Confidence factors (CNF n) are discussed later in this chapter. They indicate how "sure" the inference engine is about a particular conclusion.

Running a Consultation

To run a consultation that displays the rules and results windows, load the FROMAGE2 knowledge base file.

1. If you are continuing from the previous exercise, choose FileName from the Main Menu. (FileName lets you open a new knowledge base file.) When the list of files appears, scroll the lightbar to FROMAGE2 and press *ENTER*.

   If you start this exercise from the system prompt, type **VPX** and choose Consult. Select FROMAGE2 from the menu of knowledge base files that appears.

2. When the Main Menu appears, choose Consult, and select Go from the Consult Menu.

   This time a three-window consultation screen appears.

   Note: FROMAGE1 and FROMAGE2 knowledge base files are essentially the same. The former, however, contains the RUNTIME statement, which prevents the development windows from appearing during a consultation.

If you are in DOS and wish to go directly into a VPX consultation, type **VPX filename** *(filename is the knowledge base to use without the KBS extension).*

```
Welcome to the charming world of cheese!
Press any key to begin the consultation.
```

3. Press any key to proceed with the consultation. This time, answer
the prompts as you like.

*Note: You may choose more than one course item by pressing
ENTER by each option you want. Press the END key when all
choices have been made.*

The following illustration shows the final screen for a
consultation in which the following values were chosen:

```
Course:       Appetizer and Dessert
Preference:   Pungent
Consistency:  Firm
```

3. To find out *why* this question is being asked, type a slash (/), move the lightbar to Why?, and press *ENTER*. This is the response:

```
The question is being asked because:
The type of cheese and its complement are
determined by the course the cheese will be served
with.
(Press any key to continue)
```

4. Press any key. Then choose **Appetizer** as the course.

```
Welcome to the charming world of cheese!
Press any key to begin the consultation.
With what course will you be serving cheese?
Appetizer ◄              Salad              Dessert

What is your preference in cheese?
Mild                     Flavorful          Pungent
```

```
RULE 9 IF                          Course = Appetizer CNF 100
Complement = crackers_and_bread AND
Preference = Mild OR               Complement = crackers_and_bread CNF
Preference = Flavorful AND         100
Consistency = Soft
THEN
The_Cheese = Montrachet CNF 100

Finding Preference
```

The results window on this screen shows values for the variables *Course* and *Complement*. Before answering the next question, see how the program responds if you ask *how* it determined the value for *Complement*.

*In the Go Menu, the options Help and How? both begin with the letter H. Due to this, typing **H** to select either of these options will have no effect. Use the function keys, number keys, or the lightbar to select these options.*

See BECAUSE in Chapter 9 for information on the way Why? and How? text is generated during a consultation.

5. Type / and select How?.

   This question now appears, accompanied by a list of variable names to choose from:

   ```
   Name of variable you are asking about?
   ```

6. Choose **Complement** and press *ENTER*.

   This time *VP-Expert* responds with the following explanation:

   ```
   Complement was set because of:
   The type of cheese and its complement are
   determined by the course the cheese will be served
   with.
   (Press any key to continue)
   ```

7. Press any key and continue with the consultation. Choose **Mild** in response to the question:

   ```
   What is your preference in cheese?
   Mild                    Flavorful                Pungent
   ```

8. When the next question appears, find out *why* this question is being asked.

   VP-Expert responds with this explanation:

   ```
   The question is being asked because:
   Your preference in taste and consistency determine
   the most appropriate cheese for the course you have
   selected.
   (Press any key to continue)
   ```

9. Press any key; then respond to the question by choosing **Firm**.

```
What is your preference in cheese?
Mild ◄                    Flavorful                 Pungent

What consistency of cheese would you prefer?
Soft                    Firm ◄



The most appropriate cheese for this course is Stilton CNF 100
served with crackers and bread CNF 100.
```

```
Testing 11                          │ Course = Appetizer CNF 100
                                    │
RULE 11 IF                          │ Complement = crackers_and_bread CNF
Complement = crackers_and_bread AND │ 100
Preference = Mild OR                │
Preference = Flavorful AND          │ Preference = Mild CNF 100
Consistency = Firm                  │
THEN                                │ Consistency = Firm CNF 100
The_Cheese = Stilton CNF 100        │
                                    │ The_Cheese = Stilton CNF 100
```

```
1Help      2Go       3WhatIf   4Variable 5Rule      6Set       7Quit
Help the user
```

Consult Menu Commands

The Consult Menu appears when you choose Consult from the Main Menu and upon completion of a consultation. If you followed the previous exercise, the Consult Menu is still displayed at the bottom of your screen.

```
1Help      2Go       3WhatIf   4Variable 5Rule      6Set       7Quit
Help the user
```

You have already used Go to start a consultation. The following exercises introduce you to additional Consult options.

The WhatIf Command

After a consultation, WhatIf allows you to see how changing a response to a particular prompt affects the outcome of the consultation. In other words, WhatIf answers questions such as, "What if I had chosen *Soft* instead of *Firm* at the last prompt?"

Follow these steps to see how WhatIf works.

1. With FROMAGE2.KBS loaded, start a consultation and enter the following values at the question prompts:

   ```
   Course:         Appetizer and Salad
   Preference:     Mild
   Consistency:    Soft
   ```

   The consultation concludes with the message, "The most appropriate cheese for this course is a Montrachet CNF 100 served with crackers and bread CNF 100."

```
What is your preference in cheese?
Mild ◄                  Flavorful                 Pungent

What consistency of cheese would you prefer?
Soft ◄               Firm



The most appropriate cheese for this course is Montrachet CNF 100
served with crackers and bread CNF 100.
```

```
RULE 9 IF                              Course = Salad CNF 100
Complement = crackers_and_bread AND
Preference = Mild OR                   Complement = crackers_and_bread CNF
Preference = Flavorful AND             100
Consistency = Soft
THEN                                   Preference = Mild CNF 100
The_Cheese = Montrachet CNF 100
                                       Consistency = Soft CNF 100

Finding Preference
Finding Consistency                    The_Cheese = Montrachet CNF 100
```

```
1Help     2Go     3WhatIf   4Variable 5Rule    6Set     7Quit
Help the user
```

2. To find out the conclusion for *Firm* consistency instead of *Soft*, choose WhatIf from the Consult Menu. This displays the question:

```
Name of variable you want to change?
```

A menu of variable names appears below this prompt.

3. Choose **Consistency** and press *ENTER*.

The prompt asking for your preferred consistency reappears:

```
What consistency of cheese would you prefer?
Soft                    Firm
```

4. This time, choose **Firm**.

Now the consultation restarts. Since the welcome message is part of the execution of the knowledge base, it reappears:

```
Welcome to the charming world of cheese!
Press any key to begin the consultation.
```

5. Press any key and the new conclusion appears, this time advising you that the best choice is a *Stilton*.

Note: On this execution of the knowledge base, the variables Course *and* Preference *keep their values from the previous consultation, while* Consistency *takes the new value* Firm. *VP-Expert has all the information it needs to draw a new conclusion,* Stilton.

In another knowledge base, using WhatIf to change the response to a question might cause the inference engine to take a new logic path through the rules and to look for values for new variables. In such a case you would be prompted to provide these values (if the appropriate ASK statements were included in the knowledge base).

```
served with crackers and bread CNF 100.
What consistency of cheese would you prefer?
Soft                    Firm ◄

Welcome to the charming world of cheese!
Press any key to begin the consultation.

The most appropriate cheese for this course is Stilton CNF 100
served with crackers and bread CNF 100.
```

```
Testing 11

RULE 11 IF
Complement = crackers_and_bread AND
Preference = Mild OR
Preference = Flavorful AND
Consistency = Firm
THEN
The_Cheese = Stilton CNF 100
```

```
Consistency = Soft CNF 100

The_Cheese = Montrachet CNF 100

Consistency = Firm CNF 100

Complement = crackers_and_bread CNF

The_Cheese = Stilton CNF 100
```

```
1Help      2Go       3WhatIf  4Variable 5Rule     6Set      7Quit
Help the user
```

The Variable command can only display values after a consultation has taken place. If you start this exercise from the system prompt, follow the instructions in the previous exercise first.

The Variable Command

The fourth command option on the Consult Menu is Variable. After a consultation, Variable shows the final value of a variable. Follow these steps:

1. Choose Variable from the Consult Menu to display this prompt:

   ```
   Name of variable you want to see?
   ```

   Selecting a variable name from the menu below this prompt displays the value assigned to that variable in the previous consultation.

Final Comments

Chapter 1 has shown you how to conduct a simple *VP-Expert* consultation, making use of all the available command options. However, it has not shown you how a consultation actually works—the "behind-the-scenes" processes that make it effective. To find out how problems are solved in *VP-Expert*, it is necessary to look at the knowledge base and understand how the inference engine uses a method called "backward chaining" during a consultation.

For an introduction to the knowledge base and the inference engine, and for a detailed explanation of backward chaining, see Chapter 2.

CHAPTER TWO

The VP-Expert Inference Engine

In the language of expert systems, the "inference engine" refers to the mechanism that navigates the knowledge base and solves problems during a consultation. The inference engine is the "intelligence" that allows the expert system to make conclusions based on the "expertise" or "knowledge" stored in the knowledge base.

The method used by the inference engine to solve problems during a consultation is described in this chapter. Since the knowledge base itself is an integral part of what "drives" the inference engine towards its conclusions, we will first examine the basic structure and elements of a knowledge base.

The Knowledge Base

Knowledge base elements are also discussed in Chapter 7 under "Anatomy of a Knowledge Base," and in Chapter 9 under the keywords ACTIONS and RULE.

A knowledge base file contains three basic elements:

- The ACTIONS block.
- Rules.
- Statements.

A fourth element, clauses, are contained *within* the ACTIONS block and rules of the knowledge base.

2

"Keywords" are words that have a special function in the knowledge base, e.g., RULE, IF, THEN, etc. They may also be called "reserved words" because they are reserved for a specific use. Improper use of such words (e.g., using a keyword as a variable name) prevents knowledge base execution. See Appendix B for a complete list of VP-Expert keywords.

The ACTIONS Block

The ACTIONS block—which consists of the keyword "ACTIONS," one or more *clauses*, and a semicolon—defines the problems ("goals") of the consultation and the sequence of their solution. In other words, the ACTIONS block tells the inference engine what it needs to find out, and in what order. This is accomplished with FIND clauses that instruct *VP-Expert* to "find" the value or values of one or more "goal variables."

> *Note: Variables represent locations in memory for storing data. The value of a variable is the contents of that memory location.*

In addition to FIND clauses, the ACTIONS block can also contain other clauses—specifying database operations, spreadsheet operations, and a variety of other tasks. The knowledge bases used in this chapter contain simple ACTIONS blocks. ACTIONS blocks of greater complexity are used in later chapters of the manual.

Rules

Rules, stated as IF/THEN propositions, contain the actual "knowledge" or "expertise" of the knowledge base. For example, "If the animal has hair and bears live young, then it's a mammal."

Stated as a proper rule, this information would appear something like this:

```
RULE 1
IF      hair  = yes AND
        birth = live
THEN    animal = mammal;
```

Rules have four essential elements:

- The rule *name*.

- The rule *premise*.

- The rule *conclusion*.

- A semicolon at the end of the rule.

```
RULE 3
IF        Course = Appetizer
THEN      Complement = crackers_and_bread;

RULE 4
IF        Course = Dessert
THEN      Complement = bread_and_fruit;

ASK Course: "Is the course Appetizer or Dessert?";

CHOICES Course: Appetizer,Dessert;
```

Finding a Value for the Goal Variable

The ultimate problem, or "goal," of most consultations is defined in a FIND clause in the ACTIONS block of the knowledge base. This clause instructs the inference engine to FIND a value for a given variable—which we call the "goal variable." The goal variable named in the FIND clause of our ACTIONS block is *The_Cheese*.

```
ACTIONS
         FIND The_Cheese;
```

Once *The_Cheese* has been identified as the goal variable, the inference engine searches the knowledge base for the *first* rule that can assign a value to the goal variable. Since the goal variable is *The_Cheese*, the inference engine looks for the *first* rule containing the variable *The_Cheese* in its conclusion.

This is the rule it finds:

```
RULE 1
IF        Complement = crackers_and_bread
THEN      The_Cheese = Brie;
```

Once the rule is found, the inference engine looks at the first variable named in the premise of the rule. If it does not know the value of the variable, it looks for the first rule containing that variable in its conclusion.

The only variable named in the premise of RULE 1 is *Complement*. Since the inference engine doesn't know the value of *Complement*, it scans the knowledge base for the first rule which might provide the value—in other words, the first rule that contains the variable, *Complement*, in its conclusion.

RULE 3 is the rule the inference engine finds:

```
RULE 3
IF       Course = Appetizer
THEN     Complement = crackers_and_bread;
```

This rule shows the variable *Course* in its premise, so now the inference engine must try to find a value for *Course*. It, therefore, looks for the first rule that can assign a value to *Course* (that contains *Course* in its conclusion).

For a discussion of forward chaining, see the FIND and GET clauses in Chapter 9.

Backward Chaining

The problem-solving method used by the *VP-Expert* inference engine is called "backward chaining." The inference engine starts by identifying the goal variable and then moves through the sequence of rules until it finds a value that can help it assign a value to the goal variable.

This is the pattern it follows:

ACTIONS		
	FIND A;	The goal variable is identified as A.

RULE 1		
IF	B = value	The first rule showing *A* in its
THEN	A = value;	conclusion is found. The variable *B*—shown in its premise—is not known, so the inference engine looks for the first rule naming *B* in its conclusion.

RULE 2		
IF	C = value	This rule is found naming *B* in its
THEN	B = value;	conclusion. The variable in the premise, *C*, is unknown, so the inference engine looks for the first rule showing *C* in its conclusion.

RULE 3		
IF	D = value	This is the first rule containing the
THEN	C = value;	variable *C* in its conclusion. *D* in the premise is unknown, so a rule will be sought showing *D* in the conclusion.

This pattern continues until one of the variables being sought has a known value. Once a value is known, the inference engine can retrace its steps and test the rules that provided its original path.

When we left the inference engine, it was searching for a rule containing *Course* in its conclusion. There is no such rule in the knowledge base, but the inference engine does not give up. After scanning all the rules for one that can assign a value to the variable *Course*, it looks for an ASK statement that can provide a value for *Course*. This is what it discovers:

```
ASK Course: "Is the course Appetizer or Dessert?";
```

The ASK Statement

Whenever the inference engine can't find a variable in the conclusion of a rule, it looks for the variable in an ASK statement. ASK statements are used to prompt the user for information not contained in the knowledge base (like a human expert, if the expert system doesn't know something, it asks). It's up to the person who designs the knowledge base to make sure that appropriate questions are asked during a consultation; that is, that all variables not accounted for in rules are assigned by ASK statements.

See AUTOQUERY in Chapter 9 for information about activating VP-Expert's automatic question capability.

The CHOICES Statement

In addition to the ASK statement, the inference engine looks for a CHOICES statement. This is what it finds:

```
CHOICES Course: Appetizer,Dessert;
```

Whenever the inference engine finds an ASK statement that names a variable it is looking for, it automatically searches for a CHOICES statement naming the same variable. If present, the CHOICES statement creates a menu of options to accompany the question during a consultation. The user is required to choose from this menu. If no CHOICES statement is present, no menu will accompany the question; the user must type a response.

At this point in the consultation, the user is presented with the ASK text and a menu of options generated by the CHOICES statement:

```
Is the course Appetizer or Dessert?
Appetizer          Dessert
```

Here the user makes a choice.

RULE 3 is found.

```
RULE 3
IF        Course = Appetizer
THEN      Complement = crackers_and_bread;
```

This sends the inference engine looking for *Course*, which causes the ASK and CHOICES statements to display this prompt to the user:

```
Is the course Appetizer or Dessert?
Appetizer          Dessert
```

Up to this point, the inference engine has acted just as it did in previous consultations. But, what happens when the user chooses more than one value for *Course*?

When the user chooses both *Appetizer* and *Dessert* at the ASK prompt, the inference engine first goes back to RULE 3 (which originally sent the inference engine looking for a value for *Course*).

```
RULE 3
IF        Course = Appetizer
THEN      Complement = crackers_and_bread;
```

RULE 3 passes because *Appetizer* is one of the values assigned to *Course*. *Crackers_and_bread*, then, is assigned as a value for *Complement*.

But since *Complement* is a plural variable, the inference engine goes on to find *all other* rules that can assign a value to *Complement*. It, therefore, goes to RULE 4, which is the *next* rule showing *Complement* in its conclusion.

```
RULE 4
IF        Course = Dessert
THEN      Complement = bread_and_fruit;
```

RULE 4 passes because *Dessert* is one of the values assigned to *Course*. But if the rule looked like the following, the inference engine would be sent on a new path to search for a value for the variable *Preference*.

```
RULE X
IF        Preference = Mild
THEN      Complement = bread_and_fruit;
```

It is important to note that when a variable is declared PLURAL, every rule naming that variable in its conclusion is ultimately looked at, and every path is tested, until each of the rules either passes or fails.

Back to our example:

RULE 4 passes, assigning another value, *bread_and_fruit*, to the variable *Complement*.

If there were another rule containing *Complement* in its conclusion, the inference engine would look there next. Since there is not, the inference engine looks for an ASK statement naming *Complement*. There is none so the engine goes to the rule which required a value for *Complement*—RULE 1.

```
RULE 1
IF        Complement = crackers_and_bread
THEN      The_Cheese = Brie;
```

This rule passes because one of the values assigned to *Complement* is *crackers_and_bread*.

Brie is, therefore, determined to be the value for the goal variable *The_Cheese*.

But *The_Cheese* is also a plural variable, so now the inference engine looks for another rule naming *The_Cheese* in its conclusion. The next rule, RULE 2, is found.

```
RULE 2
IF        Complement = bread_and_fruit
THEN      The_Cheese = Camembert;
```

This rule also passes (since *bread_and_fruit* is one of the values of *Complement*), so *Camembert* is assigned as another value for *The_Cheese*.

At this point, the consultation is complete.

Confidence Factors

In real life, very little is known with absolute certainty. Even "experts" frequently resort to likely conclusions and best guesses when handing out advice. "You probably have the measles, but there is always a chance it is something else. The battery is most likely the problem, but it might be the generator." Such advice, despite a degree of uncertainty, is, nonetheless, valuable. *VP-Expert* imitates this type of real life analysis by allowing *confidence factors*. A confidence factor is an integer (between 0 and 100) indicating the degree of certainty that a particular conclusion is valid.

Confidence factors can be entered by the user when responding to a prompt, or written into the knowledge base in the conclusions of rules. For example:

```
RULE 1
IF        Complement = crackers_and_bread
THEN      The_Cheese = Brie CNF 80;
```

This rule assigns *Brie* as the value of the variable, *The_Cheese*, with 80% confidence. (Note that this should not be interpreted as a strict probability.)

But what happens if, at a prompt, the user assigns a confidence factor of 80 to *crackers_and_bread*? Will *Brie* still be assigned with 80% confidence?

No. The confidence factors will be combined in a formula (.80 x .80 = .64), and the final confidence factor assigned to *Brie* will be 64.

For more information about how confidence factors are combined and computed during a consultation, see Chapter 7.

How the Inference Engine Handles Multiple Conditions

Now that you've been introduced to the basic method of the inference engine, we'll consider the method in a more complex environment.

The following knowledge base is an elaboration of the previous knowledge base (though we've removed the PLURAL statement). This knowledge base contains two more variables, additional statements, and slightly more complicated rules. This knowledge base includes some rules containing *multiple conditions*.

```
ACTIONS
          FIND The_Cheese;

RULE 1
IF        Complement = crackers_and_bread AND
          Preference = Mild OR
          Preference = Flavorful
THEN      The_Cheese = Brie;

RULE 1A
IF        Complement = crackers_and_bread AND
          Preference = Pungent
THEN      The_Cheese = Asiago;

RULE 2
IF        Complement = bread_and_fruit AND
          Preference = Mild OR
          Preference = Flavorful
THEN      The_Cheese = Camembert;

RULE 2A
IF        Complement = bread_and_fruit AND
          Preference = Pungent
THEN      The_Cheese = Tallegio;
```

```
RULE 3
IF        Course = Appetizer
THEN      Complement = crackers_and_bread;

RULE 4
IF        Course = Dessert
THEN      Complement = bread_and_fruit;

ASK Course: "Is the course Appetizer or Dessert?";

CHOICES Course: Appetizer,Dessert;

ASK Preference: "What is your preference in cheese?";

CHOICES Preference: Mild,Flavorful,Pungent;
```

Look closely at the new knowledge base. There should be no problem understanding all the changes that were made—it is basically just more of what you've seen. But how do these changes affect the course of the inference engine during a consultation? In particular, how do the multiple conditions in some of the rules affect the engine's path?

One More Time

Once again, the inference engine begins by identifying the goal variable—*The_Cheese*—and scanning the knowledge base for the *first* rule containing *The_Cheese* in its conclusion. It finds RULE 1:

```
RULE 1
IF        Complement = crackers_and_bread AND
          Preference = Mild OR
          Preference = Flavorful
THEN      The_Cheese = Brie;
```

The inference engine looks at the first condition of the rule premise and finds that the variable *Complement* is unknown. It then moves to find the first rule that can assign a value to *Complement*—RULE 3.

```
RULE 3
IF        Course = Appetizer
THEN      Complement = crackers_and_bread;
```

This rule sends the inference engine searching for *Course*, which displays the ASK prompt to the user.

```
Is the course Appetizer or Dessert?
Appetizer          Dessert
```

If the user chooses *Dessert* for *Course*, the inference engine returns to RULE 3. But RULE 3 fails because it requires the value *Appetizer*.

```
RULE 3
IF        Course = Appetizer
THEN      Complement = crackers_and_bread;
```

So the inference engine looks for and finds the *next* rule in the knowledge base that can assign a value to *Complement*—RULE 4.

```
RULE 4
IF        Course = Dessert
THEN      Complement = bread_and_fruit;
```

So far, the engine's path is no different from previous consultations.

Now RULE 4 sends the engine to RULE 1, which originally sent the engine looking for the value of *Complement* (in order to determine whether or not the rule could assign a value to *The_Cheese*).

```
RULE 1
IF        Complement = crackers_and_bread AND
          Preference = Mild OR
          Preference = Flavorful
THEN      The_Cheese = Brie;
```

RULE 1 fails, however, because it requires that *Complement* have the value *crackers_and_bread*.

The inference engine then considers RULE 1A because it is the next rule that contains the variable *The_Cheese* in its conclusion.

```
RULE 1A
IF        Complement = crackers_and_bread AND
          Preference = Pungent
THEN      The_Cheese = Asiago;
```

A Pattern to Note

At this point a pattern should be clear:

When a rule sends the inference engine out to find a value for a variable contained in its premise, that rule is immediately returned to once the value is found. If the rule then fails (because the found value does not match the value required to satisfy the condition in the premise), the inference engine always goes immediately to the next rule (if one exists) whose conclusion assigns a value to the same variable that is named in the conclusion of the rule that just failed.

In this example, RULE 1A also fails, because it requires that *Complement* be *crackers_and_bread*. So the inference engine moves on to the *next* rule that contains *The_Cheese* in its conclusion— RULE 2.

```
RULE 2
IF          Complement = bread_and_fruit AND
            Preference = Mild OR
            Preference = Flavorful
THEN        The_Cheese = Camembert;
```

Next, the user is presented with this prompt:

```
What is your preference in cheese?
Mild                Flavorful              Pungent
```

This is because the value of *Complement* is, indeed, *bread_and_fruit*—so that portion of RULE 2's premise is valid. But now the inference engine needs to investigate the other conditions in the rule. It, therefore, finds the *next* variable in the premise, *Preference*, and sets out looking for the first rule containing *Preference* in its conclusion.

There is no such rule, so it looks for an ASK statement naming the variable *Preference*. An ASK statement is found, and, along with the CHOICES statement, produces the prompt shown above.

For the purpose of our example, suppose the user chooses *Pungent* at the prompt.

With a *Pungent* value for *Preference*, the inference engine returns to RULE 2:

```
RULE 2
IF          Complement = bread_and_fruit AND
            Preference = Mild OR
            Preference = Flavorful
THEN        The_Cheese = Camembert;
```

This time the rule fails, because *Preference* is *Pungent*, and this rule requires either *Mild* or *Flavorful*. The inference engine, therefore, scans the knowledge base for the *next* rule containing *The_Cheese* in the conclusion—which is RULE 2A.

```
RULE 2A
IF          Complement = bread_and_fruit AND
            Preference = Pungent
THEN        The_Cheese = Tallegio;
```

For a complete description of how AND/OR logic works, see "Using Logical Operators" in Chapter 4.

This rule states that IF *Complement* is *bread_and_fruit* AND the *Preference* is *Pungent*, then *The_Cheese* is *Tallegio*.

The rule passes, so *Tallegio* is assigned to the goal variable, *The_Cheese*.

Final Comments

This chapter has not shown the full range of statements and clauses that can be used in a *VP-Expert* knowledge base. The purpose here has been to show how the path of the inference engine is determined during a consultation—the path being the actual rule-by-rule course which the inference engine takes when navigating the knowledge base to solve a problem.

In order to design an effective knowledge base, it is crucial to understand how the anatomy of the knowledge base and the rules themselves affect the problem-solving process.

Summary of Terms

ACTIONS block

The ACTIONS block—consisting of the keyword ACTIONS followed by one or more clauses, and ending in a semicolon—is a required element of a knowledge base. Like a simple program, it defines the tasks to be fulfilled during a *VP-Expert* consultation. For more information on the ACTIONS block, see ACTIONS in Chapter 9.

ASK Statement

ASK statements are used in a knowledge base to generate questions during a consultation. Questions allow the user to assign values to variables that cannot be assigned values in rules. For example, the following statement asks the user to provide a value for the variable *date.*

```
ASK date: "What is your date of birth?
(Enter as yy/mm/dd).";
```

> *Note: If a CHOICES statement naming the same variable is present in the knowledge base, it generates a menu of options for the user to choose from. If no menu is displayed, a typed response is required.*

Backward Chaining

Backward chaining is the procedure that directs the inference engine's path through the knowledge base during a *VP-Expert* consultation. This chapter describes, step-by-step, how backward chaining works.

CHOICES Statement

If an ASK statement has a corresponding CHOICES statement in the knowledge base (i.e., they both name the same variable), a menu of choices (defined in the CHOICES statement) accompanies the question when it is generated during a consultation. The choices on this menu are the only values that can be assigned to the named variable by the ASK statement—hence, the term "choices." See also "ASK Statement."

Goal Variable

In a *VP-Expert* knowledge base, a goal variable—identified in a FIND clause in the ACTIONS block—is so named because finding its value(s) is the "goal" of the consultation.

When more than one goal variable is identified, each is sought in the order in which it appears in the ACTIONS block.

Inference Engine

Inference engine refers to the mechanism that navigates the knowledge base to solve problems during a *VP-Expert* consultation. It is the "intelligence" that utilizes the "expertise" or "knowledge" stored in the knowledge base. This chapter describes how the inference engine interacts with the knowledge base during a *VP-Expert* consultation.

Knowledge Base

The knowledge base contains the "knowledge" of the expert system. In addition, it shapes the course of a consultation by identifying goals, asking questions requiring user response, defining "plural" variables, etc.

For detailed information about building a knowledge base, see Chapters 3 and 4.

Logical Operators

The logical operators AND and OR can be used in a rule's premise to form complex conditions. For example:

```
RULE 1
IF   Course = Dessert OR
     Course = Salad AND
     Preference = Mild
THEN The_Cheese = Chevres;
```

AND is like the English expression "and." Both conditions must be met for the rule to pass.

OR is like the English expression ''or.'' For the rule to pass, one or both conditions must be true.

See ''Using Logical Operators'' in Chapter 4 for more examples of complex conditions.

PLURAL Statement

The PLURAL statement identifies variables in the knowledge base that can be assigned multiple values during a consultation. For example, the following statement defines the variable *Course* as ''plural.''

```
PLURAL: Course;
```

This chapter discusses how plural variables affect the path of the inference engine during a consultation.

Rule

Rules, stated as IF/THEN propositions, contain the actual ''knowledge'' or expertise of the knowledge base. Rules contain information like, ''If the sun is shining and the temperature is warm, then the weather is fair.''

Stated as a rule, this information looks like this:

```
RULE 1
IF        sun = shining AND
          temperature = warm
THEN      weather = fair;
```

Legal rules must contain the following:

- A rule name, consisting of the keyword RULE followed by a space and a unique rule label of up to 20 characters.

- A rule premise beginning with the keyword IF.

■ A rule conclusion beginning with the keyword THEN.

■ A semicolon at the end of the rule.

One or more clauses can be optionally added to the conclusion of a rule. See RULE in Chapter 9 for more information.

VP-Expert Keyword

VP-Expert keywords are words that have a special meaning and function in the *VP-Expert* knowledge base—for example, RULE, ASK, IF, THEN, PLURAL, etc. Improper use of such "reserved words" (e.g., using a keyword as a variable name) causes fatal errors during knowledge base execution.

For a complete list of *VP-Expert* keywords, see Appendix B.

CHAPTER THREE

Using Induction to Create a Knowledge Base

Chapter 2 discussed the basic structure of the knowledge base and how the inference engine operates during a *VP-Expert* consultation.

Induction is an option, not a requirement, for creating a VP-Expert knowledge base.

This chapter and Chapter 4 guide you through the process of building and using your own knowledge base. To create the initial structure, we use the Induce command on the Main Menu.

The Induce command quickly creates a simple knowledge base from "examples" stored in what we refer to as an "induction table."

The Induction Table

One of *VP-Expert's* most powerful features is its ability to generate a knowledge base from an "induction table." An induction table is a table representing examples in the form of rows and columns.

Consider this simple induction table:

Course	Consistency	The_Cheese
Appetizer	Soft	Montrachet
Appetizer	Firm	Stilton
Dessert	Soft	Camembert
Dessert	Firm	Italian_Fontina
*	Soft	Brie
*	Firm	Cheddar

Note: Placing an asterisk (*) instead of a value in an induction table column indicates that a value is not required for the corresponding variable.

3.1 USING INDUCE

3

Like an ordinary table (for example, a calendar), the top row of the induction table acts as a set of column headings. These headings define a set of variables: *Course, Consistency,* and *The_Cheese.* The rightmost variable, *The_Cheese,* is, in effect, the goal variable. Its value is determined by the values of the preceding variables.

To translate examples into rules, the rows in the body of the table can be interpreted as follows:

> IF *Course* is Appetizer and *Consistency* is Soft, THEN *The_Cheese* is Montrachet.

> IF *Course* is Appetizer and *Consistency* is Firm, THEN *The_Cheese* is Stilton.

> IF *Course* is Dessert and *Consistency* is Soft, THEN *The_Cheese* is Camembert.

> IF *Course* is Dessert and *Consistency* is Firm, THEN *The_Cheese* is Italian_Fontina.

> IF *Consistency* is Soft, THEN *The_Cheese* is Brie.

> IF *Consistency* is Firm, THEN *The_Cheese* is Cheddar.

The last two examples do not require a value for *Course,* as indicated by the asterisks in the induction table.

When using the Induce command to create a knowledge base from an induction table, *VP-Expert* interprets the rows of the table in this same manner, transforming them into a working knowledge base, complete with rules, an ACTIONS block, ASK statements, CHOICES statements, and so on.

Induce lends itself to some expert systems applications better than others, and it is limited in the complexity of knowledge base it can create. However, for many applications, Induce is the most expedient method of starting a knowledge base.

This chapter shows you how to use Induce to create a knowledge base. The next chapter guides you through the process of expanding the basic structure created here.

In response to the Induce command, VP-Expert sometimes displays a prompt recommending that a frequently occurring group of variables be combined under a single variable name. When this happens, you have the option of typing a new variable name, or pressing ENTER to indicate "no change." The former causes VP-Expert to create a less redundant, simplified knowledge base.

Creating the Induction Table

The Induce command can build a knowledge base from an induction table created in any of several different environments. An induction table can be created in a text editor, in a *VP-Info* or dBASE database file, or in a *VP-Planner* or Lotus 1-2-3 worksheet. The instructions in this chapter show you how to generate a knowledge base from a table created in a text file. For information about using database or worksheet induction tables, see Chapters 5 and 6.

Entering the Editor

1. If necessary, start the program by typing **VPX** and pressing the *ENTER* key.

```
1Help      2Induce   3Edit     4Consult  5Tree     6FileName 7Path      8Quit
Help the user
```

2. At the Main Menu, choose Induce to go to the *VP-Expert* Induce Menu.

```
1Help      2Create   3Database   4Text     5Worksht   6Quit
Help the user
```

3. At this menu, select Create. The prompt "What is the name of the examples file?" and a menu of TBL filenames (if there are any TBL files in the current directory) appear. Type **MYBASE** and press *ENTER*. You are then automatically taken into the *VP-Expert* Editor.

   Note: Whenever you type a new filename at this prompt, the file will automatically be given a TBL file extension. Later, when you give the Induce command to create a knowledge base from an induction table, VP-Expert will present a menu of TBL files to choose from.

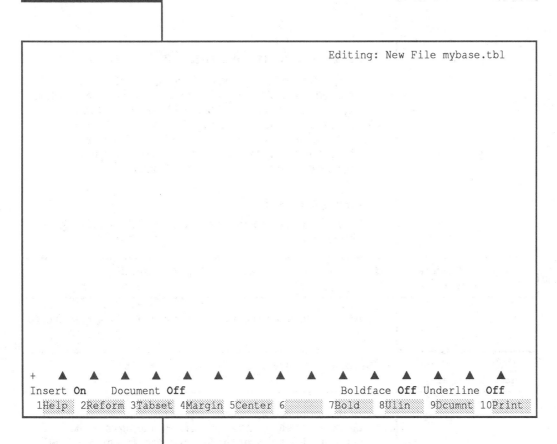

```
                                    Editing: New File mybase.tbl




+  ▲   ▲   ▲   ▲   ▲   ▲   ▲   ▲   ▲   ▲   ▲   ▲   ▲   ▲   ▲
Insert On    Document Off                     Boldface Off Underline Off
  1Help  2Reform 3Tabset 4Margin 5Center 6        7Bold   8Ulin   9Dcumnt 10Print
```

Using the Editor

The basic editing commands on the next page should be sufficient for completing the exercises in this section of the manual. However, for more information, detailed documentation of the *VP-Expert* Editor is provided in Appendix A.

Note: When using VP-Expert's built-in Editor, function key command assignments are indicated at the bottom of the editing screen. Press CTRL, SHIFT, and ALT to see how assignments change when the function keys are typed in combination with these keys.

Document mode is set to Off when you enter the VP-Expert Editor. This disables word wrap, justify (which inserts extra spaces), centering, and reformat. Function key F9 toggles Document mode.

See the EDIT command in Chapter 8 for information about using your own editor with VP-Expert.

VP-Expert Editing Commands

RIGHT/LEFT ARROW	Moves cursor right/left one character.
UP/DOWN ARROW	Moves cursor up/down one line.
INSERT	Toggles insert mode. Default is ON.
TAB	Moves cursor to next tab stop.
SHIFT-TAB	Moves cursor back one tab stop.
CTRL-ENTER	Adds a blank line.
DEL (or CTRL G)	Deletes character at cursor position.
BACKSPACE	Deletes character to left of cursor.
CTRL-T	Deletes from cursor to end of word.
CTRL-Y	Deletes line.
ALT F6	Saves file and leaves editor.
ALT F8	Abandons file without saving or changing.
ALT F5	Updates file without leaving editor.

Note: Hard carriage returns are indicated on screen with left triangles (◀).

Building the Induction Table

1. With these editing commands, create the following induction table.

   Note: Each row of the table must *end with a hard carriage return. (These are indicated on screen with a triangle (◀).)*

Course	Consistency	The_Cheese
Appetizer	Soft	Montrachet
Appetizer	Firm	Stilton
Dessert	Soft	Camembert
Dessert	Firm	Italian_Fontina

2. After you have completed the table, check it for errors; then save it by typing *ALT-F6.* At the prompt, "Save as "mybase.tbl" (Y or N)?," type **Y**.

3. When you are returned to the Induce Menu, choose Text.

   This prompt appears:

   ```
   What is the name of the examples file?
   ```

4. Choose MYBASE and press *ENTER*.

   Next, you are asked:

   ```
   What is the name of the rules file to create?
   ```

5. Press *ENTER*. The rules file will be given the default name MYBASE.KBS. (All knowledge base files are automatically given a KBS file extension.)

   The message "Inducing rules from examples" is shown followed by the Induce Menu.

6. Choose Quit from the Induce Menu.

7. Select FileName from the Main Menu and choose MYBASE from the next menu that appears.

8. Now choose Edit from the Main Menu to see the newly created knowledge base. It should look like this:

```
ACTIONS
       FIND The_Cheese;


RULE 0
IF     Course=Appetizer AND
       Consistency=Soft
THEN
       The_Cheese=Montrachet;


RULE 1
IF     Course=Appetizer AND
       Consistency=Firm
THEN
       The_Cheese=Stilton;


RULE 2
IF     Course=Dessert AND
       Consistency=Soft
THEN
       The_Cheese=Camembert;


RULE 3
IF     Course=Dessert AND
       Consistency=Firm
THEN
       The_Cheese=Italian_Fontina;


ASK Course: "What is the value of Course?";
CHOICES Course: Appetizer,Dessert;

ASK Consistency: "What is the value of Consistency?";
CHOICES Consistency: Soft,Firm;
```

8. To leave the editor and return to the *VP-Expert* Main Menu, press *ALT-F8* and then type **Y**. This abandons the file without making any changes.

3.7 USING INDUCE

9. At the Main Menu, choose Consult to run a consultation using the new knowledge base.

Note: If VP-Expert reports a syntax error, return to the induction table and make sure it matches our example. To do this, press any key and quit the Editor. Then choose Induce and select Create from the Induce Menu to edit the induction table.

Chapter 1 provides a complete introduction to the VP-Expert consultation, including information about consultation options such as Why?, How?, and WhatIf.

Consultation Guidelines

■ After choosing Consult, select Go to begin the consultation.

■ When a question appears on the screen, choose a response from the accompanying menu by moving the lightbar to the option you want (using the right and left arrow keys) and pressing *ENTER*. Then press *END* to finalize your selection. (If you change your mind before pressing *END*, press the *DEL* key with the lightbar over the option you want to "unchoose.")

When the consultation is over, the "conclusion" appears in the lower right window.

The following screen would appear after a consultation in which *Appetizer* and *Soft* were chosen at the question prompts. Note the conclusion *"The_Cheese = Montrachet CNF 100"* in the lower right window.

```
What is the value of Course?
Appetizer ◄              Dessert

What is the value of Consistency?
Soft ◄                   Firm
```

```
Testing 0

RULE 0 IF
Course = Appetizer AND
Consistency = Soft
THEN
The_Cheese = Montrachet CNF 100

Finding Course
Finding Consistency
```

```
Course = Appetizer CNF 100

Consistency = Soft CNF 100

The_Cheese = Montrachet CNF 100
```

```
1Help     2Go      3WhatIf   4Variable 5Rule    6Set      7Quit
Help the user
```

Adding to the Knowledge Base

If you have read the previous chapters, or already know about the elements of a knowledge base, you can see that the one we've created is quite basic. It provides no conclusion message in the consultation (top) window, and it asks only the generic question, "What is the value of ____?" Nevertheless, it is a working knowledge base, and using Induce to create it was certainly easier than writing the rules from scratch. Keep in mind that the table from which the knowledge base was induced was quite small. The bigger the induction table, the more time and effort you save.

To see how to develop this simple knowledge base, see Chapter 4. There, this basic structure will be turned into a more elaborate and more effective knowledge base.

Chapter Summary

Using Induce to Create a Knowledge Base

The Induce command transforms an "induction table" into a working knowledge base. The knowledge base created is quite basic, but for many applications, the Induce command is the simplest and most expedient way of starting a knowledge base.

The Induction Table

For information about creating induction tables in database and worksheet files, see Chapters 5 and 6.

An induction table represents examples in the form of rows and columns. Each row contains a set of conditions and a value, in the right-most column, that is valid if those conditions are met.

By using the Induce command, an induction table can be transformed into a working knowledge base, complete with rules, an ACTIONS block, ASK statements, and CHOICES statements.

CHAPTER FOUR

Developing the Knowledge Base

This chapter assumes you have an understanding of concepts introduced in previous chapters. It is advisable to read Chapters 1, 2, and 3 before beginning the following tutorial exercises.

Chapter 3 guided you through the process of building a simple knowledge base using *VP-Expert's* Induce command. Exercises in this chapter add to and refine the knowledge base created there. To begin this chapter without having followed the exercises in Chapter 3, use the ABASE.KBS file on the *VP-Expert* program disk.

Knowledge Base Format

This is the knowledge base created with Induce in Chapter 3:

4

```
ACTIONS
        FIND The_Cheese;


RULE 0
        Course=Appetizer AND
        Consistency=Soft
THEN
        The_Cheese=Montrachet;

RULE 1
IF      Course=Appetizer AND
        Consistency=Firm
THEN
        The_Cheese=Stilton;

RULE 2
IF      Course=Dessert AND
        Consistency=Soft
THEN
        The_Cheese=Camembert;

RULE 3
IF      Course=Dessert AND
        Consistency=Firm
THEN
        The_Cheese=Italian_Fontina;

ASK Course: "What is the value of Course?";
CHOICES Course: Appetizer,Dessert;

ASK Consistency: "What is the value of Consistency?";
CHOICES Consistency: Soft,Firm;
```

The Induce command created the knowledge base using an arbitrary format. The physical requirements of a *VP-Expert* knowledge base are quite flexible—in terms of spacing, rule names, letter case, and so on. When refining a knowledge base created with Induce, you may want to alter its appearance to a more convenient style.

Most of the knowledge bases shown in this manual conform to a particular style—one slightly different from the format used by Induce. However, your knowledge bases do not have to look exactly like the ones we suggest—or the one created by Induce in Chapter 3. With the exception of the mandatory formatting rules listed below, your knowledge bases can be structured in any way you like.

Remember that Induce is an optional method of creating a knowledge base. It is not required.

To indicate spaces in variable names or values, use the underline character; e.g., The_Cheese. VP-Expert will replace the underline character with spaces in display text.

See the end of Chapter 9 for information about adding comment lines to a knowledge base.

Mandatory Formatting Rules:

- The ACTIONS block must begin with the word ACTIONS—in upper, lower, or mixed case.

- Rules must begin with the keyword RULE followed by a space and a label that does not exceed 20 characters.

- Spaces are not allowed in rule labels, variable names, or values.

- Rule labels and variable names may contain letters, numbers, and the following special characters: _ $ % ^ |. (Remember that a variable name must begin with a letter.)

- Text specified in statements that create on-screen messages (e.g., ASK, DISPLAY, etc.) must be in double quotes.

- The ACTIONS block and every rule and statement *must* end with a semicolon. The only other place a semicolon is allowed is inside the double quotes that surround display text.

- *VP-Expert* keywords (words with special meanings in *VP-Expert*) cannot be used as variable names. See Appendix B for a complete list of *VP-Expert* keywords.

- If you want to include "comment lines" in the knowledge base (i.e., lines which should be ignored by the inference engine), each line must begin with an exclamation mark (!). Without the exclamation mark, syntax errors will result.

We suggest using upper case letters for VP-Expert keywords and using indentation to make the structure of the rules and the knowlege base easy to comprehend.

Optional Formatting

The following can be formatted as you like:

- Letter case. *VP-Expert* does not distinguish between upper and lower case letters.

- Carriage returns.

- Spacing and indentation. These have no influence and can be used in any way.

- Sequence of rules, statements, and ACTIONS block. Although sequence does affect the path of the inference engine during a consultation, rules can be listed in any order.

Refining the MYBASE Knowledge Base

For complete information about all VP-Expert menus and menu commands, see Chapter 8.

To refine and expand the knowledge base created in Chapter 3, follow these instructions:

1. To start *VP-Expert,* at the system prompt, type **VPX** and press *ENTER.* This takes you to the *VP-Expert* opening screen and Main Menu.

2. Select the Edit command at this menu.

Pressing the right arrow key scrolls past the right margin to display additional ready-made files.

   The file names shown on the bottom of the opening screen represent ready-made knowledge base files that are included on the *VP-Expert* disk. MYBASE also appears on the files list if you followed the exercise in Chapter 3.

   The tutorial exercises in this chapter refine and expand the MYBASE knowledge base. You do not have to do every exercise (although it is recommended). The ready-made files give you the option of starting any exercise with an up-to-date knowledge base. For example, ABASE.KBS can be used in the first exercise if you did not perform the exercise in Chapter 3.

3. In response to the prompt asking for the name of the knowledge base to use, use the arrow keys to move the lightbar to MYBASE and press *ENTER.* (To use the ready-made version, choose ABASE instead.)

This presents the MYBASE knowledge base created in Chapter 3.

```
ACTIONS
        FIND The_Cheese;


RULE 0
IF      Course=Appetizer AND
        Consistency=Soft
THEN
        The_Cheese=Montrachet;

RULE 1
IF      Course=Appetizer AND
        Consistency=Firm
THEN
        The_Cheese=Stilton;

RULE 2
IF      Course=Dessert AND
        Consistency=Soft
THEN
        The_Cheese=Camembert;

RULE 3
IF      Course=Dessert AND
        Consistency=Firm
THEN
        The_Cheese=Italian_Fontina;

ASK Course: "What is the value of Course?";
CHOICES Course: Appetizer,Dessert;

ASK Consistency: "What is the value of Consistency?";
CHOICES Consistency: Soft,Firm;
```

VP-Expert

*For complete
documentation of the
VP-Expert Editor, see
Appendix A.*

*The VP-Expert Editor's
automatic "word wrap"
in document ON mode
(press F9) creates line
breaks (if necessary)
when ASK text appears
during a consultation. To
override automatic
"wrapping," you can
force line breaks with
hard carriage returns.*

4. Look at the ASK statements in this "induced" knowledge base. Induce has used the generic question, "What is the value of ___?"

Using the editing commands shown in Chapter 3, edit the knowledge base to replace the existing ASK statements with more specific questions:

```
ASK Course : "With what course will you be serving
cheese?";
```

```
ASK Consistency : "What consistency of cheese would
you prefer?";
```

If you like, you can also make cosmetic changes. We recommend you change spacing slightly to make the knowledge base easier to read, as shown in the example that follows. (Note that we've also edited our knowledge base to start with RULE 1 instead of RULE 0.)

Here is the new knowledge base:

```
ACTIONS
        FIND The_Cheese;

RULE 1
IF      Course = Appetizer AND
        Consistency = Soft
THEN
        The_Cheese = Montrachet;

RULE 2
IF      Course = Appetizer AND
        Consistency = Firm
THEN
        The_Cheese = Stilton;

RULE 3
IF      Course = Dessert AND
        Consistency = Soft
THEN
        The_Cheese = Camembert;
```

```
RULE 4
IF      Course = Dessert AND
        Consistency = Firm
THEN
        The_Cheese = Italian_Fontina;

ASK Course : "With what course will you be serving cheese?";

CHOICES Course : Appetizer, Dessert;

ASK Consistency : "What consistency of cheese would you prefer?";

CHOICES Consistency : Soft, Firm;
```

5. Once all the changes to the knowledge base have been made, check it carefully. Errors prevent you from running a consultation.

   The following check-list will help you find some common mistakes.

Knowledge Base Check-List

- Do the ACTIONS block, each rule, and each statement end with a semicolon? Are there any additional semicolons out of place? The only place—besides the end of a rule, statement, or ACTIONS block—that a semicolon can be used, is *inside* the double quotes that surround display text, (e.g., the text in an ASK statement, DISPLAY clause, etc.).
- Are all *VP-Expert* keywords spelled correctly?
- Have you made sure there are no illegal characters in rule labels, variable names, or values?
- Have you used any *VP-Expert* keywords as variable names?

---

6. Once the knowledge base is checked, save it by pressing *ALT-F6*. At the prompt "Save as "mybase.kbs" (Y or N)?," type **Y**.

Running a Consultation

Having edited the MYBASE knowledge base, conduct a consultation to see if it works.

To use the ready-made knowledge base, load ABASE1.

1. To start the consultation, select Consult from the Main Menu.

   VP-Expert loads the knowledge base and checks its syntax. If there are any mistakes, you will see a message like this:

   ```
   Missing ';'
   (Press any key to go on)
   Error in line 20
   ```

See Appendix D for a complete list of VP-Expert error messages.

   This particular message would indicate that line 20 of the knowledge base is missing a semicolon. If you get such a message, press any key. You will return to the knowledge base in the Editor, and the cursor will be placed on the offending line. If you do not see any problem with the line the cursor is on, look again at the Knowledge Base Check-List to see if that helps.

   Note: VP-Expert can only guess which line contains an error. For example, if you omit a semicolon at the end of a rule, VP-Expert may assume that the rule continues past where it should end, and not recognize the mistake until it finds a semicolon several lines later. If VP-Expert reports an error in a line that looks all right, check previous lines for errors.

If you typed the knowledge base correctly, the three consultation windows appear and the message "File loaded" is displayed.

The Consultation Windows

As you can see, the screen is divided into three sections:

- The large top window, called the *consultation window*, is where questions and other display text appear.

- The lower left-hand window displays the rules as they are being executed. This is referred to as the *rules window*.

- The lower right-hand window is called the *results window*. This is where *VP-Expert* displays current values as they are determined by the inference engine.

The lower two windows are especially useful when creating or debugging a knowledge base, because they give a "behind the scenes" look at the path and intermediate conclusions of the inference engine during a consultation. For end user consultations, it's usually preferable to eliminate these windows. As you'll see in the final exercise of this chapter, this is accomplished by including the RUNTIME statement in the knowledge base.

In addition to the three windows, another menu—the Consult Menu—appears at the bottom of the screen:

```
1Help      2Go      3WhatIf   4Variable 5Rule      6Set      7Quit
Help the user
```

The Go command on this menu starts the consultation.

2. Choose Go to proceed with the consultation. When a question accompanied by a menu of choices appears, move the lightbar to the option you want and press *ENTER*. This places a triangle next to your choice. To finalize the selection and move on, press *END*. (To change a selection before pressing *END*, press the *DEL* key.)

When the consultation is finished, your screen looks something like this (this sample results from a consultation in which *Dessert* and *Firm* were chosen at the prompts):

```
With what course will you be serving cheese?
Appetizer              Dessert ◄

What consistency of cheese would you prefer?
Soft                   Firm ◄




Finding Consistency            Course = Dessert CNF 100
Testing 3
                               Consistency = Firm CNF 100
RULE 3 IF
Course = Dessert AND           The_Cheese = Italian_Fontina CNF 100
Consistency = Firm
THEN
The_Cheese = Italian_Fontina


1Help      2Go      3WhatIf    4Variable 5Rule      6Set       7Quit
Help the user
```

Notice that the conclusion of the consultation appears only in the lower right window, in the crude form, *The_Cheese = Italian_Fontina CNF 100*. To show a conclusion message in the consultation window, you need to add a DISPLAY clause to the knowledge base.

Remember, a rule is said to "pass" when its premise is determined to be true during a consultation.

Remember to move the semicolon to the new rule end whenever you add to the end of a rule, or a syntax error will result.

The DISPLAY Clause

The DISPLAY clause can be used in the ACTIONS block or in rules.

When added to a rule, a DISPLAY clause displays a given message if (and when) the rule passes. For example, we could add a clause like this to RULE 1:

```
RULE 1
IF       Course = Appetizer AND
         Consistency = Soft
THEN

         The_Cheese = Montrachet
         DISPLAY "The most appropriate cheese for this
course is Montrachet.";
```

If RULE 1 passed, the message, "The most appropriate cheese for this course is Montrachet," would be displayed in the consultation window.

> *Note: Hard carriage returns can be used to indicate line breaks in display text. For example, if you wanted the above DISPLAY clause text to appear on two lines and break at a particular word during the consultation, you would press ENTER where the first line should end. In document ON mode the VP-Expert Editor wraps the lines automatically.*

A similar DISPLAY clause at the end of each rule in our knowledge base would cause a conclusion message to appear for every possible outcome of the consultation. However, a simpler way of accomplishing the same thing is to place a single DISPLAY clause in the ACTIONS block.

The ACTIONS block of a knowledge base is like a small program. It defines an ordered list of tasks which must be accomplished during the course of a consultation.

Currently, the only task is to find a value for the goal variable *The_Cheese*. Once accomplished, the consultation is complete. However, we can add an additional task. By adding a DISPLAY clause to the ACTIONS block, we can have *VP-Expert* display a message reporting the value of the goal variable once it is found.

This clause would do the trick:

```
DISPLAY "The most appropriate cheese for this course is
{#The_Cheese}.";
```

> *Note: The variable name in curly brackets does not appear in the message during a consultation. {#The_Cheese} indicates that the value of the variable The_Cheese should be displayed. The # sign (which is optional) reports the confidence factor along with the value.*

Adding the DISPLAY Clause to the ACTIONS Block

To start this tutorial from the Main Menu, choose Edit, and then choose MYBASE.KBS. To use the ready-made knowledge base, load ABASE1.

1. If you have been following the tutorial, the Consult Menu is displayed on screen. Type **Q** to choose Quit at this menu, then type **E** to enter the editor.

   The editor will automatically load the MYBASE knowledge base file.

Use CTRL-ENTER to add blank lines to the knowledge base.

2. Edit the ACTIONS block of the knowledge base to match the following:

```
ACTIONS
        FIND The_Cheese
        DISPLAY "The most appropriate cheese for
this course is {#The_Cheese}.";
```

3. Check your work carefully. Make sure that you include the double quotes surrounding the display text, and that you move the semicolon from the original end of the ACTIONS block to the new end.

4. Before saving the knowledge base, make the consultation more interesting by adding another DISPLAY clause to the ACTIONS block. This one will precede the FIND clause, and, therefore, display a message *before* the inference engine even begins its search. Remember, tasks defined in the ACTIONS block are performed in the order in which they appear in the ACTIONS block.

Edit the ACTIONS block to match this:

```
ACTIONS
        DISPLAY "Welcome to the charming world of cheese!
Press any key to begin the consultation.~"
        FIND The_Cheese
        DISPLAY "The most appropriate cheese for this course is {#The_Cheese}.";
```

Notice the ~ symbol in the new clause. When this symbol occurs in *VP-Expert* DISPLAY text, it causes the program to pause until the user presses any key.

VP-Expert

Your new knowledge base should look like this:

```
ACTIONS
        DISPLAY "Welcome to the charming world of cheese!
Press any key to begin the consultation.~"
        FIND The_Cheese
        DISPLAY "The most appropriate cheese for this course is {#The_Cheese}.";

RULE 1
IF      Course = Appetizer AND
        Consistency = Soft
THEN
        The_Cheese = Montrachet;

RULE 2
IF      Course = Appetizer AND
        Consistency = Firm
THEN
        The_Cheese = Stilton;

RULE 3
IF      Course = Dessert AND
        Consistency = Soft
THEN
        The_Cheese = Camembert;

RULE 4
IF      Course = Dessert AND
        Consistency = Firm
THEN
        The_Cheese = Italian_Fontina;

ASK Course : "With what course will you be serving cheese?";

CHOICES Course : Appetizer, Dessert;

ASK Consistency : "What consistency of cheese would you prefer?";

CHOICES Consistency : Soft, Firm;
```

5. Check for errors; then press *ALT-F6* and type **Y** to save the new knowledge base file.

6. To see if the new knowledge base works, give the commands Consult and Go to begin a consultation. If a syntax error is reported, return to the Editor and correct the error.

Otherwise, the following screen appears:

```
Welcome to the charming world of cheese!
Press any key to begin the consultation.
```

7. Press any key, then proceed with the consultation.

The following screen shows the results of a consultation in which *Dessert* and *Soft* were chosen at the question prompts.

Note the conclusion message at the bottom of the consultation window.

```
Welcome to the charming world of cheese!
Press any key to begin the consultation.
With what course will you be serving cheese?
Appetizer              Dessert ◀

What consistency of cheese would you prefer?
Soft ◀                    Firm

The most appropriate cheese for this course is Camembert CNF 100.
```

```
Testing 3                          Course = Dessert CNF 100

RULE 3 IF                          Consistency = Soft CNF 100
Course = Dessert AND
Consistency = Soft                 The_Cheese = Camembert CNF 100
THEN
The_Cheese = Camembert CNF 100

Finding Consistency
```

```
1Help      2Go      3WhatIf   4Variable 5Rule      6Set       7Quit
Help the user
```

Note: VP-Expert also has a PDISPLAY clause that prints a message on your printer and a PRINTON clause that causes the DISPLAY clause to print the message as well as display it on screen. See PDISPLAY and PRINTON in Chapter 9 for details.

The ELSE Keyword

For some applications, the ELSE keyword is a handy device for simplifying a knowledge base. It can be used to combine two or more rules into one.

Look at the following rules:

```
RULE 1X
IF      Course = Dessert
THEN    The_Cheese = Camembert;

RULE 2X
IF      Course = Appetizer
THEN    The_Cheese = Brie;
```

According to these rules, if the *Course* is *Dessert*, then *The_Cheese* is *Camembert*; if the *Course* is *Appetizer*, *The_Cheese* is *Brie*.

Now look at this rule:

```
RULE 3X
IF      Course = Dessert
THEN    The_Cheese = Camembert
ELSE    The_Cheese = Brie;
```

This rule says, "If the *Course* is *Dessert*, then *The_Cheese* is *Camembert*—otherwise, *The_Cheese* is *Brie*." Thus, the work of two or more rules can be accomplished in a single rule.

The ELSE keyword can be useful, but it represents a "universal else." That is to say, if *Course* is *Dessert*, then *The_Cheese* is *Camembert*; but whatever else *Course* may be, *The_Cheese* will be *Brie*. If you use ELSE, make sure you clearly understand its effects. Otherwise, you may get unexpected results.

Developing the Knowledge Base Further

The MYBASE knowledge base is still fairly simple. To expand it a bit more, follow the next exercise. The new knowledge base you'll create will have an additional menu option, *Salad*, and a PLURAL statement, allowing you to choose more than one *Course* during a consultation.

See ''VP-Expert Variables'' in Chapter 7 for important distinctions between plural and single-valued variables.

The PLURAL Statement

The PLURAL statement is used in a knowledge base to define variables as ''plural,'' meaning they can be assigned more than one value during a consultation. Chapter 2 describes how the PLURAL statement affects the path of the inference engine during a consultation.

The statement is written in the following form.

```
PLURAL: variable1, variable2,...;
```

A single PLURAL statement can name up to ten variables, and a knowledge base can contain any number of PLURAL statements.

Note that this statement, like all *VP-Expert* statements, must end in a semicolon.

---

1. To expand the MYBASE knowledge base, enter the Editor and edit your knowledge base to match the following (to use the ready-made version, load ABASE2):

   Note that changes made to the knowledge base are highlighted in bold.

```
ACTIONS
        DISPLAY "Welcome to the charming world of cheese!
Press any key to begin the consultation.~"
        FIND The_Cheese
        DISPLAY "The most appropriate cheese for this course is {#The_Cheese}.";

RULE 1
IF      Course = Appetizer OR
        Course = Salad AND
        Course <> Dessert AND
        Consistency = Soft
THEN
        The_Cheese = Montrachet;

RULE 2
IF      Course = Appetizer OR
        Course = Salad AND
        Course <> Dessert AND
        Consistency = Firm
THEN
        The_Cheese = Stilton;

RULE 3
IF      Course = Dessert AND
        Course = Appetizer OR
        Course = Salad AND
        Consistency = Soft
THEN
        The_Cheese = Brie;

RULE 4
IF      Course = Dessert AND
        Course = Appetizer OR
        Course = Salad AND
        Consistency = Firm
THEN
        The_Cheese = Gouda;
```

4.19 DEVELOPING THE KNOWLEDGE BASE

```
RULE 5
IF       Course = Dessert AND
         Course <> Appetizer AND
         Course <> Salad AND
         Consistency = Soft
THEN
         The_Cheese = Camembert;


RULE 6
IF       Course = Dessert AND
         Course <> Appetizer AND
         Course <> Salad AND
         Consistency = Firm
THEN
         The_Cheese = Italian_Fontina;


ASK Course : "With what course will you be serving cheese?";

CHOICES Course : Appetizer, Salad, Dessert;

ASK Consistency : "What consistency of cheese would you prefer?";

CHOICES Consistency : Soft, Firm;

PLURAL : Course;
```

Relational operators that can be used in the premise of a rule include: =,>,<,>=,<=, and <>. Only the = sign can be used in rule conclusions.

Important things to note about this new knowledge base are:

- The first CHOICES statement now has three parameters to the right of the colon: *Appetizer*, *Salad*, and *Dessert*. *Salad* will now appear in the menu following the question, "With what course will you be serving cheese?"

- A PLURAL statement names *Course* as a plural variable.

- Rules have been changed and added to contain the new course item and accommodate *Course* as a plural variable.

- The relational operator <> (not equal) has been introduced.

- The logical operator OR has also been introduced. See the following section, "Using Logical Operators," for a detailed explanation of how AND/OR logic works.

2. Check your knowledge base carefully for errors; then save it and return to the Main Menu.

Using Logical Operators

The NOT logical operator does not exist in VP-Expert. For the same results, use AND followed by the <> (not equal) relational operator.

AND and OR are referred to as logical or "Boolean" operators. These are used in the rule premises to create complex conditions.

AND is like the English "and." Used in the premise of a rule, it indicates that the condition that follows must also be true for the rule to pass.

Look at RULE 5:

```
RULE 5
IF      Course = Dessert AND
        Course <> Appetizer AND
        Course <> Salad AND
        Consistency = Soft
THEN
        The_Cheese = Camembert;
```

This rule says, "IF the *Course* is *Dessert*, AND it is not *Appetizer*, AND it is not *Salad*, AND the *Consistency* is *Soft*, THEN *The_Cheese* is *Camembert*." In other words, *The_Cheese* will be *Camembert* if all of the stated conditions are true.

OR corresponds with the English expression "or." In order for a rule containing two conditions joined by OR to pass, one or the other or both conditions must be true. When both AND and OR are used in a rule, ORs take precedence over ANDs. It's as though parentheses surround the expressions connected by OR. RULE 3 provides a good example of a complex premise using both AND and OR.

```
RULE 3
IF      Course = Dessert AND
        Course = Appetizer OR
        Course = Salad AND
        Consistency = Soft
THEN
        The_Cheese = Brie;
```

4.21 DEVELOPING THE KNOWLEDGE BASE

This rule says, "IF the *Course* is *Dessert*, AND the *Course* is *Appetizer* OR *Salad*, AND the *Consistency* is *Soft*, THEN *The_Cheese* will be *Brie*." You cannot interpret the above rule to mean, "If the course is dessert and appetizer, or the course is salad..."

It is important to thoroughly understand the way AND/OR logic works. Look at the following complex example:

Note that in order for this rule to be valid, Main_Course would have to be a plural variable.

```
RULE 12
IF        Main_Course = Fish OR
          Main_Course = Poultry AND
          Main_Course = Beef OR
          Main_Course = Lamb AND
          Main_Course = Eggplant
THEN
          The_Cheese = Parmesan;
```

The premise would work as though it was written like this:

```
(Fish OR Poultry)  AND  (Beef OR Lamb)  AND Eggplant
```

For the rule to pass, *Main_Course* must equal one or both of the first two choices (*Fish, Poultry*), AND one or both of the next two choices (*Beef, Lamb*) AND *Eggplant*.

To use the ready-made knowledge base, load ABASE3.

See Chapter 7 for complete information about VP-Expert confidence factors.

Trying the New Knowledge Base

1. To test the new knowledge base, choose Consult and then Go to start a consultation. If an error is reported, return to the Editor to make the correction.

Entering Confidence Factors at ASK Prompts

Whenever you respond to a question accompanied by a menu during a consultation, you have the option of entering a number which reflects your level of confidence that a particular response is valid. A confidence factor of 80 represents 80% confidence, 70, 70% confidence, and so on. If no confidence factor is indicated, CNF 100 is assumed.

To enter a confidence factor at a question prompt, move the lightbar to the menu option, press the *HOME* key, type a number between 0 and 100, and press *ENTER*. Pressing *END*, as always, finalizes the selection.

Note: Entering a confidence factor of less than 50 at a prompt, in effect, negates the choice. This is due to a default "truth threshold," which requires values in rule conditions to have confidence factors of 50 or more in order for the conditions to be considered "true." See the TRUTHTHRESH clause in Chapter 9 and "Confidence Factors" in Chapter 7 for more details (including information about changing the default "truth threshold," and how multiple confidence factors are combined and computed).

---

2. When the first question prompt appears, choose more than one course item. Do so by pressing *ENTER* with the lightbar over each item you want. Press *END* when all choices have been made.

3. Proceed with the consultation.

The following screen is the result of a consultation in which *Dessert* (CNF 80) and *Salad* (CNF 50) were chosen as the *Courses*, and *Firm* was the indicated *Consistency*.

```
Welcome to the charming world of cheese!
Press any key to begin the consultation.
With what course will you be serving cheese?
Appetizer              Salad 50 ◀              Dessert 80 ◀

What consistency of cheese would you prefer?
Soft                   Firm ◀

The most appropriate cheese for this course is Gouda CNF 50.
```

```
Testing 4                              Course = Salad CNF 50

RULE 4 IF
Course = Dessert AND                   Course = Dessert CNF 80
Course = Appetizer OR
Course = Salad AND                     Consistency = Firm CNF 100
Consistency = Firm
THEN                                   The_Cheese = Gouda CNF 50
The_Cheese = Gouda CNF 100
```

```
1Help      2Go      3WhatIf   4Variable 5Rule      6Set      7Quit
Help the user
```

Adding Another Variable

To further expand the MYBASE knowledge base, add another variable to the knowledge base—*Preference*. Allow for a *Mild*, *Flavorful*, or *Pungent* taste.

This requires editing and adding some rules, plus adding new ASK and CHOICES statements to the knowledge base.

The number of rules in the knowledge base doubles as a result of introducing this new variable. However, block commands in the editor can minimize the amount of typing involved, and also the probability of introducing errors into the knowledge base.

VP-Expert Block Commands

Use the following commands to copy blocks in the *VP-Expert* Editor:

CTRL-F3	Start block.
CTRL-F4	End block.
CTRL-F7	Copy block.
CTRL-F5	Cancel block.

Follow these instructions to add the variable *Preference* to the MYBASE knowledge base.

To use the ready-made knowledge base for this exercise, load ABASE3.

1. With the MYBASE knowledge base loaded, enter the Editor.

   Your knowledge base should look like this:

```
ACTIONS
        DISPLAY "Welcome to the charming world of cheese!
Press any key to begin the consultation.~"
        FIND The_Cheese
        DISPLAY "The most appropriate cheese for this course is {#The_Cheese}.";


RULE 1
IF      Course = Appetizer OR
        Course = Salad AND
        Course <> Dessert AND
        Consistency = Soft
THEN

        The_Cheese = Montrachet;


RULE 2
IF      Course = Appetizer OR
        Course = Salad AND
        Course <> Dessert AND
        Consistency = Firm
THEN

        The_Cheese = Stilton;
```

```
RULE 3
IF      Course = Dessert AND
        Course = Appetizer OR
        Course = Salad AND
        Consistency = Soft
THEN
        The_Cheese = Brie;

RULE 4
IF      Course = Dessert AND
        Course = Appetizer OR
        Course = Salad AND
        Consistency = Firm
THEN
        The_Cheese = Gouda;

RULE 5
IF      Course = Dessert AND
        Course <> Appetizer OR
        Course <> Salad AND
        Consistency = Soft
THEN
        The_Cheese = Camembert;

RULE 6
IF      Course = Dessert AND
        Course <> Appetizer OR
        Course <> Salad AND
        Consistency = Firm
THEN
        The_Cheese = Italian_Fontina;

ASK Course : "With what course will you be serving cheese?";

CHOICES Course : Appetizer, Salad, Dessert;

ASK Consistency : "What consistency of cheese would you prefer?";

CHOICES Consistency : Soft, Firm;

PLURAL : Course;
```

2. Move the cursor to the end of the knowledge base, and add the following ASK statement:

```
ASK Preference : "What is your preference in
cheese?";
```

3. Now add this CHOICES statement:

```
CHOICES Preference : Mild, Flavorful, Pungent;
```

4. RULE 1 currently looks like this:

```
RULE 1
IF      Course = Appetizer OR
        Course = Salad AND
        Course <> Dessert AND
        Consistency = Soft
THEN
        The_Cheese = Montrachet;
```

Edit it to look like this:
(Changes are shown in bold.)

```
RULE 1
IF      Course = Appetizer AND
        Course = Salad OR
        Course <> Dessert AND
        Preference = Mild OR
        Preference = Flavorful AND
        Consistency = Soft
THEN
        The_Cheese = Montrachet;
```

Pressing the CTRL key in the Editor displays the CTRL-function key block commands along the bottom of the screen.

5. Use *CTRL-ENTER* to add some blank lines below RULE 1. Then copy RULE 1 immediately below itself using the block commands *CTRL-F3* (start block), *CTRL-F4* (end block), *CTRL-F7* (copy block), and *CTRL-F5* (cancel block).

Next, edit the copied rule to match the following:

```
RULE 1A
IF      Course = Appetizer OR
        Course = Salad AND
        Course <> Dessert AND
        Preference = Pungent AND
        Consistency = Soft
THEN
        The_Cheese = Gorgonzola;
```

6. By the same process, edit the remainder of the knowledge base to match the following:

```
RULE 2
IF      Course = Appetizer OR
        Course = Salad AND
        Course <> Dessert AND
        Preference = Mild OR
        Preference = Flavorful AND
        Consistency = Firm
THEN
        The_Cheese = Stilton;


RULE 2A
IF      Course = Appetizer OR
        Course = Salad AND
        Course <> Dessert AND
        Preference = Pungent AND
        Consistency = Firm
THEN
        The_Cheese = Kasseri;


RULE 3
IF      Course = Dessert AND
        Course = Appetizer OR
        Course = Salad AND
        Preference = Mild OR
        Preference = Flavorful AND
        Consistency = Soft
THEN
        The_Cheese = Brie;


RULE 3A
IF      Course = Dessert AND
        Course = Appetizer OR
        Course = Salad AND
        Preference = Pungent AND
        Consistency = Soft
THEN
        The_Cheese = Chevres;
```

```
RULE 4
IF      Course = Dessert AND
        Course = Appetizer OR
        Course = Salad AND
        Preference = Mild OR
        Preference = Flavorful AND
        Consistency = Firm
THEN
        The_Cheese = Gouda;


RULE 4A
IF      Course = Dessert AND
        Course = Appetizer OR
        Course = Salad AND
        Preference = Pungent AND
        Consistency = Firm
THEN
        The_Cheese = Asiago;


RULE 5
IF      Course = Dessert AND
        Course <> Appetizer AND
        Course <> Salad AND
        Preference = Mild OR
        Preference = Flavorful AND
        Consistency = Soft
THEN
        The_Cheese = Camembert;


RULE 5A
IF      Course = Dessert AND
        Course <> Appetizer AND
        Course <> Salad AND
        Preference = Pungent AND
        Consistency = Soft
THEN
        The_Cheese = Tallegio;
```

4.29 DEVELOPING THE KNOWLEDGE BASE

```
RULE 6
IF      Course = Dessert AND
        Course <> Appetizer AND
        Course <> Salad AND
        Preference = Mild OR
        Preference = Flavorful AND
        Consistency = Firm
THEN
        The_Cheese = Italian_Fontina;

RULE 6A
IF      Course = Dessert AND
        Course <> Appetizer AND
        Course <> Salad AND
        Preference = Pungent AND
        Consistency = Firm
THEN
        The_Cheese = Appenzeller;

ASK Course : "With what course will you be serving cheese?";

CHOICES Course : Appetizer, Salad, Dessert;

ASK Consistency : "What consistency of cheese would you prefer?";

CHOICES Consistency : Soft, Firm;

PLURAL : Course;

ASK Preference : "What is your preference in cheese?";

CHOICES Preference : Mild, Flavorful, Pungent;
```

7. Check the knowledge base carefully; then save it with *ALT-F6*.

8. Perform a consultation to see if the knowledge base works. If it does not, go back and make corrections.

The Why? and How? Commands

If you followed the exercises in Chapter 1, you used the Why? and How? commands to find out *why* a question was asked during a consultation and *how* a particular value was found.

The text that appeared in response to Why? and How? queries in Chapter 1 came from BECAUSE text in the rules of the knowledge base. However, you do not *have* to add BECAUSE text to your knowledge base in order to use the Why? and How? commands. The next exercises will explain.

Using Why?

1. Start a consultation using the MYBASE knowledge base. (To use a ready-made knowledge base, load ABASE4.)

2. When the prompt asks you for a course selection, type a slash (/) to display the Go Menu at the bottom of the screen.

```
Welcome to the charming world of cheese!
Press any key to begin the consultation.
With what course will you be serving cheese?
Appetizer                Salad                    Dessert




Course = Appetizer OR
Course = Salad AND
Course <> Dessert AND
Preference = Mild OR
Preference = Flavorful AND
Consistency = Soft
THEN
The_Cheese = Montrachet CNF 100

Finding Course

1Help      2How?      3Why?      4Slow      5Fast      6Quit
 Help the user
```

3. Type **W** (for Why?) to find out why this question is being asked.

   Since there is no BECAUSE text to provide an explanation, the rule that caused the question to be asked is displayed. (Seeing the rule shows you that in order to find a value for *The_Cheese*, a value for *Course* is needed.)

```
Welcome to the charming world of cheese!
Press any key to begin the consultation.
With what course will you be serving cheese?
Appetizer                    Salad                      Dessert




     Course = Salad AND
     Course <> Dessert AND
     Preference = Mild OR
     Preference = Flavorful AND
     Consistency = Soft
     THEN
     The_Cheese = Montrachet CNF 100

     (Press Any Key to Continue)



Finding Course
```

Notice that only part of the rule appears at the center of the screen. The rule is too long to fit in the window. If you want to read the entire rule, use the the Slow command on the Go Menu. Follow the next steps to try it.

4. Press any key. Then type /S to choose Slow from the Go Menu.

5. Now at the question about *Course*, type /W. This time, with slowed execution, you can read the entire rule, preceded by the phrase, "The question is being asked because:".

   Note: Give the Slow command again (and again, if necessary) if your system is not sufficiently slowed down. Repeating the command has a cumulative effect.

6. Finish the consultation. If you want, you can restore normal execution speed by typing a slash and choosing Fast from the Go Menu.

Using How?

The How? command tells you *how* a value was assigned to a given variable. If the value was assigned by the user at a prompt, a response like the one on this screen appears:

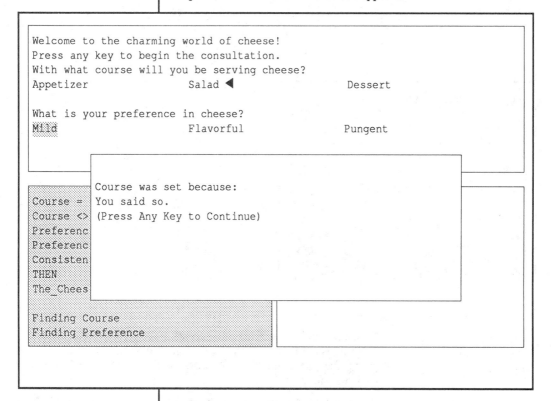

```
Welcome to the charming world of cheese!
Press any key to begin the consultation.
With what course will you be serving cheese?
Appetizer              Salad ◄                    Dessert

What is your preference in cheese?
Mild                   Flavorful                  Pungent
```

```
                Course was set because:
Course =        You said so.
Course <>       (Press Any Key to Continue)
Preferenc
Preferenc
Consisten
THEN
The_Chees


Finding Course
Finding Preference
```

If the value was assigned in a rule, the rule which assigned the value is shown.

In our knowledge base, all variables except the goal variable are assigned values at prompts. All How? queries, therefore, result in a screen like the one shown above. (How? is only available *during* a consultation. In this example, you cannot use How? to find out how *The_Cheese* got its value; once *The_Cheese* has been assigned a value, the consultation is over.)

Run another consultation to see how the How? command works.

Adding BECAUSE to the Knowledge Base

If you want to have explanatory text appear in response to the Why? and How? commands during a consultation, add BECAUSE text to your rules.

BECAUSE text is supplied in this form:

```
BECAUSE "text";
```

Since the BECAUSE text must come at the end of a rule, it must be followed by a semicolon.

Follow this exercise to add BECAUSE text to the MYBASE knowledge base.

1. Load MYBASE and enter the Editor. (Load ABASE4 to use the ready-made knowledge base.)

2. Edit the rules of the knowledge base to match the following rules and note:

   ■ All the BECAUSE text is the same, so you can write it once (for RULE 1), and use block commands to copy the text to the end of all subsequent rules. Use *CTRL-F3* to start, *CTRL-F4* at the block's end, *CTRL-F7* to copy, and *CTRL-F5* to cancel the block.

   ■ Remember to end each expanded rule with a semicolon and to remove the old semicolons.

```
RULE 1
IF       Course = Appetizer OR
         Course = Salad AND
         Course <> Dessert AND
         Preference = Mild OR
         Preference = Flavorful AND
         Consistency = Soft
THEN
         The_Cheese = Montrachet
         BECAUSE "Course, preference in taste, and consistency are needed
to determine the best cheese to serve.";
```

```
RULE 1A
IF      Course = Appetizer OR
        Course = Salad AND
        Course <> Dessert AND
        Preference = Pungent AND
        Consistency = Soft
THEN
        The_Cheese = Gorgonzola
```
**BECAUSE "Course, preference in taste, and consistency are needed
to determine the best cheese to serve.";**

```
RULE 2
IF      Course = Appetizer OR
        Course = Salad AND
        Course <> Dessert AND
        Preference = Mild OR
        Preference = Flavorful AND
        Consistency = Firm
THEN
        The_Cheese = Stilton
```
**BECAUSE "Course, preference in taste, and consistency are needed
to determine the best cheese to serve.";**

```
RULE 2A
IF      Course = Appetizer OR
        Course = Salad AND
        Course <> Dessert AND
        Preference = Pungent AND
        Consistency = Firm
THEN
        The_Cheese = Kasseri
```
**BECAUSE "Course, preference in taste, and consistency are needed
to determine the best cheese to serve.";**

```
RULE 3
IF      Course = Dessert AND
        Course = Appetizer OR
        Course = Salad AND
        Preference = Mild OR
        Preference = Flavorful AND
        Consistency = Soft
THEN
        The_Cheese = Brie
        BECAUSE "Course, preference in taste, and consistency are needed
to determine the best cheese to serve.";


RULE 3A
IF      Course = Dessert AND
        Course = Appetizer OR
        Course = Salad AND
        Preference = Pungent AND
        Consistency = Soft
THEN
        The_Cheese = Chevres
        BECAUSE "Course, preference in taste, and consistency are needed
to determine the best cheese to serve.";


RULE 4
IF      Course = Dessert AND
        Course = Appetizer OR
        Course = Salad AND
        Preference = Mild OR
        Preference = Flavorful AND
        Consistency = Firm
THEN
        The_Cheese = Gouda
        BECAUSE "Course, preference in taste, and consistency are needed
to determine the best cheese to serve.";
```

```
RULE 4A
IF      Course = Dessert AND
        Course = Appetizer OR
        Course = Salad AND
        Preference = Pungent AND
        Consistency = Firm
THEN
        The_Cheese = Asiago
        BECAUSE "Course, preference in taste, and consistency are needed
to determine the best cheese to serve.";


RULE 5
IF      Course = Dessert AND
        Course <> Appetizer AND
        Course <> Salad AND
        Preference = Mild OR
        Preference = Flavorful AND
        Consistency = Soft
THEN
        The_Cheese = Camembert
        BECAUSE "Course, preference in taste, and consistency are needed
to determine the best cheese to serve.";


RULE 5A
IF      Course = Dessert AND
        Course <> Appetizer AND
        Course <> Salad AND
        Preference = Pungent AND
        Consistency = Soft
THEN
        The_Cheese = Tallegio
        BECAUSE "Course, preference in taste, and consistency are needed
to determine the best cheese to serve.";
```

```
RULE 6
IF      Course = Dessert AND
        Course <> Appetizer AND
        Course <> Salad AND
        Preference = Mild OR
        Preference = Flavorful AND
        Consistency = Firm
THEN
        The_Cheese = Italian_Fontina
```
BECAUSE "Course, preference in taste, and consistency are needed to determine the best cheese to serve.";

```
RULE 6A
IF      Course = Dessert AND
        Course <> Appetizer AND
        Course <> Salad AND
        Preference = Pungent AND
        Consistency = Firm
THEN
        The_Cheese = Appenzeller
```
BECAUSE "Course, preference in taste, and consistency are needed to determine the best cheese to serve.";

3. When finished, check the file and save it.

Now when you ask Why? at a prompt during a consultation, a screen like this appears:

```
Welcome to the charming world of cheese!
Press any key to begin the consultation.
With what course will you be serving cheese?
Appetizer                Salad                    Dessert




The question is being asked because:
Course, preference in taste, and consistency are needed to determine the
best cheese to serve.
(Press Any Key to Continue)





Finding Course
```

4. Run a consultation and try it. (To run the ready-made knowledge base, load ABASE5.)

Creating a RUNTIME Consultation

The three-window consultation is useful for developing a working knowledge base. However, the *rules* and *results windows* are not necessary in an end-user or "runtime" consultation.

To dispense with the two lower windows during a consultation, add this simple statement anywhere in the knowledge base:

```
RUNTIME;
```

1. Add the RUNTIME statement to the MYBASE knowledge base (or load ABASE6, the ready-made knowledge base).

2. Save it and run a consultation. Instead of the three windows seen in previous consultations, a single consultation window appears:

```
Welcome to the charming world of cheese!
Press any key to begin the consultation.
With what course will you be serving cheese?
Appetizer ◀              Salad ◀                      Dessert◀

What is your preference in cheese?
Mild                     Flavorful                   Pungent ◀

What consistency of cheese would you prefer?
Soft ◀                   Firm

The most appropriate cheese for this course is Chevres CNF 100.




1Help       2Go      3WhatIf    4Variable 5Rule       6Set      7Quit
Help the user
```

Chapter Summary

In this chapter we expanded and edited a simple knowledge base created by induction.

■ First, we changed the ASK message from the Induce command's generic, "What is the value of ___?" to more appropriate text. We also changed the format of the knowledge base to make it more readable.

■ Next, we added a DISPLAY clause to the ACTIONS block that displays a conclusion message in the consultation window when the consultation is successfully completed. We also added another DISPLAY clause that displays a welcome message at the start of the consultation.

■ Then, we expanded the knowledge base. A PLURAL statement (PLURAL : *Course*;) was added to allow the user to choose more than one course item during a consultation. Rules were expanded to allow for a new course item, *Salad*. *Salad* was also added to the CHOICES statement, causing the value to appear on the menu accompanying the question, "With what course will you be serving cheese?"

■ Next, another variable, *Preference*, was introduced into the knowledge base. Rules were expanded and added to accommodate the new variable, and ASK and CHOICES statements for *Preference* were added.

■ BECAUSE text was then appended to the end of each rule. This provides explanatory text when the Why? command is given during a consultation.

BECAUSE text can also provide text for How? queries—but only when values are assigned in rules with BECAUSE text during a consultation. In our knowledge base, all values are assigned at ASK prompts—except the value of the goal variable, which is assigned at the end of, *not during*, the consultation.

■ Finally, the RUNTIME statement was added to the knowledge base to eliminate the *rules* and *results windows* from the screen during a consultation. This creates a "runtime" consultation appropriate for an end user.

Final Comments

If you followed all the exercises in this chapter, you have now completed a twelve-rule knowledge base, complete with complex rules, DISPLAY text, a PLURAL statement, BECAUSE text, and a RUNTIME statement. But you've by no means witnessed all of *VP-Expert's* important features. This section was meant to provide an easy introduction to developing a simple knowledge base. Much of *VP-Expert's* power is yet to come.

Part II of this manual discusses expanding the knowledge base to include database and worksheet files. Using such files as an "information base," *VP-Expert* can integrate large amounts of externally stored data into a consultation. Because *VP-Expert* can send as well as receive data from such files, *VP-Expert* can also be used as a "friendly" front end for adding and maintaining data.

Part III is a reference section. There you'll find detailed information about every *VP-Expert* clause, statement, function, and menu command. In addition, general topics like confidence factors, variables, and knowledge base anatomy are also discussed.

PART II

Expanding the Knowledge Base: Database and Worksheet Access

*T*his section of the manual shows you how to expand a knowledge base to include compatible database and worksheet files. Using induction with these files is also discussed.

5.2 DATABASE ACCESS

CHAPTER FIVE

Database Access

Before starting this chapter, we recommend you read sections on the MENU, GET, APPEND, PUT, and WHILEKNOWN clauses in Chapter 9. For more information about induction tables, see Chapter 3.

One of *VP-Expert's* most important and powerful features is its ability to interact with database files created using *VP-Info*, dBASE II, III, III+, or any work-alike database management system.

There are two primary ways that these database files can be used by *VP-Expert*. They can be used as "information bases," which expand the knowledge base to include data that can be accessed and altered during a *VP-Expert* consultation. They can also be used to create induction tables which, upon execution of the Induce command, are transformed into perfectly formatted, working knowledge base files. Both information bases and database induction tables are described in this chapter.

Database as Information Base

Expert systems frequently require a great amount of data that need periodic updating. Paperback Software's *Anthony Dias Blue Wines on Disk* wine advisor, for example, selects and recommends wines from among hundreds of varietals stored in a database. Suppose every wine required its own set of rules! And suppose that every time a wine needed to be added or subtracted, or a price changed, the rule base had to be modified. The task of creating and maintaining the knowledge base would be formidable. It's far more efficient to store the varying information in a database, and design the rule base to contain a single set of invariant rules. This way the rule base is kept to a manageable size, and it never (or rarely) has to change. Of course, for this to work, there has to be an effective means by which the data in the database and the rules of the rule base interact. *VP-Expert's* ability to employ this type of interaction is one of its greatest powers.

Using the GET clause, data can be retrieved from the fields of a database and assigned as values of knowledge base variables. The PUT and APPEND clauses allow data to be transferred in the opposite direction; values are copied *from* knowledge base variables *to* the fields of a database. The MENU clause makes it possible to display menus offering values extracted directly from specified database fields.

For information about how VP-Expert exchanges data with text files, see the SHIP and RECEIVE clauses in Chapter 9.

When a database is used in this fashion, it becomes an information base, and it is considered to be a part of the overall knowledge base. To distinguish between this expanded concept of knowledge base and the contents of the *VP-Expert* KBS file (previously referred to as the knowledge base), we use the term "rule base" to refer to the contents of the KBS file. This term is only used, however, when the knowledge base includes an information base, since in the absence of an information base, the rule base is, in fact, the knowledge base.

Using a Database as an Information Base

To explore the use of a database file as an information base, we've created a simple example. Look at the following information base.

	WINE	PRICE	RATING
00001	Burgundy	7.95	27
00002	Burgundy	9.95	53
00003	Burgundy	11.95	35
00004	Cabernet	12.95	96
00005	Cabernet	14.95	63
00006	Zinfandel	10.95	77
00007	Chablis	9.95	73
00008	Chablis	6.95	81
00009	Chablis	7.95	98
00010	Chablis	8.95	77
00011	Chablis	4.95	69
00012	Beaujolais	16.95	93
00013	Chardonnay	14.95	72
00014	Chardonnay	16.95	43
00015	Chardonnay	18.95	45
00016	Gewürztraminer	8.95	92
00017	Cabernet_Blanc	14.95	84
00018	Chenin_Blanc	6.95	77
00019	Chenin_Blanc	8.95	81
00020	Reisling	6.95	91
00021	Reisling	7.95	52
00022	Reisling	8.95	62

This file, named WINES.DBF, has 22 records. Its three fields are: WINE, PRICE, and RATING.

Here is a *VP-Expert* rule base that accesses the WINES.DBF information base.

```
ACTIONS
        MENU the_wine,ALL,wines,wine
        FIND the_wine
        WHILEKNOWN wine
          GET the_wine = wine,wines,ALL
          DISPLAY "Your choice, a {wine}, is priced at
${price}.
It has a rating of {rating}.~"
        END;

ASK the_wine: "For which wine do you want information?";
```

5.5 DATABASE ACCESS

In order to understand how this rule base interacts with the WINES.DBF information base, look at each clause of the rule base, in sequence.

The MENU Clause

The first clause in the ACTIONS block of the rule base is a MENU clause:

```
ACTIONS
        MENU the_wine,ALL,wines,wine
        *
        *
```

See the MENU clause and its associated system variable MENU_SIZE in Chapter 9 for more information about creating menus with the MENU clause.

The MENU clause is a particularly important feature of *VP-Expert*. Like the CHOICES statement, it creates a menu of options that accompanies a corresponding ASK question when executed during a consultation. However, the MENU clause takes its values from a field of a database file.

The syntax of the MENU clause is as follows:

MENU <*variable,ALL/database_rule, [path]DBF_filename,fieldname*>

The first parameter of the clause is the name of a *VP-Expert variable*. This is the variable that will be assigned a value when the user makes a choice from the menu created by the clause.

For more information about writing database rules, see the GET clause in Chapter 9.

The second parameter is either the keyword ALL, or a *database rule* consisting of one or more conditions by which records in the database file will be selected. If ALL is used, *all* records will contribute values to the menu. If a database rule is used (e.g., *the_wine = wine*) only those records that conform to the stated condition(s) will contribute values.

The third parameter, a *DBF_filename* (with a path optionally specified), is the name of the DBF file that is accessed by the MENU clause. Note that the DBF file extension should not be specified; it is assumed.

The last parameter, *fieldname*, specifies the field in the database that will provide the menu values.

In this example rule base, the MENU clause creates a menu containing WINE field values (wine) taken from all records (ALL) in the WINES.DBF file (wines). The value the user chooses when the menu is displayed is assigned as the value of the variable *the_wine* (the_wine).

If, instead of the keyword ALL, a database rule was specified as the second argument in the clause, only those records that matched the stated condition or conditions would contribute field values to the menu. How conditions are stated in database rules will be discussed later in this chapter with the GET clause. For now it's sufficient to understand that menus can be created that contain all or selected values taken from a given field of a database file.

Duplicate field values are omitted from MENU clause menus. This means, for example, that the menu created by our example MENU clause would display each type of wine only once, despite the fact that some wines occur more than once in the database file.

It is important to note that the menu created by the MENU clause is not necessarily displayed at the time it's executed. It is stored in memory and only displayed when a corresponding ASK or AUTOQUERY statement is executed.

The FIND Clause

```
ACTIONS
        MENU the_wine,ALL,wines,wine
        FIND the_wine
        *
        *
        *
```

See Chapter 2 for detailed information about the VP-Expert inference engine.

The second clause occurring in the ACTIONS block of our rule base is a FIND clause, instructing the *VP-Expert* inference engine to find a value for the variable *the_wine*. (Note that *the_wine* is the same variable named in the MENU clause.) The FIND clause causes the execution of the ASK statement, which occurs at the end of the rule base:

```
ASK the_wine: "For which wine do you want information?";
```

This causes the following prompt to be displayed to the user:

```
For which wine do you want information?

Burgundy           Cabernet           Zinfandel
Chablis            Beaujolais         Chardonnay
Gewürztraminer     Cabernet_Blanc     Chenin_Blanc
Reisling
```

See MRESET in Chapter 9 for information about removing menus from memory once they've been displayed.

Note that execution of the ASK statement triggers the display of the menu that was created and stored by the MENU clause. This occurs because the variable named in the ASK statement is the same variable named in the MENU clause.

The WHILEKNOWN Clause

```
ACTIONS
        MENU the_wine,ALL,wines,wine
        FIND the_wine
        WHILEKNOWN wine
            *
            *
        END;
```

The next clause in the ACTIONS block is a WHILEKNOWN clause.

The WHILEKNOWN clause is an extremely important VP-Expert feature. See WHILEKNOWN in Chapter 9 for more information.

When *VP-Expert* encounters a WHILEKNOWN clause during a consultation, it sets up a "loop" condition that causes all the clauses between the WHILEKNOWN keyword and the requisite END keyword to be repeatedly executed in loop fashion until the variable named in the WHILEKNOWN clause becomes UNKNOWN. In our example, the variable named in the clause is *wine*. This means that as long as *wine* has a known value, the clauses contained in the WHILEKNOWN-END loop will keep executing.

Note that, so far, there is no value for *wine*. Does this mean that the following clauses will not execute? No, the loop will always execute one time if the value named in the WHILEKNOWN clause is UNKNOWN. (See the UNKNOWN keyword in Chapter 9 for information about UNKNOWN variables.) This means that a WHILEKNOWN-END loop will start if the variable is UNKNOWN, and that it will execute one final time when the variable subsequently becomes UNKNOWN. The loop terminates when the END keyword is encountered, and the variable named by the WHILEKNOWN clause is UNKNOWN.

The GET Clause

```
ACTIONS
        MENU the_wine,ALL,wines,wine
        FIND the_wine
        WHILEKNOWN wine
           GET the_wine = wine,wines,ALL
           *
           *
           *
```

For a more detailed explanation of the GET clause, see Chapter 9.

The next clause in the rule base is a GET clause.

The GET clause transfers values from a database to the rule base by assigning the values in fields from a selected record to variables with the same names as the fields from which the values were taken.

Three of the most important things to realize about the GET clause are as follows:

- GET retrieves values from a database one record at a time.

If no GET clause has previously been issued, the record pointer will be at the top of the file, and the first record is considered the "next" record in the file. If you want to issue a sequence of GETs starting from this position, use the CLOSE clause to reset the record pointer to the top of the file between GETs. See the CLOSE clause in Chapter 9 for more information.

- After a GET is issued, the record accessed by the GET becomes the current record of the database file (i.e., the record pointer is positioned at that record).

- A GET always moves forward from the record pointer to the *next* record matching the selection criterion. This means that when multiple GET clauses are issued, each GET (except the first) moves forward from the record accessed by the last GET.

Look at the basic syntax of the GET clause:

GET <ALL/*database_rule*,[*path*]*DBF_filename*,ALL/*fieldname*>

The record that supplies the values that will be read into the rule base is determined by the first argument in the clause. This is either the keyword ALL or one or more conditions stated in a database rule.

In our example, a database rule is used: *the_wine = wine*. This condition instructs the GET clause to select the *next* record whose WINE field matches the value of the variable *the_wine*.

Remember, the value of *the_wine* is determined by the user's response to a question asking him or her to choose a wine from the menu generated by the MENU clause.

If the keyword ALL were used instead of a database rule, the record would be selected from among ALL the records. In other words, no special conditions would have to be met; the *next* record would be selected.

The next argument in our GET clause, *wines*, specifies that WINES.DBF is the name of the database file to access. Note that the DBF file extension is not and cannot be included in the clause.

If, instead of the keyword ALL, a fieldname was entered, only the value contained in that field would be transferred to a knowledge base variable.

The final argument, *ALL*, tells the GET clause that ALL field values of the selected record should be transferred to knowledge base variables. Each variable will have the same name as the field from which the value was taken. This means, for example, that if the user selected Burgundy from the menu, GET would find the first record. The value *Burgundy* would be assigned to a variable named *wine*; the value 7.95 would be assigned to the variable *price*, and so forth.

A GET clause can only retrieve values from one record at a time. However, used in a WHILEKNOWN-END loop, as it is here, a single GET can be used to retrieve values from ALL the records in a file (if the ALL keyword is specified as the first argument of the clause), or from all records matching the condition(s) in a database rule. This works because each time the GET clause is re-executed in the loop, it retrieves the *next* record matching the criterion specified in the first argument. Note, however, that each successive GET overwrites the values assigned by the previous GET, because values are assigned to the same variables.

The ~ character at the end of the DISPLAY clause causes the consultation to pause until the user presses any key.

The DISPLAY Clause

```
ACTIONS
            MENU the_wine,ALL,wines,wine
            FIND the_wine
            WHILEKNOWN wine
              GET the_wine = wine,wines,ALL
              DISPLAY "Your choice, a {wine}, is priced at
${price}.
It has a rating of {rating}.~"
                *
                *
```

After each execution of the GET clause, the DISPLAY clause displays its message:

```
Your choice, a {wine}, is priced at ${price}.
It has a rating of {rating}.
```

The variables shown in curly brackets will be replaced by the values that were retrieved by the GET.

If the user had chosen *Burgundy* as the wine to show information about, the first execution of the GET clause would retrieve values from the first record of the WINES file showing *Burgundy* in the WINE field. The values retrieved would be the following:

```
wine = Burgundy
price = 7.95
rating = 27
```

The DISPLAY clause would, therefore, display this message:

```
Your choice, a Burgundy, is priced at $7.95.
It has a rating of 27.
```

The next time the GET clause was executed, the *next* record containing *Burgundy* in the WINE field would be retrieved, and new values would be assigned to the variables *wine*, *price*, and *rating*. A message showing these new values would then be displayed. Messages would continue to be displayed until there were no more records containing *Burgundy* in the WINE field. Remember, the execution of the WHILEKNOWN-END loop depends on the value of the variable *wine*. Once the GET clause can find no more WINE fields to match the value of *the_wine*, the value of *wine* becomes UNKNOWN. At that point the loop executes one final time, producing this message:

```
Your choice, a , is priced at $.
It has a rating of .
```

A method of dispensing with this last message will be discussed later in this chapter.

The END Clause

```
ACTIONS
        MENU the_wine,ALL,wines,wine
        FIND the_wine
        WHILEKNOWN wine
          GET the_wine = wine,wines,ALL
          DISPLAY "Your choice, a {wine}, is priced at
${price}.
It has a rating of {rating}.~"
        END;
*
*
```

The END clause signals the end of the WHILEKNOWN-END loop. When executed, it tests the loop variable to see if it is UNKNOWN, in which case WHILEKNOWN-END loop execution ends. Since END also, in this case, is at the end of the ACTIONS block, it is followed by a semicolon.

The ASK Statement

```
ACTIONS
        MENU the_wine,ALL,wines,wine
        FIND the_wine
        WHILEKNOWN wine
          GET the_wine = wine,wines,ALL
          DISPLAY "Your choice, a {wine}, is priced at
${price}.
It has a rating of {rating}.~"
          END;

ASK the_wine: "For which wine do you want information?";
```

We've already seen that the ASK statement, executed in order to obtain a value for *the_wine*, asks the user to choose a value from a menu created by the MENU clause. The value chosen by the user is assigned as the value of *the_wine*.

The Whole Picture

Now that we've seen what each clause in the rule base does, let's look at the whole picture.

During a consultation, the user is asked to select a wine from a menu created by the MENU clause. (This selection is assigned to a variable, *the_wine*). The value selected from the menu is used by the GET clause to select a record from the WINES.DBF database file (*the_wine = wine*). The GET assigns all of the field values contained in that record to variables having the same names as the fields from which they were taken. The values of these variables are then displayed in a message created by a DISPLAY clause. Because GET and DISPLAY are contained in a WHILEKNOWN-END loop, a message will be displayed for each record that conforms to the database rule used by the GET clause to select records from the database.

Improving on the Example

As it stands, our example has two minor flaws. First, an extra, useless message is displayed at the end of the consultation. This occurs because the WHILEKNOWN-END loop always executes the loop once when the variable it names is UNKNOWN. Second, if a wine appears more than once in the information base, a separate message is displayed for each occurrence. This may be desirable. For cases where it's not, we'll show you a way to prevent multiple messages.

Preventing the Last Message

Because the WHILEKNOWN-END loop executes one final time when the value of *wine* becomes UNKNOWN, the DISPLAY clause in our example generates this message at the end of the consultation:

```
Your choice, a , is priced at $.
It has a rating of .
```

This extra message can be eliminated by taking the DISPLAY clause out of the loop and putting it into a rule, as shown below:

```
ACTIONS
        MENU the_wine,ALL,wines,wine
        FIND the_wine
        WHILEKNOWN wine
          GET the_wine = wine,wines,ALL
          RESET message
          FIND message
        END;

RULE 1
IF      wine <> UNKNOWN
THEN    message = displayed
        DISPLAY "
Your choice, a {wine}, is priced at ${price}.
It has a rating of {rating}.~"
ELSE    message = none;

ASK the_wine: "For which wine do you want information?";
```

The UNKNOWN keyword lets you account for unknown values in rule conditions. See UNKNOWN in Chapter 9 for more information.

The DISPLAY clause message will now display only if RULE 1 is executed—which will occur only while *wine* is not UNKNOWN.

Note that we've added a FIND clause to the WHILEKNOWN-END loop—FIND *message*. This is used to trigger RULE 1. We've also added another clause to the loop—RESET *message*. The RESET clause sets the variable *message* to UNKNOWN and insures that the FIND clause triggers RULE 1 with each execution of the loop. (See RESET in Chapter 9 for more information about the RESET clause.)

Eliminating Multiple Messages

In our example, if the wine chosen by the user is represented in more than one record in the database, a separate message will be displayed for each record. This may be desirable. However, if not, you can reduce the number of messages by altering the rule base to seek more specific information. For example:

```
ACTIONS
        MENU the_wine,ALL,wines,wine
        FIND the_wine
        MENU the_price,the_wine = wine,wines,price
        FIND the_price
        WHILEKNOWN wine
          GET the_wine = wine AND the_price = price,wines,ALL
          RESET message
          FIND message
        END;

RULE 1
IF      wine <> UNKNOWN
THEN    message = displayed
        DISPLAY "
Your choice, a {wine}, is priced at ${price}.
It has a rating of {rating}.~"
ELSE    message = none;

ASK the_wine: "For which wine do you want information?";

ASK the_price: "For the selected wine, which price do you choose?";
```

In this new rule base, a second MENU clause and another ASK statement have been added.

```
MENU the_price,the_wine = wine,wines,price
```

```
ASK the_price: "For the selected wine, which price do you choose?";
```

These allow the user to choose from a menu of prices. The prices are taken from the PRICE field of records which have a value in the WINE field that matches the value of *the_wine* (i.e., the value chosen by the user at the first prompt).

Note that we have also added another FIND clause—FIND *the_price*. This clause is necessary for executing the new ASK statement and for displaying the new menu.

The GET clause has also been modified:

```
GET the_wine = wine AND the_price = price,wines,ALL
```

A database rule in a GET clause can include up to ten conditions. (Both the AND and the OR logical operators can be used.)

Now it chooses only records where the WINE field matches *the_wine* and the PRICE field matches *the_price*. Adding the additional condition to the clause has the effect of ensuring that only one conclusion message is displayed, since no two records name both the same wine and the same price.

When this knowledge base is executed, the user is first asked to select a wine from a menu of wines; next they must choose a price from a menu of prices. (Only records with the selected wine name contribute prices to the second menu.) When the DISPLAY clause is executed, it will only display messages for records that contain the user-selected wine and price.

Adding Data to the Information Base: A File Update Example

In addition to extracting values from the fields of a database and reading them into knowledge base variables, *VP-Expert* can also transfer the values of knowledge base variables into the fields of a database. In other words, a database file can be updated or added to during the course of a *VP-Expert* consultation.

The clauses PUT and APPEND can be used for this purpose.

PUT is used to update fields in existing records.

APPEND appends a completely new record to the end of a database file.

Using the PUT Clause

The PUT clause is issued in the form PUT *<DBF_filename>*, where *DBF_filename* is the name of the database file to be updated.

These steps are required to update the contents of a record with PUT:

■ First, you must GET the record to be updated.

■ Second, values must be assigned to variables having the same names as the fields you want to update. This can be accomplished in the ACTIONS block, by a passing rule, or by user input. The values assigned to these variables will be transferred to the fields when the PUT is executed.

■ Finally, a PUT clause naming the file to be updated is issued; e.g., PUT wines. (The DBF file extension is assumed.)

Note in the second step, it's only necessary to assign values to variables corresponding to the fields you want to update. Note also that this step must occur *after* the GET is issued. If it comes before the GET, the values retrieved by the GET will overwrite the assigned values. Look at this example:

```
ACTIONS
        MENU the_wine,ALL,wines,wine
        FIND the_wine
        WHILEKNOWN wine
          GET the_wine = wine,wines,ALL
          RESET new_price
          FIND new_price
          price = (new_price)
          PUT wines
        END;
ASK the_wine: "Which wine's price do you want to change?";

ASK new_price: "Your choice, a {wine}, is priced at ${price}.
It has a rating of {rating}.  What is the new price?";
```

When executed, this rule base presents the user with a menu of wines and asks:

```
Which wine's price do you want to change?
```

When the user makes a choice, that wine is assigned as the value of the variable *the_wine*. The GET clause then uses the value of *the_wine* to select a record from the WINES.DBF file. This serves the purpose of moving the record pointer to the record to be updated.

Next, the user is presented with a message and question generated by the second ASK statement.

```
ASK new_price: "Your choice, a {wine}, is priced at
${price}.
It has a rating of {rating}.  What is the new price?
```

This time no menu is displayed; the user is required to type in a new price.

The price the user enters is assigned as the value of the variable *new_price*.

Next, using "indirect addressing" (*price* = (*new_price*)), the value entered by the user (which was assigned to the variable *new_price*) is assigned to the variable *price*, which is the name of the field that will be updated.

The PUT clause then transfers the value of *price* to the PRICE field of the record accessed by the GET clause.

"Indirect addressing" refers to assigning the value of one variable (shown in parentheses) to another variable. See Chapter 7 for more information.

This rule base, though simple, is a good example of how *VP-Expert* can be used to provide an expert system front-end to a database program whose interface might otherwise be less "friendly." *VP-Expert* can facilitate updating database files by asking the user meaningful questions, by checking the validity of new data, and by performing tasks in a less complex fashion than would otherwise be necessary.

Using APPEND to Add Records to a Database

Appending a record to the end of a database file is straightforward. Assign values to variables with names identical to the file's field names, and then issue an APPEND clause supplying the name of the file to receive the new record. Upon execution of the APPEND clause, *VP-Expert* adds a record containing the specified field values to the end of the database file. As with PUT, variables can be assigned values in the ACTIONS block, by a rule, or by user input. Again, *VP-Expert's* usefulness as a front-end to a database program is clear.

Look at this rule base:

```
ACTIONS
        DISPLAY "This program is used to append a record to the WINES.DBF file.
Press any key to begin.~";
        MENU the_wine,ALL,wines,wine
        FIND the_wine
        wine = (the_wine)
        FIND price
        FIND rating
        APPEND wines
        WHILEKNOWN wine
          GET all,wines,ALL
          DISPLAY "{wine} {price} {rating}"
        END;
ASK the_wine: "Choose a wine varietal:";

ASK price: "What is the wine's price?";

ASK rating: "What is the wine's rating?";
```

When this rule base is executed, first, this message is displayed to the user:

```
This program is used to append a record to the WINES.DBF
file.
Press any key to begin.
```

When the user presses any key, three questions are asked. The first question requires the user to choose a wine. The choice is restricted to wine varietals already contained in the WINES.DBF file, since the question is accompanied by a menu containing values taken from the WINE field of the WINES.DBF file. However, in response to the following two questions, which ask the user to enter values for *price* and *rating*, the user can type any numeric values (since no MENU clauses exist for these variables).

After the user answers the third prompt, the APPEND clause is executed, appending a record to the end of the WINES.DBF file. Since the variables *wine*, *price*, and *rating* (which match the field names of the database file) were assigned values by the user, these values are transferred to the new record's WINE, PRICE, and RATING fields. If no values were assigned, a blank record would be appended to the file. If only some of the fields were assigned values, those fields not assigned values would be left blank in the appended record.

The GET and DISPLAY clauses contained in the WHILEKNOWN-END loop then display the entire contents of the WINES.DBF file to the user to demonstrate that a new record has indeed been added.

Database Modification = Learning?

Since *VP-Expert* permits the user to change data or add data to the knowledge base during a consultation, it can be said that, in a limited sense, the expert system is able to learn from experience. This capability is significant, because the ability to "learn" is an important criterion in defining an expert system. For more information on this subject, see "How *VP-Expert* Can Learn" in Chapter 7.

Other VP-Expert Clauses

In addition to the clauses used in the previous examples, there are other *VP-Expert* clauses that can be used in a rule base accessing an information base. These include INDEX, which makes use of *VP-Info* and dBASE II index files; MRESET, which is used to erase obsolete menus from memory; and CLOSE, which resets the record pointer to the top of the file. For information about using these clauses, see Chapter 9. In addition, see RECORD_NUM and MENU_SIZE for information about related system variables.

Using a Database as an Induction Table

See Chapter 3 for basic information about VP-Expert induction tables.

As seen in Chapter 3, *VP-Expert's* Main Menu Induce command can transform a correctly formatted table of columns and rows into a working knowledge base. Such a table is referred to as an "induction table," or an "example base," and can be created in a text editor, in a *VP-Planner* or Lotus 1-2-3 worksheet, or in a *VP-Info* or dBASE compatible database file.

Why Induce a Knowledge Base from a Database?

Many companies have database files that contain information used for decision making. Sales information, customer information, numbers, locations, dollar amounts, dates, figures, employee data, all kinds of data are stored in databases and later used in making decisions. Should an employee be given a raise? Should a line be continued or discontinued? Should sales efforts be expanded in a particular sales region? With *VP-Expert's* Induce command, many of these kinds of database files can easily be transformed into working knowledge base files. And remember, once a knowledge base is created, it can be elaborated with clauses, such as GET, PUT, MENU, and APPEND, that can be used to access and maintain other company database files.

Database File as Induction Table

To use the records and fields of an existing database as an induction table (described in Chapter 3), several changes must typically be made to the database file.

First, fields that are not relevant in decision making must be
eliminated from the database. Second, a column will usually have to
be added at the extreme right of the file. This column contains data
representing the conclusion or decision indicated for each row of
"decision making" data. Third, fields containing additional relevant
data may need to be added. (All these operations can be performed
quickly and easily using *VP-Info*.)

A Simple Example

Suppose a company called Mouse Manufacturing, Inc. has a *VP-Info*
database file containing the following employee records:

	NAME	DEPT	SALARY	SALES	HIRED	PHONE	OFFICE
00001	Robert Morgan	HR	31100.00	31	78	x123	143
00002	Joann Bickley	SA	40500.00	20	82	x558	244
00003	Jenny Shapiro	CSA	41000.00	31	85	x145	232
00004	Artie Fluffkin	CSA	42300.00	29	71	x223	113
00005	Mark Thomas	SA	39100.00	41	75	x338	152
00006	Susan Jackson	CSA	42000.00	40	79	x218	222
00007	Danny Reyes	SA	44050.00	28	82	x166	243
00008	Janet Schwartz	CA	28700.00	44	83	x331	305

Mouse Manufacturing's personnel manager wants to use a *VP-Expert*
system to decide when to increase employee salaries. With some
modification, the employee file can be transformed into an induction
table and then used to induce a knowledge base to help make such
decisions.

Obviously, some information contained in the original employee file
is irrelevant to salary decisions. It's not necessary to know the
employee's telephone extension or office number, for example.

After careful analysis, the personnel manager decides that the fields
shown in the following database are the ones relevant to the decision-
making process.

	NAME	SALARY	SALES	HIRED	RAISE
00001	Robert Morgan	31100.00	31	78	YES
00002	Joann Bickley	40500.00	20	82	NO
00003	Jenny Shapiro	41000.00	31	85	YES
00004	Artie Fluffkin	42300.00	29	71	YES
00005	Mark Thomas	39100.00	41	75	NO
00006	Susan Jackson	42000.00	40	79	NO
00007	Danny Reyes	44050.00	28	82	YES
00008	Janet Schwartz	28700.00	44	83	YES

Note that an additional field has been added on the far right of the database, with the field heading, RAISE. In this field, the personnel manager will enter a *Yes* or a *No*, indicating whether the employee named in that record qualifies for a raise.

There are a couple of different methods she could use for determining which to enter. She could apply company policy to each record and determine, on that basis, whether or not each employee qualifies for a raise. Or, she could use historical data; e.g., was the employee actually given a raise or not? This method could shed light on how salary decisions have typically been made. Perhaps company policy is not reflected in reality. (See ''Decision Checking'' later in this chapter for a discussion of how ''reality'' can be analyzed using *VP-Expert.*)

A knowledge base created from an induction table is only as good as the data from which it was induced. In other words, if crucial decision-making factors are absent from the induction table, then the resulting knowledge base will be of questionable value.

Since the Induce command creates a rudimentary knowledge base, the knowledge base will typically require some elaboration and fine-tuning. See Chapter 4 for information about the kinds of enhancements which are generally advisable.

So, before Mouse Manufacturing's personnel manager actually uses the Induce command to create the knowledge base from the induction table, she should think carefully about whether or not any additional fields should be added to the database; perhaps, for example, she should add a field containing last year's salary review ratings (e.g., poor, fair, good, excellent). Of course, rules can always be added to the knowledge base once it's created—but the more information included in the induction table, the less the knowledge base will have to be altered later.

Decision Checking

In addition to using induction tables to create knowledge bases that can help make decisions, induction tables can also be used to help analyze how decisions are actually made. Sometimes there may not be an apparent pattern to decision making. In such cases, collecting data into an induction table and inducing a knowledge base may bring patterns into focus.

By using an induction table for ''decision checking,'' it's possible to identify negative as well as positive decision-making patterns. For example, knowledge bases created using induction tables, upon review, can answer questions like, ''Has the company's promotion history indicated a bias with respect to sex, race, or age?'' Or, ''Has our decision making been consistent with our written policy?'' In addition, other kinds of patterns can be identified. For example, rules created using induction can shed light on questions like, ''Is an employee's level of education a relevant factor in his or her job performance?'' or ''Does a bonus system improve employee performance?'' and so on.

SUMMARY

Knowledge bases can be expanded to include information bases consisting of *VP-Info*, dBASE II, III, III+, or other work-alike database files. When an information base is used, the collective clauses and statements contained in the KBS file are referred to as the rule base.

By using the GET and MENU clauses, data can be transferred from the information base to the rule base.

The PUT and APPEND clauses transfer data in the opposite direction. They transfer values assigned to knowledge base variables to the fields of a database file. These clauses can be useful for creating rule bases that serve as friendly front-ends for database files that require periodic updating.

Database files can also be used to create induction tables from which knowledge bases can be induced using *VP-Expert's* Induce command. (Chapter 3 discusses using induction to create knowledge bases.) This capability makes it possible to create basic knowledge bases from pre-existing database files.

CHAPTER SIX

Worksheet Access

Much of Chapter 5's general discussion regarding the use of database files applies to worksheet files as well. To avoid repetition, we refer you to that chapter.

In addition to using *database* files, as described in Chapter 5, *VP-Expert* can also interact with *worksheet* files created with *VP-Planner*, Lotus 1-2-3, and Lotus work-alike spreadsheet programs. Like database files, worksheet files can be used both as "information bases" and as "induction tables" for use with *VP-Expert's* Induce command.

Chapter 3 of this manual describes how the *VP-Expert* Induce command creates a knowledge base from an induction table. The table used in that chapter was created using the *VP-Expert* Editor, but *VP-Planner* or Lotus 1-2-3 worksheet tables can also be used as "induction tables." Tables created in worksheets have a few restrictions that don't apply to "text" tables, however. They must contain a blank row under the column headings, and they can contain no blank columns. Also, there may be no blank rows above or to the left of the table. See "Using a Database as an Induction Table" in Chapter 5 for information regarding the advantages of using pre-stored data to create knowledge bases.

Worksheets as Information Bases

See the SHIP and RECEIVE clauses in Chapter 9 for information about transferring data between a rule base and text files.

In Chapter 5 we saw how to use a database as an "information base"—which we defined as a store of data that can be accessed and altered during a *VP-Expert* consultation. *VP-Planner* and Lotus 1-2-3 worksheets can also be used as information bases. Using the WKS clause, data can be transferred from the cells of a worksheet to knowledge base variables. With the PWKS clause, values can be transferred from *VP-Expert* variables directly to the cells of a worksheet.

Reading Worksheet Data

Assume that you have the following sales information stored in a *VP-Planner* worksheet:

	A	B	C	D	E
1	Rep No	March	April	May	Quarter
2	S489	$9,100	$8,425	$3,119	$20,644
3	J099	$3,099	$5,225	$6,007	$14,331
4	R123	$8,888	$7,777	$6,666	$23,331
5	A701	$1,442	$9,876	$2,376	$13,694
6	Q011	$5,432	$6,543	$7,654	$19,629
7	TOTAL	$27,961	$37,846	$25,822	$91,629
8					
9					

6

Using this worksheet and the following two-rule rule base, we can demonstrate the use of a worksheet as an information base.

```
ACTIONS
        FIND sales_volume;

RULE 1
IF      source = cell
THEN    info = found
        WKS Sales,B7,Q1sales;

RULE 2
IF      info = found
THEN    sales_volume = found
        DISPLAY "The March sales volume was ${Sales}.~";

ASK source: "Is data to be fetched from a worksheet cell,
column, or range?";

CHOICES source: cell,column,range;
```

When a knowledge base has been expanded to include an information base, the contents of the KBS file are referred to as the "rule base."

Read Chapter 2 for a thorough description of how the VP-Expert inference engine navigates the rules of a knowledge base during a consultation.

The purpose of this rule base is to demonstrate the retrieval of data from a single worksheet cell to a single knowledge base variable. The DISPLAY clause in RULE 2 is used to prove that the retrieval has occurred:

```
DISPLAY "The March sales volume was ${Sales}.~";
```

The consultation is directed by the FIND clause contained in the ACTIONS block. This clause instructs the inference engine to find a value for the variable *sales_volume*.

The first rule the inference engine finds that can assign a value to *sales_volume* is RULE 2. But RULE 2 requires a value for the variable *info*, so the inference engine looks for the first rule that can assign a value to *info*. This variable is assigned the value *found* in RULE 1 if *source* has the value *cell*. *Source* acquires its value from a user response to an ASK statement.

This two-rule sequence acts as a framework to which we can add clauses that will fetch and display data from the worksheet.

Notice the WKS clause at the end of RULE 1:

```
WKS Sales,B7,Q1sales
```

This clause causes the contents of cell B7 in the worksheet file called Q1SALES.WKS to be assigned to the variable *Sales*.

The DISPLAY clause at the end of RULE 2 displays the value of *Sales* at the end of the message, ''The March sales volume was ____.''

This, then, is what happens when this knowledge base is executed:

First, the user is asked where data is to be fetched from:

```
Is data to be fetched from a worksheet cell, column or
range?
cell                   column                   range
```

If the user answers anything other than "cell," the consultation terminates, because in this simple rule base, "cell" is the only answer accounted for in a rule.

Assuming the user chooses *cell* at the prompt, the value contained in cell B7 of the file Q1SALES.WKS will be assigned as the value of the variable *Sales*, as directed by the WKS clause in RULE 1.

Proving that the data has been retrieved, the DISPLAY clause in RULE 1 displays the message: "The March sales volume was $27961."

This ends the consultation.

*Note: VP-Expert cannot read formulas in worksheet cells. A variable named in a WKS clause which accesses a cell with a formula will remain UNKNOWN. Within the spreadsheet program, there are two ways to convert formulas to retrievable values. First, you can place the lightbar over the cell and key in F2-F9-ENTER (Edit-Recalc). This replaces the formula with the literal value. The second way is to extract values and store them in another file that can be accessed by the WKS clause. (Type /**FXV** (File-Xtract-Values), enter the new filename, and specify the range.)*

Our example rule base could actually be made simpler by eliminating the two rules and moving the WKS and DISPLAY clauses into the ACTIONS block. The simplified rule base would look like this:

```
ACTIONS
    WKS Sales,B7,Q1sales
    DISPLAY "The March sales volume was ${Sales}.~";
```

Though this rule base doesn't do very much, it is, nonetheless, perfectly valid. When executed, it opens the file called Q1SALES.WKS, extracts the value of cell B7, stores it to the variable *Sales*, and displays the value along with a text message. The consultation ends when the user presses any key (as determined by the ~ character in the DISPLAY clause, which causes the consultation to pause until any key is pressed.)

A More Complex Example

In addition to data in a single cell, data contained in an entire row, column, or range of a worksheet can also be retrieved using a single WKS clause. The second argument in the WKS clause determines the location of the data to be retrieved. To demonstrate, we'll expand our sample rule base to include all three methods of data retrieval.

```
ACTIONS
        FIND sales_volume;


RULE 1
IF      source = cell
THEN    go = ok
        WKS Sales,E7,q1sales;


RULE 1A
IF      source = column AND
        info <> UNKNOWN
THEN    go = ok
        WKS Sales,column=(info),q1sales;


RULE 1B
IF      source = range
THEN    go = ok
        WKS Sales,B2..E7,q1sales;

RULE 2
IF      go = ok AND
        source = cell
THEN    sales_volume = found
        DISPLAY "March Sales volume was ${Sales}.";


RULE 2A
IF      go = ok AND
        source = column
THEN    sales_volume = found
        DISPLAY "The Sales are:
{Sales[1]},{Sales[2]},{Sales[3]},{Sales[4]},{Sales[5]},
{Sales[6]}";
```

```
RULE 2B
IF     go = ok AND
       source = range
THEN   sales_volume = found
       DISPLAY "The Sales are:
{Sales[4]},{Sales[8]},{Sales[12]},{Sales[16]},Sales[20]},
{Sales[21]},{Sales[22]},{Sales[23]},{Sales[24]}";

ASK source: "Is data to be fetched from a worksheet cell,
column, or range?";

ASK info: "Which month do you want to see?";

CHOICES info: March, April, May, Quarter;

CHOICES source: cell, column, range;
```

Look carefully at RULES 1, 1A, and 1B. Each has a different WKS clause:

RULE 1:   WKS Sales, E7,q1sales;

RULE 1A: WKS Sales, column = (info),q1sales;

RULE 1B: WKS Sales, B2..E7,q1sales;

RULE 1 reads information from a single *cell* (E7); RULE 1A reads information from a spreadsheet *column* (column=(info)); and RULE 1B reads data from a spreadsheet *range* (B2..E7).

Which rule gets executed depends on the user's response to the question:

```
Is data to be fetched from a worksheet cell, column or
range?
cell                    column                  range
```

Dimensioned Variables

See ''Creating Dimensioned Variables'' later in this chapter for more information about VP-Expert dimensioned variables.

When data is retrieved from more than one cell—as from a range, column, or row—the data is stored by *VP-Expert* as a *dimensioned variable*. A dimensioned variable is a variable that stores multiple values as a one dimensional array of *elements*. Each element of the array is represented by the dimensioned variable name followed by a bracketed number corresponding to its placement in the array. For example, if the range B2..C5 were read into the dimensioned variable *var*, *VP-Expert* would retrieve data as follows (note that data are transferred row-wise):

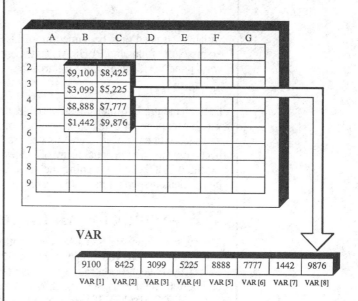

VAR

9100	8425	3099	5225	8888	7777	1442	9876
VAR [1]	VAR [2]	VAR [3]	VAR [4]	VAR [5]	VAR [6]	VAR [7]	VAR [8]

By creating dimensioned variables that give a unique name to each retrieved element, *VP-Expert* makes it possible to access and manipulate each element just like any other *VP-Expert* variable. For example, the following DISPLAY clause would display the value of the element *var*[2]:

```
DISPLAY "Display the value of the element here:
{var[2]}."
```

Don't confuse dimensioned variables with plural variables. Plural variables are variables (named in a PLURAL statement) that can be assigned multiple values during a consultation. Unlike the elements of dimensioned variables, plural variable values cannot be named or manipulated independently. (See the POP clause in Chapter 9 for an exception.)

Any time a WKS clause transfers data from more than one cell to a variable, the variable created is a dimensioned variable. When data is transferred from a single cell, a single-valued variable is created.

However, any element of a dimensioned variable can also be a plural variable—it need only be named in a PLURAL statement. For example, the following PLURAL statement names the elements *var[1]* and *var[2]* as PLURAL variables.

```
PLURAL: var[1], var[2];
```

Each element of a dimensioned variable, then, is an independent variable, capable of being single-valued or plural. A dimensioned variable, with each of its elements declared plural, could, in effect, become a two-dimensional array of values. A number of sequentially executed WKS clauses naming the same dimensioned variable with plural elements would have this result.

WKS Syntax for Multi-Cell Retrieval

The syntax of the WKS clause is straightforward for a cell or range address. For a cell, you simply give the cell address (e.g., WKS Sales,C9,q1sales). For a range, you give the addresses of the top left and bottom right cells, separated by two periods (e.g., WKS Sales,C3..D7,q1sales). If you've used *VP-Planner* or Lotus 1-2-3, this syntax may be familiar to you, since it's identical to the syntax used to reference cell ranges inside a worksheet.

Specifying a column, row, or named range in a WKS clause is a bit more complicated.

The following syntax is used to specify a column in a WKS clause.

COLUMN = *<heading>*

VP-Expert is not case sensitive. The heading may be in upper, lower, or mixed case.

Here, the string supplied as the *heading* should match the contents of the worksheet cell that is the "heading" of the column to be retrieved. If the string is enclosed in parentheses (e.g., COLUMN = (info)), indicating indirect addressing, it is the name of a variable whose value matches the heading of a column. In either case, when the WKS clause is executed, the first cell *below* the indicated "heading" and all subsequent cells in that column are retrieved. Blank cells that may occur in the specified column are ignored.

Consider these two WKS clauses:

```
WKS Sales,COLUMN = March,q1sales;
```

```
WKS Sales,COLUMN = (info),q1sales;
```

The first retrieves data from the column with *March* as its heading; the second retrieves a column whose heading matches the value of the variable *info*.

If a column or row "heading" indicated in a WKS clause occurs more than once in a worksheet, the first occurrence will be used when the clause is executed.

The syntax for retrieving a row of data is the same as for retrieving a column, except instead of the word COLUMN, the word ROW is used, indicating that the string or variable that follows specifies the heading of a row to be retrieved.

Thus, the following WKS clause would retrieve a row of data beginning with the cell to the *right* of the cell containing the string *RepNo*.

```
WKS Sales,ROW = RepNo,q1sales
```

The data would be written from the worksheet to the dimensioned variable *Sales*. As with column access, any blank cells contained in the retrieved row are ignored (blank elements are not created to correspond with blank cells).

Now consider this clause:

```
WKS Sales,ROW = (info),q1sales
```

Naming a variable instead, this WKS clause retrieves a row of data beginning with the cell to the right of the cell whose contents match the value of the variable *info*.

The ability to use a variable to specify a row or column heading adds a great deal of flexibility to the WKS clause. This flexibility can be applied to range access also, if the range is identified using a *range name* instead of cell coordinates (as described earlier.)

Range names must be assigned from within the spreadsheet program. For information about naming ranges, see the VP-Planner or Lotus 1-2-3 documentation.

The following syntax is used in a WKS clause to access a range by a range name:

NAMED = <*range_name*>

Here, *range_name* can be a string matching a worksheet range name. If parentheses are added, a variable can be used. For example, look at the following WKS clauses:

```
WKS Sales,NAMED = Month,q1sales
```

```
WKS Sales,NAMED = (range_name),q1sales
```

The first clause reads data from a range of cells that have been given the range name *Month*. The second reads data from a range of cells whose name matches the value of the variable *range_name*. Both create a dimensioned variable named *Sales* with elements *Sales[1]*, *Sales[2]*, and so forth. Blank cells contained within the range are ignored.

Writing Information to Worksheets: The PWKS Clause

In addition to extracting data *from* a worksheet, *VP-Expert* can also transfer data *to* a worksheet using the PWKS clause. The syntax of the PWKS clause is virtually identical to the syntax of WKS. The only difference between the two clauses is the direction in which data is transferred.

For example, look at the following PWKS clause:

```
PWKS Sales,Column = March,q1sales
```

This clause would transfer the contents of the dimensioned variable *Sales* into the column with the heading *March* in the Q1SALES worksheet.

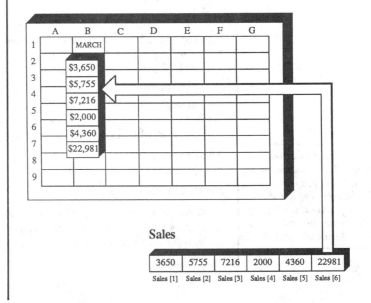

It's important, when using PWKS, to make sure that the number of elements in the dimensioned variable to be transferred to the worksheet matches the number of cells indicated in the second argument of the clause. If the receiving cells indicated are too few, additional worksheet cells will be overwritten. It's also important to make sure that the data in the dimensioned variable are arranged in such a way that they will be transferred to the intended worksheet cells.

Creating Dimensioned Variables

As you've seen, dimensioned variables are created when a WKS clause copies the contents of more than one cell into a knowledge base variable. However, the WKS clause is not the only means of creating dimensioned variables. They can be created in a rule base by simply assigning values to subscripted variables. This can be accomplished using the FIND clause, or through direct value assignment in the ACTIONS block. For example:

```
ACTIONS
    Week[1] = Megan
    Week[2] = John
    Week[3] = Susan
    FIND Week[4]
*
*
*
```

The clauses in this ACTIONS block create the dimensioned variable *Week*. The first three elements of the variable are assigned the values *Megan* (*Week[1]*), *John* (*Week[2]*), and *Susan* (*Week[3]*). A fourth element will be created if the inference engine is successful in FINDing a value for *Week[4]*.

Some Restrictions

Transferring data to a worksheet is subject to limitations that do not apply to similar database operations. These restrictions result from the fact that spreadsheet cells, unlike database fields, are precisely delineated with codes that describe the type of data in a cell, and the cell width. *VP-Expert* does not modify the cell description. It merely writes data into the cell within the description that already exists.

■ First, *VP-Expert* will only write data to a cell that already contains data.

■ Second, the length of the data being written to a worksheet must not exceed the length of the data already contained in the cell. If it does, it will be truncated. For example, if a PWKS clause attempts to transfer the string *STEVE* to a worksheet cell containing the text string *RON*, only the letters *STE* will be transferred. (The cell containing *RON* is encoded as a text cell that is 3 characters long. Since *VP-Expert* does not change the cell description, only the 3 characters *STE* can be written into this cell.) This does not apply to numeric values.

■ Third, the data being written to the worksheet cell must be of the same data type as the data previously contained in that cell. If you were to write text to a cell with numeric data, the contents of the cell would become zero. If you tried to write a number to a cell with text, the number would appear in the cell in a label format, not a numeric format.

In short, *VP-Expert* will not make any structural changes to a worksheet. It will only replace existing data with data of an identical type that is no longer than the original data.

It should be noted also that blank cells are ignored in PWKS operations. This means that empty cells inside the recipient row, column, or range will be skipped when values are transferred from a dimensioned variable to a worksheet.

Note: If you're using VP-Planner and such restrictions are problematic, write the data to a database file instead of a worksheet (database operations place no restrictions on what VP-Expert can write to them). Then call VP-Planner using the WORKON clause. (See WORKON in Chapter 9 for more information.) Using an auto-executing macro, you can import the database file to the worksheet, and then return to VP-Expert.

Writing to a Worksheet: An Example

The following small rule base demonstrates how the PWKS clause writes data to a worksheet. The worksheet to which data is transferred, Q1SALES.WKS, was shown at the beginning of this chapter.

```
ACTIONS
    X = 1
    WKS old_sales,COLUMN = March,q1sales
    WHILEKNOWN old_sales[X]
        FIND updated_sales
        new_sales[X] = (updated_sales)
        X = (X+1)
        RESET updated_sales
    END
    PWKS new_sales,COLUMN = March,q1sales;

ASK updated_sales: "Sales value {X} is {old_sales[X]}.
Enter the new amount here.";
```

The WKS clause in this rule base transfers the entries from the *March* sales column of the worksheet Q1SALES.WKS to the elements of a dimensioned variable *old_sales*.

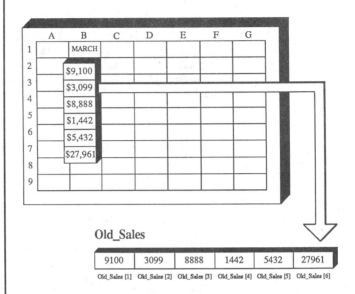

Old_Sales

9100	3099	8888	1442	5432	27961
Old_Sales [1]	Old_Sales [2]	Old_Sales [3]	Old_Sales [4]	Old_Sales [5]	Old_Sales [6]

Next, a WHILEKNOWN-END loop is executed. Note in the WHILEKNOWN-END loop that a "counter," represented by the variable *X*, is used to change the subscript numbers attached to the elements of the dimensioned variables with each iteration of the loop. Though the counter has its initial value set to 1 outside the loop (X=1), it is incremented with each execution of the loop (X=(X+1)) so that the loop executes once for each element of the dimensioned variable *old_sales*.

Each time the loop executes, the FIND clause triggers the ASK statement, which presents a message to the user. The message shows the value of one of the elements of the dimensioned variable created by the execution of the WKS clause, and asks the user to provide an updated value. The value provided is then assigned as the "updated" value of the element. The counter variable, *X*, is subsequently incremented by 1 so that the next time the question is presented, it will show the "old value" of the next element of the dimensioned variable. When the loop stops executing, the user will have assigned new values to each element of the dimensioned variable *new_sales*. The PWKS clause is then executed, transferring all the "updated" values back to the worksheet column.

Observe that the variable *updated_sales* must be RESET for each iteration of the WHILEKNOWN-END loop. If it were not, the ASK statement would only execute on the first pass through the loop. On the next pass, the variable *updated_sales* would already have a value and the FIND statement would not be triggered. (Remember, the ASK statement is only executed if the variable named in the FIND clause is UNKNOWN and there are no rules which are able to assign a value to it.) The result would be that the value entered at the first (and only) ASK prompt would be assigned to all elements of the dimensioned variable *new_sales*. The PWKS clause would subsequently transfer this value to every cell of the March column of the Q1SALES worksheet.

Summary

Using Worksheets with VP-Expert

VP-Expert can interact with worksheet files created with *VP-Planner*, Lotus 1-2-3, and other Lotus work-alike spreadsheet programs. Like database files, worksheet files can be used both as information bases and as induction tables for use with *VP-Expert's* Induce command.

Chapter 3 describes how the *VP-Expert* Induce command creates a knowledge base from an induction table created using the *VP-Expert* Editor. You can also create an induction table in a *VP-Planner* or Lotus 1-2-3 worksheet, but there are two restrictions that don't apply to text tables: they must contain a blank row under the column headings, and they must contain no blank columns.

Worksheets as Information Bases

For more information about the WKS and PWKS clauses, see Chapter 9.

In Chapter 5 you saw how to use database files as an information base—which we have defined as a store of data that can be accessed and altered during a *VP-Expert* consultation. *VP-Planner* and Lotus 1-2-3 worksheets can also be used as information bases. Using the WKS clause, data can be transferred from the cells of a worksheet to knowledge base variables. Using the PWKS clause, values can be written from *VP-Expert* variables directly to the cells of a worksheet.

Dimensioned Variables

When the WKS clause retrieves data from more than one cell—as from a range, column, or row—the data is stored by *VP-Expert* as a *dimensioned variable*. A dimensioned variable is a variable that stores multiple values as a one dimensional array of *elements*. Each element of the array is represented by the dimensioned variable name followed by a bracketed number corresponding to its placement in the array. For example, individual worksheet cells copied into a dimensioned variable called *Week* would be assigned as variable elements *Week[1]*, *Week[2]*, and so forth.

The PWKS clause also uses dimensioned variables; it transfers elements *from* a dimensioned variable *to* the cells of a worksheet.

Dimensioned variables used by PWKS need not have been created by a WKS clause. Dimensioned variables can also be created by simply assigning values to subscripted variables. For example, the following ACTIONS block creates the dimensioned variable *Month* containing 3 elements: *Month[1]*, *Month[2]*, and *Month[3]*.

```
ACTIONS
  Month[1] = Jan
  Month[2] = Feb
  Month[3] = Mar
  *

  *
```

PART III

The VP-Expert Reference Section

*C*hapters 7 through 10 comprise the reference section of this manual.

Chapter 7, the "Topical Reference," covers numerous subjects under seven broad topics.

Chapter 8, the "Menu Command Reference," documents each of VP-Expert's menu commands, in alphabetical order.

Chapter 9, the "Alphabetical Keyword Reference," documents each and every "keyword" that can be used in the construction of a VP-Expert knowledge base. These include the words that begin every clause and statement, special words used in rule construction, and other words reserved for special use in the knowledge base.

Chapter 10, the "Math Function Reference," explains how math can be used in a knowledge base, and describes VP-Expert's ten available math functions.

7.1 **TOPICAL REFERENCE**

7.2 TOPICAL REFERENCE

CHAPTER 7

Topical Reference

This chapter deals with a number of subjects fundamental to creating and using *VP-Expert* systems, organized under these seven broad topics:

- **Topical Keyword Reference**
- **Anatomy of a Knowledge Base**
- **External Program Calls: Using DOS COM, EXE, and BAT Files**
- **VP-Expert Variables**
- **VP-Expert Confidence Factors**
- **How VP-Expert Can Learn**
- **Creating an Effective Knowledge Base**

7

The first section, the "Topical Keyword Reference," groups the *VP-Expert* keywords by function in order to help you make more effective use of the *Alphabetical Keyword Reference* in Chapter 9. "Anatomy of a Knowledge Base" describes all the major elements that can be combined to create a knowledge base. The next section, "External Program Calls," discusses how *VP-Expert* can call and make use of other DOS programs. "VP-Expert Variables" includes everything you should know about *VP-Expert* variables. The next topic, "VP-Expert Confidence Factors," covers the use of confidence factors in *VP-Expert,* including information about how confidence factors are calculated by the program. "How VP-Expert Can Learn" illustrates how *VP-Expert* systems can be designed to, in a sense, learn during a consultation. The final section, "Creating an Effective Knowledge Base" provides tips for building an effective, error-free knowledge base.

Topical Keyword Reference

Chapter 9, the "Alphabetical Keyword Reference," gives detailed information on how to use each of *VP-Expert's* keywords. These include system variables, special words used in rule and ACTIONS block construction, and the names that identify every *VP-Expert* clause and statement.

The pages that follow here deal briefly with these keywords by topic. Rather than appearing alphabetically, keywords are listed and described under headings relating to how they're used. This treatment is intended to help you know what to look for in the Alphabetical Keyword Reference.

ACTIONS Block Construction

Though the FIND clause is used to identify the goal variable(s) of a consultation, many other clauses can also be used in an ACTIONS block. The complete list of available clauses appears in Appendix B. For details about each clause, see Chapter 9.

ACTIONS: Identifies the mandatory "ACTIONS block," which sets the agenda for a *VP-Expert* consultation. [STATEMENT]

FIND: Used in the ACTIONS block or in rules to instruct the inference engine to find a value for a given variable. When used in the ACTIONS block, the variable is referred to as a "goal variable," because finding the value is a "goal" of the consultation. [CLAUSE]

Chaining Knowledge Bases

CHAIN: Used for "chaining" together two KBS files for use in a single consultation. This clause permits the use of knowledge bases that would otherwise be too large to be contained in memory.

[CLAUSE]

EXECUTE: Makes for a seamless transition from one knowledge base to another. [STATEMENT]

LOADFACTS: In knowledge base chaining, LOADFACTS facilitates the transfer of variable values from one KBS file to the next.

[CLAUSE]

SAVEFACTS: In knowledge base chaining, SAVEFACTS saves the values from one knowledge base so that they can be loaded (using LOADFACTS) into the new knowledge base file. [CLAUSE]

Confidence Factors

RULE: Identifies a knowledge base rule (where confidence factors can be assigned to conclusion values). [STATEMENT]

SORT: Sorts the values of plural variables into descending order of confidence factors. [CLAUSE]

TRUTHTHRESH: Sets the minimum confidence factor required for values in rule conditions (in order for the condition to be considered "true"). [CLAUSE]

Database Access

ALL: Used in GET and MENU clause syntax.

AND: Logical operator used to combine conditions in rules and in database rules in GET and MENU clauses.

APPEND: Adds a record to the end of a database file. [CLAUSE]

CLOSE: Closes a database file and moves the record pointer to the top of the file. Used between GET clauses to reset the record pointer.

[CLAUSE]

GET: Used to transfer field values in database files to knowledge base variables. [CLAUSE]

INDEX: Makes use of *VP-Info* or dBASE II index files to change the order in which database records can be accessed. [CLAUSE]

MENU: Creates a menu consisting of field values taken from all or selected records of a database file. [CLAUSE]

MENU_SIZE: A system variable whose numeric value corresponds to the number of items on the last menu created by a MENU clause.

MRESET: Erases a MENU clause menu from memory. [CLAUSE]

OR: Logical operator used to combine conditions in rules or in database rules in GET and MENU clauses.

PUT: Transfers values from knowledge base variables to the fields of the current record of a given database file. [CLAUSE]

External Program Calls

BCALL: Executes a DOS batch (*BAT*) file, then resumes the consultation. [CLAUSE]

CALL: Executes a DOS *EXE* file, then resumes the consultation. [CLAUSE]

CCALL: Executes a DOS *COM* file, then resumes the consultation. [CLAUSE]

WORKON: Executes *VP-Planner* and displays a given worksheet, allowing the user to perform normal worksheet operations; then resumes the consultation. [CLAUSE]

Inference Engine

ASK: Creates a message requiring the user to input a value for a given variable. This statement is executed when the inference engine cannot assign a value to the variable with a passing rule. [STATEMENT]

FIND: Instructs the inference engine to find a value for a given variable. [CLAUSE]

PLURAL: Identifies variables that can be assigned multiple values during a consultation. [STATEMENT]

Loop Construction

END: Identifies the end of a WHILEKNOWN-END loop construction. [CLAUSE]

RESET: Resets a named variable to UNKNOWN. [CLAUSE]

WHILEKNOWN: Identifies and controls the execution of a command loop contained in a rule or ACTIONS block. [CLAUSE]

Menu Creation

CHOICES: Creates a menu of options that will accompany a
question generated by the ASK or AUTOQUERY statement.

[STATEMENT]

MENU: Creates a menu consisting of field values taken from all or
selected records of a database file. [CLAUSE]

MENU_SIZE: A system variable whose numeric value corresponds
to the number of items on the last menu created by a MENU clause.

MRESET: Erases a MENU clause menu from memory. [CLAUSE]

Message Displays

ASK: Creates a message requiring the user to input a value for a
given variable. This statement is executed when the inference engine
cannot assign a value to the variable with a passing rule.

[STATEMENT]

AUTOQUERY: Automatically addresses a question to the user when
the inference engine requires a value for a variable for which there is
no passing rule or ASK statement. [STATEMENT]

BECAUSE: Provides text for display in response to the Why? and
How? menu commands.

BKCOLOR: Determines the background color of the consultation
screen. [STATEMENT]

COLOR: Determines consultation text color. [CLAUSE]

DISPLAY: Displays a given message to the user during a
consultation. [CLAUSE]

FORMAT: Sets the format for numbers displayed using DISPLAY
and PDISPLAY. [CLAUSE]

PDISPLAY: Like DISPLAY, except instead of displaying a message
on screen, the message is sent to a printer. [CLAUSE]

PRINTOFF: Disables PRINTON clause, causing subsequent
DISPLAY commands to execute normally. [CLAUSE]

PRINTON: Causes all subsequent DISPLAY text to be printed by a
printer as well as displayed on the screen. [CLAUSE]

Plural (Multiple-Value) Variables

PLURAL: Identifies variables that can be assigned multiple values during a consultation. [STATEMENT]

POP: Used to manipulate the values of a plural variable separately. [CLAUSE]

SORT: Sorts the values of plural variables into descending order of confidence factors. [CLAUSE]

Printing Messages on a Printer

EJECT: Used with continuous form paper, causes the printer head to move to the top of the next page. [CLAUSE]

PDISPLAY: Like DISPLAY, except instead of displaying a message on the screen, the message is sent to a printer. [CLAUSE]

PRINTOFF: Disables PRINTON clause, causing subsequent DISPLAY commands to execute normally. [CLAUSE]

PRINTON: Causes all subsequent DISPLAY text to be printed by a printer as well as displayed on screen. [CLAUSE]

Question Generation

ASK: Creates a message requiring the user to input a value for a given variable. This statement is executed when the inference engine cannot assign a value to the variable with a passing rule.
[STATEMENT]

AUTOQUERY: Automatically addresses a question to the user when the inference engine requires a value for a variable for which there is no passing rule or ASK statement. [STATEMENT]

CHOICES: Creates a menu of options that will accompany a question generated by the ASK or AUTOQUERY statement.
[STATEMENT]

MENU: Creates a menu consisting of field values taken from all or selected records of a database file. The menu is displayed when a corresponding ASK or AUTOQUERY statement is executed.
[CLAUSE]

See Chapter 2 and RULE in Chapter 9 for information about rule construction.

Rule Construction

AND: Logical operator used to combine conditions in a rule premise or in a database rule in a GET or MENU clause.

BECAUSE: Provides text for display in response to the Why? and How? menu commands.

ELSE: Provides an alternate rule conclusion to be used in the event that the premise of a rule is found to be false.

IF: Identifies the premise of a rule.

OR: Logical operator used to combine conditions in a rule premise or in a database rule in a GET or MENU clause.

RULE: Identifies the beginning of a knowledge base rule.

[STATEMENT]

THEN: Identifies the conclusion of a rule.

Runtime Consultations

BKCOLOR: Determines the background color of the consultation screen.   [STATEMENT]

COLOR: Determines consultation text color.   [CLAUSE]

ENDOFF: Eliminates the need to press the *END* key to finalize a selection from menus created by the CHOICES statement or MENU clause. Affects only single-valued variables.   [STATEMENT]

EXECUTE: Causes a consultation to begin immediately upon execution of the Main Menu Consult command.   [STATEMENT]

RUNTIME: Eliminates the two bottom windows that are used for development of the knowledge base, thus creating a "runtime" consultation screen.   [STATEMENT]

Screen Appearance

BKCOLOR: Determines the background color of the consultation screen.   [STATEMENT]

COLOR: Determines consultation text color.   [CLAUSE]

System Variables

MENU_SIZE: A system variable whose numeric value corresponds to the number of items on the last menu created by a MENU clause.

RECORD_NUM: A system variable whose numeric value corresponds to the number of the last record accessed by a GET clause.

UNKNOWN: A keyword used in *VP-Expert* to identify variables that have unknown values.

Text Files

LOADFACTS: Retrieves variables and values stored in a text file. Used in knowledge base chaining. [CLAUSE]

RECEIVE: Imports the current line of a given text file into a knowledge base variable. [CLAUSE]

SAVEFACTS: Stores all currently known variables and values in a text file. Used in knowledge base chaining. [CLAUSE]

SHIP: Exports the value of a knowledge base variable to the last line of a given text file. [CLAUSE]

SHOWTEXT: Imports a page of text with a heading equal to the value of a knowledge base variable. [CLAUSE]

Variables and Values

ASK: Creates a message requiring the user to input a value for a given variable. This statement is executed when the inference engine cannot assign a value to the variable with a passing rule.
[STATEMENT]

AUTOQUERY: Automatically addresses a question to the user when the inference engine requires a value for a variable for which there is no passing rule or ASK statement. [STATEMENT]

CHOICES: Creates a menu of options that will accompany a question generated by the ASK or AUTOQUERY statement.
[STATEMENT]

FIND: Instructs the inference engine to find a value for a given variable. [CLAUSE]

GET: Used to transfer field values in database files to knowledge base variables. [CLAUSE]

LOADFACTS: In knowledge base chaining, LOADFACTS facilitates the transfer of variable values from one KBS file to the next.
[CLAUSE]

MENU: Creates a menu consisting of field values taken from all or selected records of a database file. [CLAUSE]

PLURAL: Identifies variables that can be assigned multiple values during a consultation. [STATEMENT]

POP: Used to manipulate the values of a plural variable separately.
[CLAUSE]

PUT: Transfers values from knowledge base variables to the fields of the current record of a given database file. [CLAUSE]

PWKS: Transfers values from variables into a *VP-Planner* or Lotus 1-2-3 worksheet. [CLAUSE]

RECEIVE: Imports the current line of a text file into a knowledge base variable. [CLAUSE]

RESET: Resets the value of a named variable to UNKNOWN.
[CLAUSE]

RULE: Identifies beginning of a knowledge base rule. [STATEMENT]

SAVEFACTS: In knowledge base chaining, SAVEFACTS saves the values from one knowledge base so that they can be loaded (using LOADFACTS) into the new knowledge base file. [CLAUSE]

SHIP: Exports the value of a knowledge base variable to the last line of a text file. [CLAUSE]

SORT: Sorts the values of plural variables into descending order of confidence factors. [CLAUSE]

UNKNOWN: A keyword used by *VP-Expert* to identify variables that have unknown values.

WHILEKNOWN: Identifies and controls the execution of a command loop contained in a rule or ACTIONS block. [CLAUSE]

WKS: Transfers cell values from a *VP-Planner* or Lotus 1-2-3 worksheet into a single-valued variable (for single cell transfer) or into the elements of a dimensioned variable. [CLAUSE]

Worksheet Access

PWKS: Transfers values from variables into a *VP-Planner* or Lotus 1-2-3 worksheet. [CLAUSE]

WKS: Transfers cell values from a *VP-Planner* or Lotus 1-2-3 worksheet into a single-valued variable (for single cell transfer) or into the elements of a dimensioned variable. [CLAUSE]

WORKON: Executes *VP-Planner* and displays a given worksheet, allowing the user to perform normal worksheet operations; then resumes the consultation. [CLAUSE]

Anatomy of a Knowledge Base

The following illustration represents all of the major elements that can be combined to create a *VP-Expert* knowledge base. They are not all required. Strictly speaking, the only element that is actually *required* in a knowledge base is an ACTIONS block. Some perfectly reasonable knowledge bases don't contain a single rule—they simply consist of an ACTIONS block, an information base, and maybe, but not necessarily, some statements.

Each of the elements in the illustration is described elsewhere in the manual, but in order to provide a more concise, integrated approach, we will review them briefly here. In addition, for each topic, we will direct you to other places in the manual where further information can be found.

VP-Expert Knowledge Base

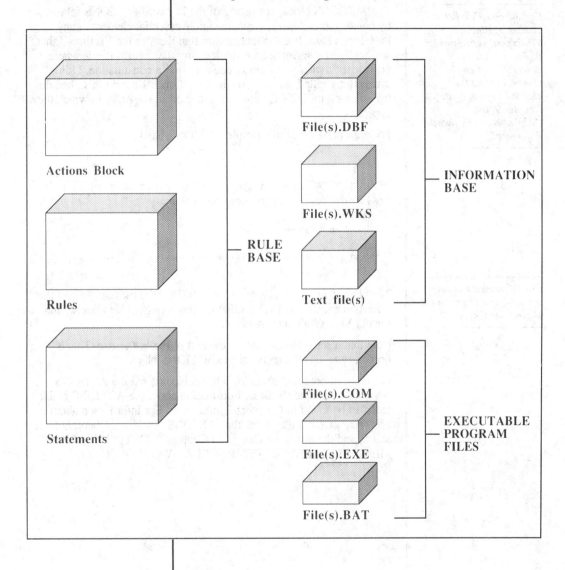

For the complete list of clauses available in VP-Expert, see Appendix B. For a detailed description of any clause, look up the clause "keyword" in Chapter 9, the "Alphabetical Keyword Reference."

The ACTIONS Block

The ACTIONS block, consisting of the keyword ACTIONS followed by one or more *clauses*, is an absolutely essential element in any knowledge base. It is the mechanism that dictates the "actions" that will take place during a consultation. In other words, this is where you identify what you want to occur during a consultation. Using instructions called clauses, you, in effect, say, "First do this, then do this, then do this...." Clauses are executed in the order in which they appear.

For example, look at this simple ACTIONS block:

```
ACTIONS

   DISPLAY "Welcome to the charming world of cheese!
Press any key to begin the consultation. ~"

   FIND The_Cheese

   DISPLAY  "The most appropriate cheese for this course
is {#The_Cheese}.";
```

The clauses in this ACTIONS block DISPLAY a message, direct the inference engine to FIND a value for the variable *The_Cheese*, and then DISPLAY another message.

For information about the VP-Expert inference engine, see Chapter 2.

Note that a semicolon occurs at the end of the last clause. This is necessary to signal the end of the ACTIONS block.

For more information about ACTIONS blocks, see the ACTIONS keyword in Chapter 9. Basic information about the ACTIONS block can also be found in Chapters 2 through 4. For information about accessing external files from the ACTIONS block, see Chapters 5 and 6, and the following clauses in Chapter 9: GET, PUT, APPEND, MENU, WKS, PWKS, SHIP, RECEIVE, WORKON, CALL, CCALL, BCALL.

See Chapter 2 for information about how rule order affects a VP-Expert consultation.

Rules

The "knowledge" or "expertise" of the expert system is contained in the form of IF-THEN rules. "IF this is true, THEN that is true." For example:

```
RULE 1
IF    Complement = crackers_and_bread
THEN  The_Cheese = Brie;
```

This rule says, in effect, "If the complement is crackers and bread, then the cheese will be Brie."

The IF portion of the rule, which contains one or more *conditions*, is called the rule premise. The THEN portion, which contains one or more *conclusions*, is called the rule conclusion.

> *Note: Rules can also contain elements identified by the keywords ELSE and BECAUSE. If used, ELSE supplies conclusions that will execute in the event that the conditions in the premise are determined to be false. BECAUSE is followed by text that will be displayed in response to the Why? and How? menu commands during a consultation. For more information, see ELSE (under RULE) and BECAUSE in Chapter 9.*

Rules can also contain clauses—just like the ACTIONS block. But these clauses, placed in the rule conclusion, only execute if the rule "passes" (is found to be true). "If A is true, then B is true and do this."

```
RULE 3
IF    Course = Appetizer
THEN  Complement = crackers_and_bread CNF 80;
      DISPLAY "The complement will be crackers and
bread."
      FIND Preference;
```

See "VP-Expert Confidence Factors" in this chapter for an explanation of confidence factors.

This rule says, "IF the *Course* is an *Appetizer*, THEN the *Complement* will be *crackers_and_bread* (with a confidence factor of 80). If *Course* is, in fact, *Appetizer*, DISPLAY this message to the user. 'The *complement* will be *crackers_and_bread*.' Then FIND a value for the variable *Preference*."

*Variables are discussed
later in this chapter
under the heading
"VP-Expert Variables."*

Notice that the English-like *variables* (*Course, Complement*) and *values* (*Appetizer, crackers_and_bread*) used in rules make the rules easy to understand and compose.

The relational operators shown below are used to compare variables and values in rule conditions. Only the equal sign can be used in rule conclusions.

=	equals	>	greater than
<	less than	>=	greater than or equal to
<=	less than or equal to	<>	not equal to

For more explicit information about writing rules, see the RULE keyword in Chapter 9. See also Chapters 2, 3, and 4. Chapter 2 discusses both rule construction and how the inference engine uses rules to solve problems during a consultation. Chapters 3 and 4 provide basic information about writing and expanding rules.

Statements

While the rules of a knowledge base contain the "expertise" of the expert system, *statements* typically contain information relating to the consultation itself. The RUNTIME statement, for example, removes windows used during knowledge base development from the screen, creating a "runtime" or "end user" consultation. The BKCOLOR statement controls the background color of the consultation screen. Many statements affect knowledge base variables. For example, the ASK statement identifies a variable whose value must come from the user, and specifies text that will be used to ask the user for the value. A CHOICES statement naming the same variable can be used to provide a menu of values from which the user will choose in response to the ASK query.

Unlike clauses, which must occur within the ACTIONS block or be contained in a rule, statements stand alone. For example:

```
RUNTIME;

BKCOLOR = 5;

ACTIONS

   DISPLAY "Welcome to the charming world of cheese!
Press any key to begin the consultation.~"

   FIND The_Cheese

   DISPLAY "The most appropriate cheese for this course is {#The_Cheese}.";

RULE 1
IF    Complement = crackers_and_bread
THEN  The_Cheese = Brie;

RULE 2
IF    Complement = bread_and_fruit
THEN  The_Cheese = Camembert;

RULE 3
IF    Course = Appetizer
THEN  Complement = crackers_and_bread;

RULE 4
IF    Course = Dessert
THEN  Complement = bread_and_fruit;

ASK Course: "Is the course an Appetizer or Dessert?";

CHOICES Course: Appetizer, Dessert;
```

Notice that like rules and ACTIONS blocks, statements must end in a semicolon. Notice also that they can be placed almost anywhere in the knowledge base. Unlike clauses and rules, placement of statements in a knowledge base has no affect on how they're executed. They can be placed anywhere outside of the ACTIONS block or the rules. This manual, by convention, places them at the beginning and at the end of the KBS file.

The complete list of *VP-Expert* statements appears in Appendix B. For detailed information about using each statement, look up the statement "keyword" in Chapter 9, the "Alphabetical Keyword Reference." Basic information about statements is also provided in Chapters 2 through 4.

Using an Information Base

VP-Expert is one of the first expert system tools for personal computers which permits the total integration of information contained in database, worksheet, and text files with the rules and other control structures inherent in the rule base. When such files are used, the KBS file is referred to as the "rule base."

VP-Expert is compatible with database files created in VP-Info, dBASE II, III, III+, or any work-alike database program. Worksheet files can be created in VP-Planner, Lotus 1-2-3, or a work-alike spreadsheet program. Text files can be created by any text editor which creates ASCII files.

There are a number of advantages to using external files as an information base. For example:

■ Data contained in these files can be transferred to and from knowledge base variables.

■ The knowledge base can make use of existing data files.

■ Since large amounts of easily changeable data can be stored separately from the rule base, the rule base can be kept relatively simple.

■ *VP-Expert* can be used to create an expert system "front end" to the external programs, making modification of the data files even easier.

Chapters 5 and 6 deal explicitly with the subject of using database files and worksheet files as *VP-Expert* information bases. SHIP and RECEIVE in Chapter 9 discuss exchanging data with text files.

For more information about the specific *VP-Expert* clauses used for exchanging data with database files, see: GET, PUT, APPEND, MENU, and INDEX. The clauses used for exchanging data with worksheet files are WKS, PWKS, and WORKON.

Calling External DOS Files

In addition to its ability to exchange data with compatible database and worksheet files, *VP-Expert* also has the ability to "call" other external files. This allows *VP-Expert* to, in effect, borrow the capabilities of other programs.

The next section in this chapter deals specifically with this topic.

External Program Calls: Using DOS COM, EXE, and BAT Files

One of *VP-Expert's* most outstanding features is its ability to call external programs. This capability allows *VP-Expert* to, in effect, perform the functions and operations of other software. You can make a *VP-Expert* system include sophisticated math analysis programs or advanced telecommunications; you can invoke a Pascal routine, or *VP-Planner* or Lotus 1-2-3, where the user can perform worksheet operations.

There are four *VP-Expert* clauses that are used to make outside program calls: CALL, CCALL, BCALL, and WORKON.

CALL is used to execute DOS files with an *EXE* extension.

CCALL is used to call DOS *COM* files.

BCALL executes DOS batch (*BAT*) files.

WORKON executes *VP-Planner* and calls a given worksheet to screen.

Each of these clauses is discussed in detail in Chapter 9. The discussion here will deal broadly with some of the tasks these clauses can be used to perform.

Complex Math Programs

Although *VP-Expert* offers a number of advanced mathematical functions (described in Chapter 10), its capabilities may be limited for certain highly technical needs. In such cases, external programs can be called to perform the required operations.

Suppose you wanted to design an engineering-oriented expert system requiring the calculation of heat fluctuation data using numerical analysis. You could create the analysis programs in C or Pascal (or another high-level language), compile them into executable DOS files, and call them, when needed, from within *VP-Expert*. The results could be stored in an ASCII file and then retrieved by the expert system using the LOADFACTS or RECEIVE clause.

Telecommunications Links

Telecommunications links can also be established using *VP-Expert*.

Suppose you are working on a *VP-Expert* stock portfolio analyzer, and you want the system to access information stored in a remote database (e.g., the current Dow Jones stock data) to ensure that recommendations are based on the most current information available. You could set up a commercial telecommunications package to handle the task, store its instructions in an executable file, and then simply call the program file from within *VP-Expert*.

General Considerations

When designing expert systems that make external program calls, you should be aware of the following:

Program calls can be "interactive" or "transparent." Interactive calls require the user to interact with the external program and then return to the consultation. Transparent calls are carried out "behind the scenes," without the awareness of the user.

■ The memory of the computer for which the consultation is designed must be sufficient to handle the extra memory required by the external program.

■ In order for *VP-Expert* to make use of data from an external program call, the program should load the data into a compatible database, worksheet, or text file.

■ BCALL is the only "call" clause with the ability to pass parameters to an externally called program via the command line interface.

VP-Expert Variables

Variables are a fundamental and essential component of a knowledge base. In fact, the key to *VP-Expert's* problem solving ability is the "intelligent" assignment of values to variables during a consultation.

Practically every clause, rule, and statement makes use of variables. They're used in the ACTIONS block to identify the "goals" of a consultation, and in rules to encode the "knowledge" or "expertise" of the expert system. DISPLAY clauses use variables to indicate where associated values should be displayed in text. ASK statements identify variables whose values must be supplied by the user at question prompts, and so on.

This section examines many uses and facets of *VP-Expert* variables, covering such topics as:

- How variables are assigned values.

- The different types of variables.

- Indirect addressing.

- How dimensioned variables are used and created.

- Using variables as "counters."

- How variables are used to transfer data to and from database, worksheet, and text files.

- Variable lengths and limitations.

How Variables Are Assigned Values

During a consultation, variables can be assigned values by passing rules, user input, direct value assignment in the ACTIONS block, indirect variable addressing, and transferring data from external files. Each of these methods will be examined in turn.

Passing Rules

Whenever a rule passes during a consultation, at least one variable is assigned a value.

For example, in the following rule, the variable *animal* is assigned the value *mammal* if the values named in the rule premise match the current values of the variables *backbone, birth,* and *blood.*

```
RULE 1
IF    backbone = yes AND
      birth = live AND
      blood = warm
THEN  animal = mammal;
```

In a rule, values can also be assigned to variables following the ELSE keyword. An expression following ELSE in a rule assigns a value to a variable if the premise of the rule is determined to be false. For example, if the conditions stated in the following rule are not met, *animal* is assigned the value *reptile*.

```
RULE 2
IF    backbone = yes AND
      birth = live AND
      blood = warm
THEN  animal = mammal
ELSE  animal = reptile;
```

User Input

Most knowledge bases, when executed, require the user to answer questions. Through questions requiring a user response, information which is not contained in the knowledge base can be integrated into the consultation.

The statements used to generate questions are ASK and AUTOQUERY.

ASK identifies a variable and supplies text that is used during a consultation to obtain a value from the user. The CHOICES statement or MENU clause can be used to display, along with the question, a menu of values from which the user can choose. For example, look at the following ASK and CHOICES statements.

```
ASK month: "For which month do you want sales
information?";
```

```
CHOICES month: Jan, Feb, Mar, Apr;
```

These would produce the following prompt when executed during a consultation:

```
For which month do you want sales information?
Jan                   Feb                   Mar
Apr
```

If the user were to choose *Jan* at the prompt, the value *Jan* would be assigned to the variable *month*.

The AUTOQUERY statement can also be used to address questions to the user. When executed, it generates a generic question any time the inference engine cannot find a value for a variable through any other means. For example, if the inference engine could not find a value for the variable *month*, AUTOQUERY would display the question, *"What is the value of month?"* The user's response would then be assigned as the value of *month*.

The AUTOQUERY statement is not typically used in a runtime knowledge base. It's primarily used during knowledge base development to identify variables that require ASK statements.

For more information, see AUTOQUERY in Chapter 9.

ACTIONS Block Direct Value Assignment

In rules, "direct value assignment" occurs following the keyword THEN or ELSE. If certain conditions are met, a variable is directly assigned a value through an equation like *variable = value*. Direct value assignment can also be accomplished in the ACTIONS block—only in the ACTIONS block, no conditions need be met. When the assignment expression is executed, the variable takes the given value.

For example, the following ACTIONS block uses direct value assignment to assign the value *DOS* to the variable *operating_system*.

```
ACTIONS
    operating_system = DOS
    FIND best_computer
    DISPLAY "The best computer for your needs is a
{best_computer}." ;
*
*
*
```

Indirect Addressing

In the ACTIONS block and in the conclusion of rules, expressions like the following are used to assign values to variables.

variable = value

The variable always occurs on the left side of the expression, the value on the right.

However, variables can occur on both sides of the expression if the variable on the right is enclosed in parentheses—like this:

variable = (variable)

This expression assigns the value of the variable named in parentheses to the variable named on the left (the variable on the left cannot be enclosed in parentheses). This method of indirectly accessing a value is called indirect addressing.

In the following ACTIONS block, the variable *best_month* is assigned the value of the variable *month*.

```
ACTIONS
  FIND month
  best_month = (month)
  *
  *
```

The following rule assigns the value of the variable *difference* to the variable *profit* if the condition stated in the premise is true:

```
RULE 21
IF   difference > 0
THEN profit = (difference);
```

Variables enclosed in parentheses can also be used to indirectly represent values in rule conditions. For example:

```
RULE 4
IF    profit >= (March_profit)
THEN  strategy = successful;
```

Indirect Addressing in the GET Clause

Indirect addressing can also be used in a "database rule" in a GET clause. Instead of a field name on the right side of a database rule condition, a field name can be specified indirectly using a variable name in parentheses.

Use indirect addressing in cases where you're not sure which field or fields the database rule will access.

For example, look at the following rule base:

```
ACTIONS
  FIND pick
  WHILEKNOWN profit
    GET  pick = (period),sales,ALL
    DISPLAY "The profit for the month of {month},
{year}, was {profit}";
  END;

RULE a
IF   period = month
THEN MENU info1,ALL,sales,month
     FIND info1
     pick = (info1);

RULE b
IF   period = year
THEN MENU info2,ALL,sales,year
     FIND info2
     pick = (info2);

ASK period: "Do you wish to view the profit history for a
particular month or year?";
CHOICES period: MONTH, YEAR;

ASK info1: "Select the month.";

ASK info2: "Select the year.";
```

When this is executed, the user will be asked to choose a value for the variables *period* and *info1* or *info2*. The value of *period* will be used in the database rule of the GET clause to determine which record is selected. The value chosen for *info1* or *info2*, which is assigned to *pick*, is the value that will be compared to the value of *period* in the GET clause. For example, if the user were to choose *MONTH* and *JAN* at the ASK prompts, the database rule, *pick=(period)*, would cause the GET to search for all the records with the value *JAN* stored in the field *MONTH*.

Double Indirect Addressing

Another kind of indirect addressing, "double indirect addressing" can also be used to assign values to variables.

Consider the following sequence of expressions:

PET = Dog
DOG = Whippet
ANIMAL = (@Pet)

The @ "at" sign in the last expression indicates that the value of the variable *Pet* is the name of the variable whose value should be assigned to *ANIMAL*. The value assigned to the variable *ANIMAL* would be *Whippet*.

To explain how this works, it's useful to think about how variables and values are dealt with in memory.

The first expression, *PET = Dog*, creates a place in memory, PET, and stores in it the value *Dog*.

PET

The second expression *DOG = Whippet*, creates a place in memory, DOG, and stores in it the value *Whippet*.

DOG

The third expression *ANIMAL = (@Pet)*, creates a place in memory called *ANIMAL*. To find a value to store there, *VP-Expert* looks first to the location PET. PET contains the value *Dog*, so the location DOG is examined next. The value contained in DOG is *Whippet*, so *Whippet* is assigned to *ANIMAL*.

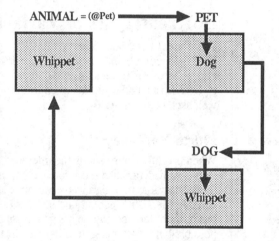

These levels of indirect addressing can be particularly useful when accessing database files. Using only one variable name, one could indicate a field name and the value stored in that field (after a GET has been executed).

Transferring Data To and From External Files

One of *VP-Expert's* greatest strengths is its ability to assign values stored in compatible text, database, and worksheet files to knowledge base variables. Values can also be transferred in the opposite direction—from variables to text, database, and worksheet files. Since this capability is well documented in other parts of the manual, it won't be repeated here. Instead, refer to the following sections:

For information about transferring data between *VP-Info* or dBASE database files and knowledge base variables, see Chapter 5 and the GET, MENU, PUT, and APPEND clauses in Chapter 9.

For information about copying data to and from the cells of a *VP-Planner* or Lotus 1-2-3 worksheet, see Chapter 6 and the WKS and PWKS clauses in Chapter 9.

For information about transferring data between variables and text files, see the SHIP, RECEIVE, SHOWTEXT, LOADFACTS, and SAVEFACTS clauses in Chapter 9.

Different Types of Variables

There are 3 basic variations of the *VP-Expert* variable. Variables can be *single-valued, plural,* or *dimensioned.* Each type is examined briefly here. For further information about plural variables, see PLURAL in Chapter 9. For more information about dimensioned variables, see Chapter 6.

Plural Variables

A single PLURAL statement can name up to 10 variables. See PLURAL in Chapter 9 for more information specific to the PLURAL statement.

When a FIND clause sends the inference engine to find a value for a single-valued variable, the inference engine stops looking after it finds one value to assign to the variable. But if the variable is a plural variable (i.e., if it's named in a PLURAL statement in the knowledge base), the inference engine assigns as many values to the variable as possible before stopping. In other words, the inference engine will only stop looking for values for a plural variable when all possible paths have been explored.

Rules can name more than one of the values assigned to a plural variable in conditions, but only one variable name is used. For example:

```
RULE 1
IF    Course = Appetizer OR
      Course = Salad AND
      Course <> Dessert
THEN The_Cheese = Gouda;
```

Rules can also assign more than one value to a plural variable in its conclusion. For example:

```
IF    Course = Appetizer OR
      Course = Salad AND
      Course <> Dessert
THEN The_Cheese = Gouda CNF 80
      The_Cheese = Brie CNF 60;
```

You cannot refer to the separate values of plural variables by separate names. However, there is a clause that lets you manipulate the values one at a time. See the POP clause in Chapter 9 for more information.

Plural Variables and Display Text

If a plural variable name enclosed in curly brackets is included in ASK or DISPLAY text, each of the values assigned to the plural variable will be displayed. For example, if *The_Cheese* was a plural variable, the following DISPLAY clause would display each of its assigned values when executed:

The # sign displays the corresponding confidence factor with each value of the plural variable.

```
DISPLAY "Any of the following cheeses would be
appropriate for the meal you've indicated:
{#The_Cheese}."
```

If a SORT clause were to precede this DISPLAY clause, the different values assigned to the plural variable would be displayed in the descending order of confidence factor. See SORT in Chapter 9 for more information.

If you wanted to display a separate message for each value of a plural variable, you could do so using the POP clause and a WHILEKNOWN-END loop:

```
*
*
WHILEKNOWN sample
   RESET sample
   POP The_Cheese, sample
   DISPLAY "{sample} is one of several appropriate
cheeses for the meal you've described.
END;
*
*
PLURAL: The_Cheese;
*
```

See POP, WHILEKNOWN, PLURAL, and RESET in Chapter 9 for more information about using the above clauses.

Dimensioned Variables

A dimensioned variable is a variable that stores multiple values as a one-dimensional array of elements.

VARIABLE

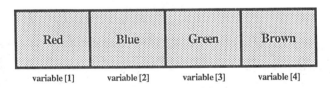

| variable [1] | variable [2] | variable [3] | variable [4] |

Each element of the array can be addressed and manipulated separately using the variable name and a bracketed number representing the element's placement in the array.

Dimensioned variables are created when multiple cell values are read from a worksheet to a rule base with the WKS clause. Chapter 6 and the WKS clause in Chapter 9 give detailed information about how this works.

Dimensioned variables can also be created by simply assigning values to variables with subscripted numbers. For example, the following expressions in an ACTIONS block would create the dimensioned variable *Dog*, with three elements, *Dog[1]*, *Dog[2]*, and *Dog[3]*.

```
ACTIONS
 Dog[1] = Bloodhound
 Dog[2] = Beagle
 Dog[3] = Boxer
 *
 *
```

DOG

Bloodhound	Beagle	Boxer
dog [1]	dog [2]	dog [3]

Each element of the dimensioned variable is like any other (non-dimensioned) variable. They can be single-valued or plural; they can be named in clauses or statements (though in some cases subscripts cannot be specified with counter variables); their values can be displayed separately, and so on.

The PWKS clause copies the values in dimensioned variables to the cells of a worksheet.

Dimensioned variables are useful for transferring multiple values to and from worksheet files. But there are other uses for them as well.

Dimensioned variables can be used in some instances to significantly cut down on the number of rules in a knowledge base. For example, look at this rule:

```
RULE 11
IF    stock_price_1 > (buy_price)  AND
      stock_price_1 < (10_wk_average)
THEN  response = sell;
```

This rule applies to one stock price only, represented by the variable *stock_price_1*.

Using ''counters'' for incrementing variables is common practice in WHILEKNOWN-END loops. See ''Writing to a Worksheet'' in Chapter 6 and the PWKS clause in Chapter 9 for additional examples of using counters.

Now look at this rule and ACTIONS block:

```
ACTIONS
*
*
    X = 1
    WHILEKNOWN stock[X]
       RESET response
       FIND response
       action[X] = (response)
       X = (X + 1)
    END;
*
*

RULE 11
IF     stock_price[X] > (buy_price[X]) AND
       stock_price[X] < (10_wk_average)
THEN   response = sell
*
*
```

Using an index counter—in this case, X—you can generalize a rule to accommodate an array of stocks, their corresponding prices and the suggested actions.

Single-Valued Variables

Now that ''plural'' and ''dimensioned'' variables have been defined, single-valued variables can be described as variables that are not named in a PLURAL statement and are not dimensioned. Quite simply, a single-valued variable is a variable that can only have one value assigned to it at a time.

We stated previously that when the FIND clause sends the inference engine to find a value for a plural variable, it assigns as many values as it possibly can to the variable before it ends the search. When the inference engine seeks a value for a single-valued variable, it stops the search after a single value has been found. It should be noted, however, that if at some later point in the consultation another value is assigned to that single-valued variable, the new value will replace the old one—even if the confidence factor is less than the original confidence factor.

Variable Lengths and Limitations

The following rules apply to *VP-Expert* variables:

- Variable names must begin with a letter.

- Variable names are restricted to 20 characters, which can include letters, numbers, and the following special characters:

    _ $ ^ | %

- Spaces are not allowed in variable names. Instead of spaces, use the underline character (e.g., *The_Cheese*).

- *VP-Expert* keywords cannot be used as variable names. If they are, errors may occur when the consultation is executed. Keywords can, however, be included within variable names. For example, *color* cannot be used as a variable name, because COLOR is a keyword. But *the_color* is a perfectly legal variable name. The complete list of *VP-Expert* keywords is provided in Appendix B.

- Most variables can be assigned values of no more than 20 characters. However, there are cases where variables can be assigned longer values. Variables created by the RECEIVE clause (which reads a line of text from a text file into a variable) can be assigned a maximum of 80 characters. Variables created by the GET clause can have values of up to 256 characters in length.

The SHIP and PUT clauses can send variable values of up to 80 and 256 characters to text or database files, respectively, but the variables must have been created by a RECEIVE or GET clause (respectively).

VP-Expert Confidence Factors

In expert systems created with *VP-Expert*, numbers referred to as "confidence factors" are used to account for varying levels of certainty. These numbers can be entered into the conclusions of rules in the knowledge base, or entered by the user in response to questions accompanied by menus.

The confidence factor of 75 attached to the conclusion in the following rule, for example, indicates that the conclusion is drawn with 75% confidence. (Note that this is not the same as assigning a 75% probability—75 is a subjective, not a statistical, value.)

```
RULE 1
IF    today = Tuesday
THEN  city = Belgium CNF 75;
```

Note that the letters *CNF* are used to identify the confidence factor in the rule.

If a question is not accompanied by a menu, no confidence factor can be specified, and 100% confidence is assumed.

See the keywords RULE, TRUTHTHRESH, and DISPLAY in Chapter 9 for more information about confidence factors.

Confidence factors cannot be directly written into the conditions of a rule premise; when constructing rules, confidence factors can only be used in rule conclusions (including the conclusions following the ELSE keyword).

If the user wants to specify a confidence factor when choosing from a menu during a consultation (to indicate that they're less than 100% certain that their response is valid), they can press the *HOME* key and type a number between 0 and 100 before pressing *ENTER* to make the choice. If no confidence factor is entered, 100% confidence is assumed.

How Confidence Factors Are Calculated

The direct entry of confidence factors into the knowledge base is straightforward. However, the subject gets more complicated when you begin to examine how confidence factors are combined and computed during the course of a *VP-Expert* consultation. For example, consider the following rule:

```
RULE 8
IF    Travel_Budget = Low
THEN  Country = Mexico CNF 80;
```

This rule assigns a confidence factor of 80 to the conclusion value *Mexico* if the variable *Travel_Budget* is assigned the value *Low*. But the confidence factor in the conclusion assumes that a confidence factor of 100 is assigned to the value in the premise. Suppose at a prompt, the user assigns a confidence factor of 50 to *Low*?

In such a case, the confidence factor of the premise value would be multiplied by the confidence factor of the conclusion value:

.50 x .80 = .40

The new confidence factor assigned to the conclusion value, *Mexico*, would be 40.

For simplicity, we've shown the numbers multiplied as fractions of 100. This is in keeping with the concept of ''percents'' (although, remember these numbers do not represent real statistical probabilities), and it simplifies the equation, which would otherwise look like:

$$\frac{50 \times 80}{100} = 40$$

Now consider a rule in which no confidence factor is explicitly specified:

```
RULE 11
IF    Season = Summer
THEN  Weather = Hot;
```

If no confidence factor is written into the conclusion, 100% confidence is assumed.

But what happens if *Season* is assigned the value *Summer* with 75% confidence? Again, the same formula applies; the two confidence factors (expressed here as percents) are multiplied:

.75 x 1.0 = .75

The variable *Weather* would be assigned the confidence factor 75 (the confidence factor of the premise value).

If another rule naming *Weather* in its premise was subsequently executed, the confidence factor of 75 for the premise value would be used to compute a new confidence factor for the conclusion value in that rule. For example, if the rule shown below was executed, the confidence factor would be 60 (.75 x .80 = .60).

```
RULE 14
IF    Weather = Hot
THEN    Air_Conditioning = Yes CNF 80;
```

Confidence Factors and the AND Logical Operator

Now consider a more complicated rule. What, for example, happens when confidence factors are assigned to more than one value in a rule's premise?

First, we'll look at a rule whose premise contains three conditions connected by the AND logical operator.

```
RULE 17
IF   Travel_Budget = Low_to_Med AND
     Mexico = Yes AND
     Preferred_Climate = Tropical
THEN Area = Yucatan CNF 70;
```

This rule will only pass if all of the conditions in the premise are true. For information about how the logical operators AND and OR are used in rules, see ''Using Logical Operators'' in Chapter 4 and the keywords AND and OR in Chapter 9.

If one or more of the values named in the premise of this rule are assigned confidence factors of less than 100, the *lowest* confidence factor will be multiplied by .70 (the conclusion confidence factor) to arrive at the final confidence factor for the value *Yucatan*.

This means that if the confidence factors 50, 70, and 60 were assigned to the values *Low_to_Med*, *Yes*, and *Tropical*, respectively, the final confidence factor assigned to *Yucatan* would be 35, since .50 x .70 = .35.

The VP-Expert ''Truth Threshold''

It's important to be aware of the fact that a condition containing a value that has a confidence factor of less than 50 is considered ''false.'' This means, for example, that if any of the values named in the premise of the following rule were assigned a confidence factor of less than 50, the rule would fail (because in order for the rule to pass, all the conditions must be ''true'').

```
RULE 17
IF    Travel_Budget = Low_to_Med AND
      Mexico = Yes AND
      Preferred_Climate = Tropical
THEN Area = Yucatan CNF 70;
```

If this is unsatisfactory for your purposes, the TRUTHTHRESH clause can be used to change the ''truth threshold'' from 50 to any other number between 0 and 100. See TRUTHTHRESH in Chapter 9 for more information.

Note: The ''truth threshold'' applies only to confidence factors for premise *values. If the confidence factor of a conclusion value falls below the ''truth threshold,'' the rule will not be prevented from passing.*

If a variable is assigned the same value more than once in a consultation, we say that the variable was assigned the value through "multiple paths."

Confidence Factors, the OR Logical Operator, and Multiple Paths

For conditions connected by OR in rule premises, the formula for computing the final confidence factor is different. If both conditions connected by an OR are true, a conclusion confidence factor is computed using each premise value (by multiplying each premise confidence factor by the conclusion confidence factor); then a formula is used to combine the two results. It's as though two separate rules have assigned the same value to a variable—and any time a variable is assigned the same value through "multiple paths," all the individual confidence factors are combined to determine the final confidence factor.

The formula used (if written using decimals) is:

CNF1 + CNF2 - (CNF1 x CNF2) = final_CNF

Take a look at this rule:

```
RULE 27
IF      Country = Brazil OR
        Country = Argentina
THEN    Airline = SouthAir CNF 80;
```

Suppose the values named in the premise of this rule were assigned the following values during a consultation:

```
Country: Brazil CNF 80
Country: Argentina CNF 50
```

The final confidence factor for the conclusion, *Airline = SouthAir*, would be 78. The three formulas used are:

.80 x .80 = .64

.50 x .80 = .40

.64 + .40 - (.64 x .40) = .78

Notice that the resulting confidence factor is higher than either of the original confidence factors. This will be the case any time a variable is assigned the same value by multiple paths. (This is logical, because if the same conclusion is drawn more than once, the conclusion is reinforced, and, therefore, "more certainly true.")

Note: If more than two conditions are connected by ORs in a rule, or if more than two "paths" assign a particular value to a variable, this formula still applies:

$CNF1 + CNF2 - (CNF1 \times CNF2) = final\_CNF$

However, it is applied like this: First, the confidence factor values from two paths are used in the formula. Then, the resulting value is used in the formula with the confidence factor value from a third path, and so on.

Computing Complex Conditions

Now let's look at a rule where both the AND and the OR logical operators are used.

VP-Expert allows a great deal of flexibility in rule formatting. For example, the rule to the right— written in such a way as to highlight the AND and OR logical operators—is perfectly legitimate.

```
RULE 31
IF     Area = Hawaii OR
       Country = Japan AND
       Budget = Low_to_Med
THEN   Airline = TravelPacific CNF 80;
```

In a case like this, the conclusion confidence factor would be computed as though there were two rules (like we showed previously for conditions separated by OR):

```
RULE X
IF    Area = Hawaii AND
      Budget = Low_to_Med
THEN Airline = TravelPacific CNF 80;
```

and:

```
RULE Y
IF    Country = Japan AND
      Budget = Low_to_Med
THEN Airline = TravelPacific CNF 80;
```

As you can see, each condition on either side of the OR is compared, separately, to the condition following AND.

The values resulting from these "rules" are then used in the formula that computes confidence factors for multiple paths.

For this example, suppose the values named in the premise of the rule have been assigned the following confidence factors:

```
Area: Hawaii CNF 50
Country: Japan CNF 70
Budget: Low_to_Med CNF 60
```

Remember, the rule for the AND logical operator is: If two "true" conditions are combined by an AND, the lesser confidence factor value will be multiplied by the confidence factor identified in the conclusion of the rule to determine the final confidence factor of the conclusion value.

The two formulas that compute the confidence factors for the "separate rules," then, are:

.50 x .80 = .40

.60 x .80 = .48

Now, if we plug the two resulting values into the "multiple path" formula, we get the final confidence factor—69.

.40 + .48 - (.40 x .48) = .69

Confidence Factors and Single-Valued Variables

As we mentioned before, if the same value is assigned to a variable through multiple paths, the final confidence factor is determined by a formula that takes all of these confidence factors into account.

It should be noted, however, that if at any time another path assigns a *different* value to that variable (and the variable is single-valued), that value with that confidence factor will become the new value of the variable—even if the confidence factor assigned to the new value is less than the confidence factor assigned to the previous value.

For information about transferring data to and from database files, see Chapter 5 and the GET, PUT, APPEND, and MENU clauses in Chapter 9. For information about transferring data to and from worksheet files, see Chapter 6 and the WKS and PWKS clauses. See also SHIP, RECEIVE, SAVEFACTS, and LOADFACTS for information about exchanging data with text files.

How VP-Expert Can Learn

There are those in the field of expert systems technology who maintain that a true expert system must have the ability to "learn" from experience. Just what constitutes learning is, of course, a complicated and somewhat controversial topic. However, it can reasonably be stated that, in some respect, *VP-Expert* has the ability to learn from experience.

Most expert systems can "learn" in the sense that their knowledge base can be modified and expanded to contain additional knowledge or data. But a *VP-Expert* system, because it can be designed to access and input data stored in database, worksheet, and text files, can actually be modified during the course of a consultation. The following examples will illustrate.

A Training System Example

A training system could track a student's progress so that each time he/she signed on, the system would bypass those lessons already successfully completed. The system could also evaluate the student's performance and determine whether or not more exercises were in order. This is an example of the system learning from experience.

A Restaurant Advisor

Imagine a "Restaurant Advisor" that uses a rule base and a database containing information about eating establishments to recommend reputable local restaurants.

The user would be required to answer prompts like:

```
What kind of food are you interested in having?
American          Chinese           French
Mexican           Greek             Italian
Seafood           Soul food         Thai
```

And:

```
Do you wish to have breakfast, lunch, or dinner?
Breakfast         Lunch             Dinner
```

And:

```
Please choose a dollar-per-meal price range from the
following list:
4 to 6               5 to 8              7 to 10
10 to 14             12 to 17            15 to 24
```

And:

```
Choose a preferred atmosphere from the following list:
Well lit modern     Romantic            Family style
Ethnic              New wave
```

Based on the user's answers to these and other questions, the Restaurant Advisor recommends, if possible, a restaurant meeting the chosen specifications.

Now, it's obvious that the advisor can only recommend restaurants that are present in the restaurant database. This means that if any local restaurants have been left out, or if any new ones have opened since the database was assembled, they cannot be recommended—unless the rule base is constructed in such a way that allows the user to "teach" the knowledge base about additional restaurants.

Suppose after a restaurant is recommended, the user is asked this question:

```
Is there a restaurant you'd like to add to the database?
Yes                 No
```

If the user answers *Yes*, a whole sequence of questions would follow, the first of which would be:

```
Please enter the name of the restaurant.
```

If the restaurant is already present in the database, a message would appear indicating that this is the case.

If the restaurant is not present in the database, a number of questions would follow. For example:

```
What is the dollar range of the average meal?
4 to 6               5 to 8              7 to 10
10 to 14             12 to 17            15 to 24
```

And:

```
How would you characterize the atmosphere of the
restaurant?
Well lit modern      Romantic              Family style
Ethnic               New wave
```

When the user has answered all the questions, a record containing values provided by the user would be APPENDed to the restaurant database, and the knowledge base will have "learned" a new restaurant. The next time a consultation is run, this new restaurant would be among the restaurants that could be recommended.

Adding Comments

The Restaurant Advisor could also elicit comments about restaurants that have been visited by the user. For example, during a consultation the following questions could be asked:

```
Would you care to comment about a restaurant you've
visited lately?
Yes                      No
```

And:

```
What is the name of the restaurant?
```

And:

```
Please enter your comments here:
```

The comments entered by the user could be sent to a data file (using PUT), or to a text file (using SHIP). The next time the corresponding restaurant is recommended, the comments could be displayed to the user. For example:

```
We recommend you try The Best Restaurant located at 2314
Andrew Drive, tel: 767-3970. Comments about this
restaurant include:

  We had a marvelous time there. The food was great,
  reasonably priced, and the atmosphere was warm and
  friendly. Our only complaint was that we had to wait
  an hour to get a table.  If you go on a weekend, make
  reservations in advance.
```

Conclusion

This has been a simple example, but the following should be clear: *VP-Expert's* ability to transfer user input to external files allows the person designing the knowledge base to create expert systems that can be said to, in some sense, learn during a consultation. Of course, this type of "learning" is only as good as the data the user enters. If a user enters incorrect information, the reliability of the database will be compromised. Despite this drawback, it's not hard to think of applications for which the ability of the user to enter input would be of great value. Consider an expert system used by a group of doctors that permits physicians to input data for statistical analysis, or add comments to an attached file. Such a system would allow the compilation of medical information reflecting the experience of tens, perhaps hundreds, of doctors. This type of system could be created for use by scientists, lawyers, engineers, teachers, students.... The possibilities are virtually limitless.

Creating an Effective Knowledge Base

The following techniques and rules of thumb may help you to create an effective knowledge base.

- Before starting the knowledge base, think carefully about the subject you've chosen to make sure it's appropriate for an expert system. Can "knowledge" about the subject be stated in IF-THEN rules?

- Design the knowledge base in such a way that it's easy to read.

A list of mandatory knowledge base formatting rules is provided in Chapter 4.

- We recommend that you choose variable names which are meaningful, document your code with comments, and use BECAUSE text in the knowledge base.

- Read Chapter 9 before starting the knowledge base. It describes all the clauses and statements that can be used in constructing a knowledge base.

- For problems which are suited to it, use induction. This is a fast way to create an initial knowledge base which can later be refined.

- Give each rule a unique rule label following the keyword RULE. Numbering rules is advisable.

■ Build the knowledge base in small increments, testing it thoroughly at each step (by running trial consultations). If you try to do too much too fast, it will be more difficult to find and correct errors in the knowledge base.

■ Use the AUTOQUERY statement to identify variables that may require ASK statements for eliciting user input.

■ Make use of the Slow command to observe the path of the inference engine during trial consultations.

The Trace command will be discussed in greater detail in this chapter under the heading "Displaying a Graphics Tree."

■ If your knowledge base is running, but seems to contain some logical errors, use the Trace command to record the search pattern used by the inference engine. Then, using one of the Tree commands (Text or Graphics), take a look at the "trace" to see what's taking place in the knowledge base during a consultation.

■ Remember not to use any of the *VP-Expert* keywords as a variable name. If you do, the knowledge base will probably run, but the consultation will hang up when the variable is encountered by the inference engine.

■ Make sure you understand how to use the AND and OR logical operators to combine conditions in rule premises (and "database rules" contained in some clauses). Remember, ORs take precedence over ANDs. This means that conditions connected by the OR operator are treated as though they were surrounded by parentheses. For example, look at RULE 1. It is interpreted as if it is written like the rule next to it.

```
RULE 1                        RULE X
IF      A = 1 AND             IF      A = 1
        B = 2 OR                     AND
        C = 3 AND                    (B = 2 OR C = 3)
        D = 4 AND                    AND
        E = 5 OR                     D = 4
        F = 6                        AND
THEN    G = 7;                       (E = 5 OR F = 6)
                             THEN    G = 7;
```

Note: The parentheses in the above rule are used only to demonstrate how the AND and OR operators are figured. Parentheses cannot be used this way in rules.

■ Make sure you understand the affect of the "truth threshold" on a consultation. The default truth threshold number is 50, meaning that if the confidence factor of a value contained in a rule condition is less than 50, the condition will be considered "false." (This applies only to values in rule *conditions*. If a value in a rule conclusion falls below the truth threshold number, the rule will not be prevented from passing.) See the TRUTHTHRESH clause in Chapter 9 for more information— including instructions for changing the default truth threshold number.

See Chapter 5 for information about using VP-Expert to create friendly front ends for compatible database and worksheet files.

■ If your knowledge base requires a great deal of data that is likely to require updating, store the data in a database or worksheet "information base." Storing such data apart from the "rule base" allows the data to be modified and updated more easily. Using an information base also allows you to create a much simpler rule base. See Chapters 5 and 6 for more information.

■ If your knowledge base requires lengthy DISPLAY text, use the RECEIVE command to read text into a consultation from external text files. This prevents the rule base from becoming cluttered with excess verbiage. See the RECEIVE command in Chapter 9 for more information.

Displaying a Graphics Tree

If your knowledge base is running, but seems to contain some logical errors, you may want to perform a "trace" on a consultation to see what's going on behind the scenes.

To perform a trace, issue the Trace command (on the Set Menu) prior to running a consultation. This saves the search pattern subsequently used by the inference engine to a file with the same name as the knowledge base, but with a TRC file extension. This file can be viewed in one of two ways: as a "text tree" or as a "graphics tree." (The Text and Graphics commands on the Tree Menu are used to create the two types of display.)

In Chapter 1, a text tree was demonstrated under "The Set Commands." This section will show you how to view and interpret a graphics tree.

In order to use the Graphics command to produce a graphics tree, a trace must have previously been performed on a consultation using the active knowledge base. (When the Graphics command is issued, *VP-Expert* looks for a TRC file with the same name as the currently loaded knowledge base.)

If such a trace has been performed, the Graphics command displays a screen that resembles this:

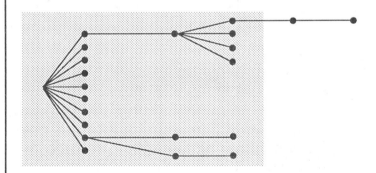

In order to use the Graphics command to produce a graphics tree from a TRC file, your system must have an IBM EGA, CGA, Hercules, or compatible graphics card. Hercules or compatible cards must be in "full" or "half" mode prior to starting VP-Expert.

The graphics tree shown here was created using the sample knowledge base FROMAGE1.KBS.

As you can see, this display contains no text. However, using a number of simple keyboard commands, you can scroll to and enlarge any portion of the tree for closer examination.

When you first display a graphics tree, a highlighted box appears at the upper left corner of the tree. Pressing the spacebar enlarges the area inside this box, making that portion of the display legible. Pressing the spacebar again returns the previous screen display.

To zoom in on other areas of the tree, the box can be moved. The arrow keys move the box up, down, left, or right. The *PgUp* and *PgDn* keys move the box in larger, box-size steps. By moving the box and pressing the spacebar, you can zoom in on any section of the graphics tree for closer examination.

The following screen shows the display that results when the spacebar is pressed with the box in the upper-left location shown in the previous illustration.

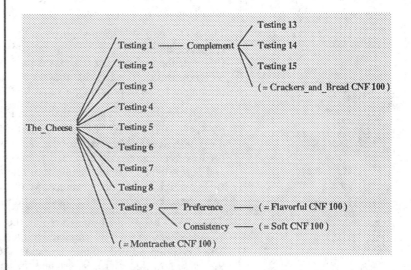

This display represents most of the search pattern that was used by the inference engine during a consultation with the FROMAGE1 knowledge base.

The variable shown on the left, *The_Cheese*, is the goal variable of the consultation. This is the variable for which the inference engine must find a value to successfully complete a consultation.

To the right, the tree shows which rules were tested by the inference engine and the results from each test.

Testing a rule is not the same as executing a rule. When a rule is initially "tested," it is simply looked at by the inference engine to see if its conclusion contains the variable the inference engine is currently seeking a value for. A passing rule is "executed."

The first "Testing" line shows RULE 1 being tested (indicated by the message "Testing 1"). The horizontal line to the right culminating in the variable name *Complement* shows that as a result of testing RULE 1, the inference engine is searching for a value for the variable *Complement*. The group of "Testing" lines to the right of *Complement* show the inference engine testing rules to find a value for that variable. The value *crackers_and_bread*, preceded by an = sign and contained in parentheses, indicates that a value has been found. Since it appears directly below the phrase "Testing 15," RULE 15 is identified as the rule that supplied the value.

It should be noted here that since the right-most portion of the graphics tree is not displayed in this enlargement, there are a couple of steps missing. In order to see the rest of the tree, it would be necessary to return to the normal tree, move the highlighted box to the right, and zoom into that portion of the tree.

The next group of "Testing" lines in this enlargement shows that RULEs 2 through 8 were subsequently tested by the inference engine (to see if the variable *The_Cheese* is named in their conclusions), but with no results. (The fact that they were tested indicates that RULE 1 ultimately failed to provide the value for *The_Cheese*.)

The enlarged tree next shows that when RULE 9 was tested, the inference engine set out to find values for the variables *Preference* and *Consistency* (because these variables were discovered in the premise conditions of RULE 9). To the right, the values *Flavorful* and *Soft* are indicated as having been found. Since the tree shows no rules being tested for those values, we can assume that those values were assigned by the user at question prompts.

The bottom line of the tree shows that the value *Montrachet* has been assigned to the goal variable with a confidence factor of 100. Since this line is lined up directly below the line which says "Testing 9," we know that RULE 9 assigned the value to the goal variable.

Pressing the spacebar causes the tree to return to normal size. (Pressing any of the arrow keys, or *PgUp* or *PgDn*, has the same effect.) Pressing *ESC* at the "normal" tree returns you to the Tree Menu.

CHAPTER EIGHT

Menu Command Reference

VP-Expert contains six built-in command menus. While using *VP-Expert*, one of these menus is usually displayed at the bottom of the screen, offering a number of different command options. This chapter describes the purpose and operation of each of these options, in alphabetical order. For information about how the commands relate to one another hierarchically, see the menu tree supplied in Appendix C.

Note: The descriptions in this chapter include the names of the menus in which the commands are contained, e.g., the Main Menu, the Set Menu, the Consult Menu, and so on. With the exception of the Main Menu, which is VP-Expert's top-level menu, each menu name identifies the command that makes the menu available.

Command Conventions

There are a number of ways to give *VP-Expert* menu commands. You can:

- Type the first letter of the command.
- Type the number that precedes the command on the menu.
- Type the function key corresponding to the command number.
- Use the arrow keys to scroll the lightbar to the command and press the *ENTER* key.

One *VP-Expert* command menu works differently from the others. The Go Menu, which offers commands while a consultation is in progress, requires you to type a slash (**/**) before issuing a command. In addition, neither the How? nor the Help command on this menu can be chosen by typing the first letter of the command (since the first letters are the same for both). Any of the other described methods can be used instead.

CONSULT

8

Menu:

Main Menu

Description:

The Consult command loads the current knowledge base into memory and displays the Consult Menu. If a knowledge base is not already in use, a menu of KBS files appears before the Consult Menu is presented. Choose a knowledge base file from this menu, or type in the name of a knowledge base file to load.

Notes:

- When the Consult command loads the current knowledge base file into memory, the file is scanned for syntax errors. If an error is detected, it's reported in an error message. Pressing any key takes you to the line in the knowledge base where the error occurs. (Sometimes *VP-Expert* can only approximate the correct line. For example, if a semicolon is missing from the end of a rule, an error may not be detected until later in the knowledge base.)

- Choosing the Go command on the Consult Menu starts a consultation.

CREATE

Menu:
Induce Menu

Description:
The Create command allows you to create or edit an induction table in the *VP-Expert* Editor.

When Create is selected, a menu of files with TBL extensions is presented (if there are TBL files in the current directory). Choose one of these files from the menu, or type in a new filename. (You need not type a TBL file extension; it is assumed.) After a filename is indicated, you're transferred to the given file in the Editor.

Notes:
- The Induce command transforms induction tables into working knowledge base files. See Chapter 3 and the Induce command for more information.

DATABASE

Menu:
Induce Menu

Description:
The Database command, contained in the Induce Menu, informs *VP-Expert* that the induction table from which the knowledge base will be induced is contained in a *VP-Info* or dBASE file with a DBF extension. When the command is given, *VP-Expert* displays a list of DBF files from which to choose (if there are DBF files in the current directory). If the desired file is not listed, the filename can be typed at the prompt. (A DBF file extension need not be typed; it is assumed.)

Notes:

- See Chapter 5 for more information about creating a knowledge base from a table stored in a DBF file.

- Knowledge bases can also be induced from tables created in text files and *VP-Planner* or Lotus 1-2-3 worksheet files. See Chapter 3 for information about using the Induce command with text files. For specific information about using worksheet induction tables, see Chapter 6.

EDIT

See Appendix A for complete documentation of the VP-Expert Editor.

If you replace the VP-Expert Editor with another editor, it must operate in non-document mode.

Menu:

Main Menu

Description:

The Edit command invokes the *VP-Expert* Editor and loads the currently active knowledge base for display and/or modification. If no knowledge base file is currently loaded, a menu of KBS files is presented. A filename can be chosen from this menu or typed in. (If no file extension is typed, a KBS extension is assumed.)

Notes:

- *VP-Expert* comes with a built-in Editor (created from Paperback Software's *Paperback Writer* word processor). However, *VP-Expert* can be modified to use any text editor that creates straight ASCII files. To make such a modification, create a one-line file called EDNAME. This file will contain merely the name of the calling program file of the new text editor. For example, to use WordStar, the line would read "WS.COM". If necessary, additional command line parameters can be added to the end of the EDNAME file.

- If you replace the *VP-Expert* Editor with your own editor, *VP-Expert* will no longer be able to take you directly to lines containing errors when syntax errors are detected upon execution of the Consult command.

FAST

The Slow command is used during knowledge base development to slow down the scrolling in the rules *and* results *windows located at the bottom of the consultation screen.*

Menu:

Go Menu and Set Menu

Description:

If the Slow command has been used to slow down the execution of a non-runtime consultation, the Fast command resumes normal consultation speed.

Notes:

■ The Fast and Slow commands don't work in a runtime consultation (a consultation using a knowledge base that includes the RUNTIME statement).

■ The Fast and Slow commands are available on both the Go and the Set Menus. Thus, speed of knowledge base execution can be altered prior to, or at any time during, a consultation.

■ If the Slow command is not issued prior to a Fast command, the latter will have no affect on consultation speed.

■ See Chapter 1, Chapter 4, and the Slow command in this chapter for more information about altering consultation speed.

FILENAME

Menu:

Main Menu

Description:

The FileName command allows you to load a new knowledge base file to consult or edit.

Notes:

■ In response to this command, *VP-Expert* presents the same KBS file menu that it presents when the Consult or Edit command is chosen for the first time. A file can be chosen from the menu, or typed. (If no file extension is indicated, a KBS extension is assumed.)

■ The file menu that appears in response to this command can contain up to 100 filenames. The right and left arrow keys scroll the filenames across the bottom of the screen.

GO

GRAPHICS

When the Trace command is given prior to running a consultation, the path used by the inference engine during the consultation is saved to a disk file.

Menu:
Consult Menu

Description:
The Go command initiates a consultation session after the Consult command has successfully loaded a knowledge base file.

Notes:
■ When you give the Go command to start a consultation, a new menu becomes available (the Go Menu). In order to choose a command from this menu, a slash (/) must first be typed to suspend the consultation.

■ If the EXECUTE statement is included in a knowledge base, the Go command is bypassed, and the Consult command starts the consultation.

Menu:
Tree Menu

Description:
The Graphics option on the Tree Menu is used to graphically display the results of a consultation Trace. See "Creating an Effective Knowledge Base" in Chapter 7 for an example of a graphics tree.

Notes:
■ This command can only be used in systems containing an IBM CGA, EGA, Hercules, or an equivalent graphics card. Hercules or compatible cards must be set in "full" or "half" mode prior to starting *VP-Expert*.

■ The Text command on the Tree Menu can be used to present a search pattern display that does not require a graphics card.

■ Using the spacebar and the number pad arrow keys, different sections of the graphic tree can be selected and enlarged for closer inspection. See "Creating an Effective Knowledge Base" in Chapter 7 for details.

HELP

Menu:

All menus

Description:

The Help command, available on all *VP-Expert* command menus, provides on-screen information about the commands offered by the currently active menu.

Notes:

- To give the Help command from the Go Menu, you must first suspend the consultation by typing a slash (**/**).

HOW?

Menu:

Go Menu

Description:

The How? command is used while a consultation is in progress to determine how a particular variable's value was found. When the command is first issued, *VP-Expert* presents a question asking for a variable name. The program responds in one of 3 ways:

If the variable was given a value by user input, or in the ACTIONS block of the knowledge base, the message "Because you said so" is displayed.

If the variable was assigned a value in the conclusion of a rule containing BECAUSE text, the BECAUSE text is displayed.

If the variable was assigned a value by a rule with no BECAUSE text, the rule itself is presented.

See the BECAUSE keyword in Chapter 9 for more information about BECAUSE text.

INDUCE

See Chapter 5 for a discussion of some of the advantages of inducing knowledge bases from existing database and worksheet files.

PATH

Notes:

■ Before giving the How? command, you must type a slash (/) to suspend the consultation.

■ After giving the How? command, pressing any key resumes the consultation.

Menu:

Main Menu

Description:

The Induce command creates a working knowledge base from a properly formatted induction table contained in a database, worksheet, or text file. After giving the Induce command, a submenu appears offering the choices Text, Worksht, and Database. Choosing from this menu tells *VP-Expert* what type of file the knowledge base will be created from.

Notes:

■ See Chapter 3 for a general discussion of knowledge base induction. For specific information about using induction on database and worksheet tables, see Chapters 5 and 6, respectively.

■ Induce is compatible with *VP-Info* and dBASE database (DBF) files, and *VP-Planner* and Lotus 1-2-3 worksheet (WKS) files.

Menu:

Main Menu

Description:

The Path command changes the default directory path that *VP-Expert* uses to access files. For example, if you wanted *VP-Expert* to access files on the C drive in the VPX directory, you'd give the Path command, and then type **c:\vpx**. If the Path command is not used, the directory from which the program was started is the default directory.

Notes:

- Pressing *ESC* before completing this command leaves the path unchanged.

- When you exit the *VP-Expert* program, the Path command is canceled.

- *VP-Expert* clauses that access external files (e.g., GET, PUT, CALL, etc.) allow you to specify paths with filenames. Paths specified in these clauses override the path set with this command.

QUIT

Menu:

All menus

Description:

The Quit command, included in every *VP-Expert* command menu, quits the current menu and redisplays the previous menu. From the Main Menu, the Quit command quits the program and returns the system prompt to screen.

Notes:

- Before you can give the Quit command on the Go Menu (to quit a consultation before completion), you must first type a slash (/).

RULE

Menu:

Consult Menu

Description:

The Rule command permits you to examine rules of the currently active non-runtime knowledge base.

In response to this command, *VP-Expert* asks which rule should be examined. A menu of rule labels will appear. Scroll the light bar to the label of the rule you wish to view and press *ENTER*. For example, choosing 1 would display RULE 1.

Notes:

■ This command works only if the knowledge base does not contain the RUNTIME statement.

SET

Menu:

Consult Menu

Description:

The Set command displays a submenu containing commands used to alter the execution of the subsequent consultation. These options include: Slow, which slows down the scrolling in the rules and results windows so that you can follow the activity of the inference engine during a consultation; Fast, which resumes normal consultation speed; and Trace, which records the path of the inference engine during the consultation for later examination.

Notes:

■ The Slow and Fast commands work only if the active knowledge base does *not* contain the RUNTIME statement.

■ The Slow and Fast options on the Set Menu are also available on the Go Menu. This allows consultation speed to be altered both prior to and during a consultation.

■ See Fast, Slow, and Trace for more information about Set Menu commands.

SLOW

Menu:

Go Menu and Set Menu

Description:

If the Slow command is given prior to or during a non-runtime consultation, the scrolling in the rules and results windows is slowed down, allowing you to observe the behind-the-scenes activity of the inference engine.

Notes:

■ The Slow command has a cumulative effect. If giving the command once does not slow the consultation sufficiently, the command can be repeated until the desired speed is achieved.

■ The Fast command resumes normal consultation speed after the Slow command has been issued. Returning to the Main Menu after a consultation also cancels the Slow command.

■ Since the Slow and Fast commands are available on both the Set and Go menus, consultation speed can be controlled both prior to and during a consultation.

■ This command does not work if the active knowledge base contains the RUNTIME statement.

TEXT

There are two VP-Expert Text commands. Unlike the Slow and Fast commands, which are also contained on two different menus, the two Text commands do not perform the same function.

Menu:

Induce Menu

Description:

The Text command on the Induce Menu informs *VP-Expert* that the induction table from which the knowledge base will be induced is contained in a text file with a TBL extension. When the command is given, *VP-Expert* displays a list of TBL files from which to choose (if there are TBL files in the current directory). If the desired file is not listed, the filename can be typed at the prompt. (A TBL extension need not be typed; it is assumed.)

Notes:

■ See Chapter 3 for more information about inducing a knowledge base from an induction table created in a text file.

■ See Chapters 5 and 6 for information about inducing knowledge bases from tables created in database (DBF) and worksheet (WKS) files.

TEXT

See the EDIT command for information about using your own text editor with VP-Expert.

Menu:

Tree Menu

Description:

This command is used in combination with the Trace command, which records the path of the inference engine during a consultation. Choosing Text from the Tree Menu displays a "text tree" representing the consultation recorded by the Trace.

Notes:

- The text tree is displayed in the *VP-Expert* Editor (or your own editor, if you've created the EDNAME file). Typing *ALT-F8* leaves the Editor without updating the file and returns to the Main Menu. When you type *ALT-F6* to exit the Editor, you're given the opportunity to rename the file containing the text tree. Do so if you want to execute another Trace of the same knowledge base without overwriting the file.

- See "The Set Commands" in Chapter 1 for an example of a text tree.

- This command is one of two different *VP-Expert* Text commands. The other Text command, appearing on the Induce Menu, is used to induce a knowledge base from an induction table stored in a text file.

TRACE

Menu:

Set Menu

Description:

The Trace command records the path of the inference engine during the next consultation and stores it in a file with the same name as the active knowledge base (with a TRC file extension.) This file can be viewed using the Text or Graphics commands on the Tree Menu. See the Text and Graphics commands for more information. See also "The Set Commands" in Chapter 1 and "Creating an Effective Knowledge Base" in Chapter 7.

Notes:

- During the debugging phase of expert system development, this command is useful for checking the logic constructions of the knowledge base.

- Each time a Trace is performed on the same knowledge base, the previously saved Trace file is overwritten. To avoid overwriting a file, give it a new name before running another Trace. (See "Notes" for the Text command for more information.)

TREE

Menu:

Main Menu

Description:

The Tree command is used to view the file created by the last execution of the Trace command which records the behind-the-scenes search pattern of a consultation.

When you give the Tree command, another menu is presented, offering two options: Text and Graphics. If you choose Text, a "text tree" is displayed. If you choose Graphics, a graphic representation of the consultation is presented. See the Trace, Text, and Graphics commands for more information.

Notes:

- During the debugging phase of expert system development, this command is useful for checking the logic constructions of the knowledge base.

- The Graphics command on the Tree Menu requires an IBM CGA, EGA, Hercules, or an equivalent graphics card. Hercules or compatible cards must be in "full" or "half" mode prior to starting *VP-Expert*.

- Each time a Trace is performed on the same knowledge base, the previously saved Trace file is overwritten. To avoid overwriting a file, give it a new name before running another Trace. (See "Notes" for the Text command for more information.)

- See "The Set Commands" in Chapter 1 and "Creating an Effective Knowledge Base" in Chapter 7 for examples of each type of Tree display.

VARIABLE

Menu:

Consult Menu

Description:

The Variable command permits you to examine the values that were assigned to specified variables during the last consultation. Confidence factors assigned to values are also displayed.

When you give this command, you're asked to choose a variable name. The value (or values) assigned to that variable during the last consultation is displayed.

Notes:

■ Unlike the Rule command (which only operates in non-runtime consultations), the Variable command can be used in both runtime and non-runtime consultations.

WHATIF

Menu:

Consult Menu

Description:

The WhatIf command allows you to find out how the last consultation would be affected if you had responded differently to a question prompt. In other words, it answers questions like, "What if I had chosen *yes* instead of *no* at the first prompt?"

See the UNKNOWN keyword in Chapter 9 for information about UNKNOWN variables.

When you give this command at the end of a consultation, *VP-Expert* asks which variable's value you want to change. A menu of variable names appears for you to choose from. When the prompt asking for a value for the chosen variable appears, a new value can be entered. All other values remain as they were assigned during the last consultation and the knowledge base is re-executed. The new value may cause the execution of questions not asked in the previous consultation. These must be responded to before a new conclusion value is reported. Otherwise, *VP-Expert* will immediately report the conclusion value resulting from the new input.

Notes:

■ This command can only be used to change values assigned by user input.

WHY?

In order to give any command on the Go Menu, you must first type a slash (/) to suspend the consultation.

Menu:

Go Menu

Description:

The Why? command is used during a consultation to find out why a particular question is being asked. When a question appears, you simply type a slash (/), issue the Why? command, and one of two responses results. If the rule which caused the question to execute contains BECAUSE text, that text is displayed. If the rule does not contain BECAUSE text, the rule itself is displayed.

Notes:

■ See the BECAUSE keyword in Chapter 9 for more information about BECAUSE text.

■ After giving the Why? command, pressing any key resumes the consultation.

WORKSHT

Menu:

Induce Menu

Description:

The Worksht command, contained in the Induce Menu, informs *VP-Expert* that the induction table from which the knowledge base will be induced is contained in a *VP-Planner* or Lotus 1-2-3 WKS file. In response to the command, *VP-Expert* displays a list of WKS files from which to choose (if there are WKS files in the current directory). If the desired file is not listed, the filename can be typed at the prompt. (A WKS file extension need not be typed; it is assumed.)

Notes:

■ For general information about using induction to create a knowledge base, see Chapter 3. For specific information about using induction tables created in worksheet files, see Chapter 6.

CHAPTER NINE

Alphabetical Keyword Reference

This chapter contains detailed information on how to use each of *VP-Expert's* keywords. In *VP-Expert*, "keywords" are those words which have special meaning in the knowledge base. These include the words which begin every clause and statement, special words used in rule construction, system variables such as MENU_SIZE, RECORD_NUM, and so forth.

Note: Keywords are sometimes referred to as "reserved words" because they are reserved for a particular use in the knowledge base. Improper use of keywords can result in errors during knowledge base execution and may even prevent execution.

This section does not include commands that appear on VP-Expert menus. For information on menu commands, see Chapter 8. Mathematical functions available in VP-Expert are detailed in Chapter 10.

Reference Section Conventions

Throughout this chapter, clause and statement parameters are indicated inside left and right angle brackets. Optional parameters are shown in square brackets. These brackets should not be typed. They are used here only for differentiation.

If a "/" appears in a parameter description, it should be taken to mean "or."

ACTIONS

INSTRUCTION TYPE:
Statement

USAGE:
ACTIONS
<clause1>
[clause2]
[clause3]
etc.
;

PARAMETERS:
The ACTIONS keyword must be followed by one or more valid *VP-Expert* clauses. After the final clause, a semicolon must be added to signal the end of the ACTIONS block.

Variables can be assigned values in the ACTIONS block using direct value assignment, e.g., variable = value.

DESCRIPTION:
The keyword ACTIONS identifies the beginning of an ACTIONS block. The ACTIONS block in a *VP-Expert* knowledge base sets the agenda for the *VP-Expert* consultation by listing one or more clauses to be executed, in order, during a consultation. When each clause has been executed to completion, the consultation is finished.

In short, the ACTIONS block is the "program" that drives the consultation. It, in effect, says "First do this, then do this, then do this...."

Typically, an ACTIONS block contains at least one FIND clause. The FIND clause is an indispensable part of most expert system applications because this is the clause used to direct the *VP-Expert* inference engine. The inference engine is the mechanism that utilizes the "expertise" contained in the rules and statements of a knowledge base to solve problems during a consultation. For more information, see the FIND clause in this chapter.

9

EXAMPLE:

```
RUNTIME;

ACTIONS
        DISPLAY "Welcome to the charming world of
cheese!
Press any key to begin the consultation.~"
        FIND The_Cheese
        DISPLAY "The best cheese for this meal is a
{#The_Cheese}.";

RULE 1
IF      Course = Appetizer
THEN    Consistency = Soft
        BECAUSE "The consistency of the cheese is
determined by the course.";
*
*
*
```

The ACTIONS block in this example prescribes the following agenda for the consultation:

First, DISPLAY a welcome message.

Next, FIND a value for the variable *The_Cheese*.

Finally, DISPLAY a conclusion message.

NOTES & CAUTIONS:

■ Though it is not mandatory, the ACTIONS block is best placed above the rules in the knowledge base.

MORE INFORMATION:

See Chapter 2 and Chapter 7 for more information.

ALL

INSTRUCTION TYPE:
Reserved word

USAGE:
Used in the GET clause and MENU clause.

PARAMETERS:
None required or permitted.

DESCRIPTION:
The keyword ALL is reserved for use in the GET and MENU clauses. See GET and MENU for more information.

EXAMPLE:
```
*
*
GET ALL,cheeses,ALL
*
*
MENU cheese_price,ALL,cheeses,price
*
*
```

In this example, the GET clause retrieves ALL fields from the next record (starting from the record pointer) in the CHEESES.DBF database file. Retrieved field values will be assigned to variables with the same names as the fields from which they were taken.

The MENU clause creates a menu containing the contents of the PRICE field from ALL the records in the CHEESES.DBF file. Duplicate field values are excluded from the menu.

NOTES & CAUTIONS:
■ Note in the previous example that the first ALL in the GET clause means that the next record (starting from the record pointer) should be accessed—not that all records should be accessed at once. The ALL keyword is used simply to indicate that no special conditions need to be met by the record; it should be selected from among ALL the records.

MORE INFORMATION:
See the GET and MENU clauses for more information.

AND

*See the RULE keyword
for a list of the relational
operators.*

INSTRUCTION TYPE:

Logical operator

USAGE:

<condition1> AND <condition2>

PARAMETERS

The AND logical operator always occurs between two *conditions*. A
condition is an expression that compares a variable to a value using
one of the relational operators, e.g., *price > 15000*.

DESCRIPTION:

The AND logical operator is used to combine conditions in rule
premises, and in database rules contained in GET and MENU
clauses. When AND is present in a rule, the conditions on either side
of the AND must both be true in order for the rule to pass. When
used in a database rule, the record selected by the GET or MENU
clause must meet both conditions connected by the AND operator.

EXAMPLE:

```
*
*
RULE feasibility4
IF        capital_gains <= 15000 AND
          bid >= 95000 AND
          bid <= 140500 AND
          down_payment >=60000
THEN      purchase = feasible;
*
*
*
```

In order for the above rule to pass, the value of the variable *capital_gains* must be less than or equal to *15,000*, AND the value of *bid* must fall between *95,000* AND *140,500*, AND the value of *down_payment* must be greater than or equal to *60,000*. If any of these conditions are not met, the rule will fail.

NOTES & CAUTIONS:

■ When both the AND and the OR operators occur in the same rule premise or database rule, OR takes precedence over AND. See OR in this chapter or "Using Logical Operators" in Chapter 4 for more information.

■ Using the AND and OR logical operators, you can combine up to ten conditions in a rule premise or database rule. However, you should make sure you understand how complex conditions will be interpreted by *VP-Expert* when the rule is tested.

MORE INFORMATION:

See the OR logical operator in this chapter and "Using Logical Operators" in Chapter 4. For information about database rules, see GET in Chapter 9.

APPEND

INSTRUCTION TYPE:
Clause

USAGE:
APPEND <[*path*]*DBF_filename*>

PARAMETERS:
A path can optionally be specified using the same format as that used by DOS (e.g.,\files\data). This tells *VP-Expert* where to find the named file. The default is the current directory.

The DBF filename supplied to the APPEND clause must be the name of an existing database file with a DBF extension. However, the extension must not be explicitly provided, or a syntax error will result.

DESCRIPTION:
APPEND appends a record to the end of database file. To add values to the fields of the record, values should be assigned to variables having the same names as the fields in the database file before the APPEND clause is executed. If no field values are assigned, a blank record will be appended to the file.

EXAMPLE
Assume a file in the directory STOCK named PARTS.DBF with a structure consisting of two fields: a part number (PARTNO) and a part name (PTNAME). This ACTIONS block APPENDs a record to the end of PARTS.DBF using field values supplied by the FIND clauses.

```
ACTIONS
  FIND PARTNO
  FIND PTNAME
  APPEND \STOCK\PARTS
  *
  *
```

NOTES & CAUTIONS:

■ When the APPEND clause is executed, any field in the new record that has not been supplied a value (by a knowledge base variable) is set to a blank.

MORE INFORMATION:

Refer to Chapter 5 for additional examples of the APPEND clause. See the PUT clause for another method of writing data to a database file.

ASK

INSTRUCTION TYPE:

Statement

USAGE:

ASK *<variable>*: ''*<text>*'';

PARAMETERS:

The variable supplied to the ASK statement can be any valid *VP-Expert* variable name.

The text parameter of the ASK statement can be any text enclosed within double quotation marks. (Double quotation marks are the only keyboard character that cannot be used as text.)

ASK text can contain up to 1,000 characters, including spaces.

DESCRIPTION:

Whenever the *VP-Expert* inference engine cannot find a rule which assigns a value to a particular variable, it looks for an ASK statement naming that variable. If found, the ASK statement displays the text string enclosed in double quotation marks, then pauses for the user's response. The user's response is assigned as the value of the named variable. See ''Notes & Cautions'' for important details regarding the ASK statement.

EXAMPLE:

```
RUNTIME;
ACTIONS
    FIND use
    *
    *

ASK use:  "Will this computer be for home
use, business use, or both?";

CHOICES use: Home,Business,Both;
*

*
```

If, in this example, the *VP-Expert* inference engine could not find a rule to assign a value to the variable *use*, the ASK statement and corresponding CHOICES statement would cause this prompt to be displayed to the user:

```
Will this computer be for home use, business
use, or both?
Home                    Business            Both
```

The user's menu choice would be assigned as the value of the variable *use*.

NOTES & CAUTIONS:

■ If the knowledge base contains a CHOICES statement or a MENU clause for the variable named in the ASK statement, a menu of choices accompanies the ASK text when it is displayed.

■ If the user does not know how to answer an ASK prompt, a question mark can be typed to indicate "don't know." This leaves the variable UNKNOWN and allows the consultation to continue. See UNKNOWN in this chapter for more information.

Although spaces cannot be used in values specified in the knowledge base, they can be included in user input.

■ If no menu accompanies ASK text when it is displayed, the user needs to type a response. Typed responses are restricted to 20 characters, including spaces. When this limit is reached, the system stops accepting input.

■ If an ASK statement has no corresponding CHOICES statement or MENU clause (meaning that no menu will be displayed with the question), the user is only allowed to enter one value at the prompt, even if the variable taking the value is named in a PLURAL statement.

■ Unless line breaks are specifically indicated with hard carriage returns in ASK text, *VP-Expert* automatically formats the text to the appropriate screen-width when it is displayed.

■ Variables enclosed in curly brackets in text (e.g. {name}) will be replaced by their values when displayed.

■ If the variable named in an ASK statement is a dimensioned variable, the statement will not execute. If it is an *element* of a dimensioned variable (e.g., price[2]) the statement will execute, but only if the subscript is indicated with a digit (a variable cannot be used).

■ When a menu is displayed with ASK text, the user can enter a confidence factor with their menu choice (or choices). If ASK text is not accompanied by a menu, a confidence factor cannot be entered. See Chapter 7 and the TRUTHTHRESH clause in this chapter for more information about confidence factors.

■ The AUTOQUERY statement can be used in the early stages of knowledge base development to help identify variables that require ASK statements. See AUTOQUERY for more information.

■ The usual restriction on "reserved words" does not apply to ASK text. Any *VP-Expert* keyword can be included in ASK text as long as it appears between the double quotes.

MORE INFORMATION:
The ASK statement is widely used in the examples in this manual. See also the MENU clause and the AUTOQUERY, CHOICES, and PLURAL statements. For information about dimensioned variables, see the WKS clause. Confidence factors are discussed in Chapter 7.

AUTOQUERY

INSTRUCTION TYPE:
Statement

USAGE:
AUTOQUERY;

PARAMETERS:
None required or permitted.

DESCRIPTION:

The AUTOQUERY statement is issued once in a program, typically at or near the beginning of the file. Its purpose is to automatically address a question to the user in the event that the inference engine requires a value for a variable for which there is no passing rule or ASK statement. The question posed is, "What is the value of *variable*?" (where *variable* is the name of variable for which a value is needed).

EXAMPLE:
```
*
AUTOQUERY;
*
*
RULE 1
IF    temp >= 100
THEN weather = hot;
*
*
```

RULE 1 in this example requires a value for the variable *temp* before it can be determined whether or not it can assign a value to *weather*. If there is no rule in the knowledge base that can assign a value to *temp*, and if there is no ASK statement naming the variable *temp*, AUTOQUERY will generate this question:

```
"What is the value of temp?"
```

NOTES & CAUTIONS:

- AUTOQUERY questions can be accompanied by menus just like questions generated by the ASK statement. (The CHOICES statement and MENU clause work the same for AUTOQUERY as they do for ASK.) See the MENU clause and the CHOICES and ASK statements for more information.

- This statement is useful in the early stages of developing a knowledge base because it helps to identify variables which require ASK statements.

- If the *VP-Expert* inference engine cannot assign a value to a goal variable during a consultation, AUTOQUERY will generate a question asking for the value of the goal variable. This is true even if you have supplied a rule to account for an UNKNOWN value. This is remedied by the removal of the AUTOQUERY statement when the runtime knowledge base is finalized.

BCALL

MORE INFORMATION:

See the ASK and CHOICES statements and the MENU clause. For information about the UNKNOWN keyword, see UNKNOWN in this chapter.

INSTRUCTION TYPE:

Clause

USAGE:

BCALL <[*path*]*filename*>

PARAMETERS:

A path can optionally be specified using the same format as that used by DOS (e.g.,\files\data). This tells *VP-Expert* where to find the named file. The default is the current directory.

The filename supplied to the BCALL clause must be the name of an existing DOS file with a BAT extension. However, the extension must not be explicitly provided, or an error condition will result.

DESCRIPTION:

This clause executes a DOS batch (BAT) command file. At the conclusion of the file's execution, the *VP-Expert* consultation resumes where it left off. This clause operates identically to CALL and CCALL.

EXAMPLE:

```
*
*
BCALL MAKE
*
*
```

This clause in a rule or ACTIONS block executes the file, MAKE.BAT, and then resumes the consultation where it left off.

NOTES & CAUTIONS:

■ The file COMMAND.COM must reside in your root directory.

■ For information about calling DOS EXE and COM files, see CALL and CCALL, respectively.

- The BAT file named in the clause need not be contained in the current directory. A path and/or drive can be included with the BAT filename, e.g., BCALL c:filename.

- When using this clause, make sure that the DOS program being executed does not conflict with *VP-Expert's* memory requirement.

MORE INFORMATION:
See Chapter 7 for more information about DOS program calls. See also CALL and CCALL.

BECAUSE

INSTRUCTION TYPE:
Rule keyword

USAGE:
BECAUSE "*<text>*";

BECAUSE text can contain up to 1,000 characters, including spaces.

PARAMETERS:
The BECAUSE keyword is followed by a text string enclosed inside double quotation marks. (Double quotes are the only keyboard characters not allowed in BECAUSE text.) Because it must come at the end of a rule, BECAUSE text must be followed by a semicolon.

DESCRIPTION:
The BECAUSE keyword is used to provide explanatory text for display in response to the Why? or How? command given by the user during a consultation.

When the Why? or How? command is given, *VP-Expert* displays BECAUSE text taken from the rule which either caused the question to be asked, (Why?), or assigned a value to a given variable (How?). If no BECAUSE text is present in the rule, the rule itself is displayed.

Since Why? and How? are both supplied text by BECAUSE, BECAUSE text should be written to provide an appropriate response for either query.

EXAMPLE:

```
*
*
RULE 43

IF   temp >= 101 AND
     activity = resting

THEN fever = yes

BECAUSE "A 101 or greater temperature in a
child who's been resting for an hour should
be considered a fever. If the child has been
active prior to having his/her temperature
taken, 101 does not necessarily indicate a
fever.";
*
*
ASK activity: "Was the child resting or
active during the hour prior to having
his/her temperature taken?";

CHOICES activity: Resting, Active;
*
*
```

Suppose the rule shown in this example was designed to cause the ASK and CHOICES statements to display the following prompt to the user:

```
Was the child resting or active during the
hour prior to having his/her temperature taken?
Resting              Active
```

Before answering the prompt, the user could give the Why? command to find out why the question was being asked. In response, the text supplied by the BECAUSE would appear on screen.

NOTES & CAUTIONS:
- BECAUSE can only be used at the end of a rule. You must, therefore, remember to follow BECAUSE text with a semicolon.

■ The usual restriction on "reserved words" does not apply to BECAUSE text. Any *VP-Expert* keyword can be included in BECAUSE text as long as it appears between the double quotes.

MORE INFORMATION:
See Chapters 1 and 4 for examples of BECAUSE in action. See also Why? and How? in Chapter 8.

BKCOLOR

INSTRUCTION TYPE:
Statement

USAGE:
BKCOLOR=<*integer*>;

PARAMETERS:
The integer supplied in the BKCOLOR statement must be from 0 to 7.

DESCRIPTION:
When the BKCOLOR statement is included in a knowledge base, it sets the background display to the color corresponding to the given number. The integer values and their corresponding colors are as follows:

Value	Color
0	Black
1	Blue
2	Green
3	Light Blue
4	Red
5	Magenta
6	Brown
7	White

On a monochrome display, values 0-6 display a black background.

EXAMPLE:

```
BKCOLOR=5;
RUNTIME;
ACTIONS
  DISPLAY "Welcome to the Child Illness
Assistant, an expert system created using
VP-Expert.

Press any key to begin the consultation.~"
    *
    *
    *
```

The BKCOLOR statement in this example would set the background on a color monitor to magenta. (A monochrome monitor would have a black background.)

NOTES & CAUTIONS:

■ If you specify an integer outside the legal range of 0-7, an error message indicating that you have specified an ''illegal background color'' will result.

■ Remember that BKCOLOR is a statement and not a clause. This means that it cannot be used to switch colors during a consultation (unless knowledge base files are ''chained'' using the CHAIN clause). If a knowledge base contains more than one BKCOLOR statement, all but the last will be ignored.

MORE INFORMATION:

See the COLOR clause for information about setting text color.

CALL

INSTRUCTION TYPE:

Clause

USAGE:

CALL <[*path*]*DOS_filename*>

PARAMETERS:

A path can optionally be specified using the same format as that used by DOS (e.g.,\files\data). This tells *VP-Expert* where to find the named file. The default is the current directory.

The DOS filename parameter must be the name of an existing DOS file with an EXE extension. However, the extension must not be explicitly provided, or a syntax error will result.

DESCRIPTION:

The CALL clause suspends a *VP-Expert* consultation and loads an EXE program file. When execution of the program is finished, the consultation resumes where it left off. More RAM memory than is normally needed for the external program may be required.

To make data derived from the execution of an external program available, store the data in an ASCII text file and use LOADFACTS or RECEIVE to read the data into the knowledge base. Worksheet and database files can also be used for this purpose.

EXAMPLE:
```
*
ACTIONS
   *
   *
   DISPLAY "Press any key to display a graph of
the plant design.~"
   CALL graphic1
   *
   *
```

In this example, the CALL clause is used to interrupt the consultation and display a graphic design contained in the file GRAPHIC1.EXE. When the user quits the graph, the consultation will resume where it left off.

NOTES & CAUTIONS:

- See CCALL and BCALL for information about calling DOS COM and BAT files, respectively.

- The DOS file named in the clause need not be contained in the current directory. A path and/or drive can be included with the EXE filename, e.g., CALL a:filename.

- When using this clause, make sure that the DOS program being executed does not conflict with *VP-Expert's* memory requirement.

CCALL

MORE INFORMATION:
See Chapter 7 for more information about DOS program calls. See
also the CCALL and BCALL clauses.

INSTRUCTION TYPE:
Clause

USAGE:
CCALL <[*path*]*DOS_filename*>

PARAMETERS:
A path can optionally be specified using the same format as that
used by DOS (e.g.,\files\data). This tells *VP-Expert* where to find the
named file. The default is the current directory.

The DOS filename supplied to the CCALL clause must be the name
of an existing DOS file with a COM extension. However, the
extension must not be explicitly provided, or an error condition will
result.

DESCRIPTION:

*To make data derived
from the execution of an
external program
available, store the data
in an ASCII text file and
use LOADFACTS or
RECEIVE to read the
data into the knowledge
base. Worksheet and
database files can also
be used for this purpose.*

This clause suspends the *VP-Expert* consultation and executes the
named file. When execution of the external program is completed, the
consultation is resumed where it left off. More RAM memory than is
normally needed for the external program may be required.

EXAMPLE:
```
*
*
RULE 13
IF     worksheet = yes
THEN   add = yes
CALL VP;
*
*
```

If this example rule were to pass during a consultation, the CCALL
clause would call the VP.COM file (*VP-Planner*). The user could
then perform any normal worksheet operations. After quitting
VP-Planner, the consultation would resume where it left off.

NOTES & CAUTIONS:

- See CALL and BCALL for information about calling DOS EXE files and BAT files, respectively.

- The DOS file named in the clause need not be contained in the current directory. A path and/or drive can be included with the COM filename, e.g., CCALL c:\am\filename.

- It is the responsibility of the person designing the knowledge base to ensure that the DOS program being executed does not conflict with *VP-Expert's* memory requirement.

MORE INFORMATION:
See Chapter 7 and the BCALL and CALL clauses in this chapter.

CHAIN

INSTRUCTION TYPE:
Clause

USAGE:
CHAIN <[*path*]*KBS_filename*>

PARAMETERS:
A path can optionally be specified using the same format as that used by DOS (e.g.,\files\data). This tells *VP-Expert* where to find the named file. The default is the current directory.

The KBS filename parameter given in the CHAIN clause is the name of a knowledge base file with a KBS extension. However, the extension must not be explicitly provided, or an error will result.

DESCRIPTION:
The CHAIN clause, used in combination with the SAVEFACTS and LOADFACTS clauses, permits the use of knowledge bases that would otherwise be too large to be contained in memory. With these clauses you ''chain'' together two or more knowledge bases for use in a single consultation. Here are the basic steps required.

- Use SAVEFACTS to save the known values (facts) from the current consultation.

- Issue a CHAIN clause naming a new knowledge base file. (The old knowledge base file will be closed and this file will take its place in the current consultation.)

- Use LOADFACTS to load the values saved by SAVEFACTS into the new knowledge base.

SAVEFACTS and CHAIN should occur in the first knowledge base file. LOADFACTS must be contained in the new knowledge base file.

EXAMPLE:

Assume a consultation that diagnoses faulty air conditioners.

In this first knowledge base segment (contained in a file FIXAC1.KBS), the SAVEFACTS and CHAIN clauses are used to save the values assigned to the variables up to this point in the consultation, and load a new knowledge base file, FIXAC2.KBS.

```
ACTIONS
   *
   *
   SAVEFACTS fixvalue
   CHAIN fixac2;
*
*
```

This next segment shows a section of the new knowledge base file, FIXAC2.KBS. Note the EXECUTE statement. This allows a smooth transition from one knowledge base to another (see EXECUTE for more information). Note also that the LOADFACTS clause is the first clause contained in the ACTIONS block. This placement ensures that the saved values will be loaded immediately upon execution of the new knowledge base.

```
EXECUTE;
RUNTIME;
ACTIONS
   LOADFACTS fixvalue
   *
   *
   *
```

NOTES & CAUTIONS:

- If SAVEFACTS is not executed prior to a CHAIN clause, all the values obtained up to that point in the consultation will be lost.

- SAVEFACTS saves *all* assigned values to a text file. You cannot use SAVEFACTS to save selected values.

■ Do not forget that the LOADFACTS clause should be contained within the new knowledge base file. Placing it in the old file does not achieve the desired effect.

■ In order to achieve a smooth transition when chaining from one knowledge base file to another, place the EXECUTE statement in the knowledge base file named in the CHAIN clause.

■ You can also pass data between chained knowledge bases via database files. Data written to a file by one knowledge base can be accessed subsequently by any chained modules.

MORE INFORMATION:
See SAVEFACTS and LOADFACTS. See also Chapter 7 for a discussion of knowledge base chaining techniques.

CHOICES

INSTRUCTION TYPE:
Statement

USAGE:
CHOICES <*variable1*[,*variable2*,...]:*value1*[,*value2*,...]>;

PARAMETERS:
The first parameter in the CHOICES statement is the name of one or more knowledge base variables. Up to 10 variables are allowed. See ''Notes & Cautions'' following.

The *value* parameters (one required and as many additional as desired) are values which are presented to the user as a menu if the statement is executed during a consultation. These must be separated by commas. Spaces surrounding the commas are optional.

DESCRIPTION
The CHOICES statement works together with the ASK statement. When a question generated by an ASK statement is displayed during a consultation, the values given in a corresponding CHOICES statement (i.e., a CHOICES statement naming the same variable as the ASK statement) are presented to the user as a menu of choices.

The CHOICES statement can also generate menus to accompany questions caused by the AUTOQUERY statement. See AUTOQUERY for more information.

EXAMPLE:

```
*
*
ASK age_range: "In what age range do you fall?";

CHOICES age_range: 18_to_30,31_to_55,56_or_older;
*
*
```

These statements, if executed during a consultation, would present the following question and menu to the user (the underscore character will display as a space during a consultation):

```
In what age range do you fall?
18 to 30        31 to 55        56 or older
```

NOTES & CAUTIONS:

- A single CHOICES statement can name up to ten variables. This is convenient when you have a number of variables that can be assigned values from the same menu—for example, variables that will be assigned *Yes* or *No* values, e.g:

  ```
  CHOICES married,employed: Yes, No;
  ```

- Corresponding CHOICES and ASK statements need only name the same variable. They do not have to be physically adjacent in the knowledge base.

- When a CHOICES menu is presented during a consultation, the values on the menu are the only choices available to the user—with one exception. The user can type a question mark to indicate that they do not know the answer to the question. This leaves the variable UNKNOWN and allows the user to proceed with the consultation. See UNKNOWN in this chapter for more information.

Before pressing END, the user can cancel a choice by moving the lightbar to the selection and pressing DEL.

- To select an option from a menu generated by the CHOICES statement, the user must move the lightbar to the option (using the arrow keys) and press the *ENTER* key. A triangle will appear next to the chosen value. Pressing the *END* key finalizes the selection.

■ If an ENDOFF statement is present in the knowledge base, an option is selected in the manner described above, except that for single-valued variables, the *ENTER* key finalizes the selection (there is no need to follow by pressing the *END* key). For plural variables the *END* key must still be pressed, and ENDOFF has no effect.

■ If a plural variable is named in a CHOICES statement, then the user may select more than one option when the question and menu appear. (If the variable is *not* plural, *VP-Expert* allows only one selection.)

■ Confidence factors can be assigned to menu choices by pressing the *HOME* key and typing a number between 0 and 100 before pressing *ENTER* to make the selection. If no confidence factor is indicated, CNF 100 is assumed. See Chapter 7 and the TRUTHTHRESH clause for more information about confidence factors.

■ If a knowledge base contains a MENU clause for a particular variable, a CHOICES statement for the same variable is not normally present. In the event that both are contained in a knowledge base, the CHOICES statement will be ignored if the MENU clause is executed. See the MENU clause for more information.

MORE INFORMATION:

See the ASK, PLURAL, and AUTOQUERY statements, and the MENU and TRUTHTHRESH clauses in this chapter.

CLOSE

INSTRUCTION TYPE:
Clause

USAGE:
CLOSE <[path]DBF_filename>

PARAMETERS:
A path can optionally be specified using the same format as that used by DOS (e.g.,\files\data). This tells *VP-Expert* where to find the named file. The default is the current directory.

The filename supplied to the CLOSE clause must be an existing database file with a DBF extension. However, the extension must not be explicitly provided, or a syntax error will result.

DESCRIPTION:
The CLOSE clause closes an open database file and resets the record pointer to the first record of the file. This clause is useful for resetting the record pointer before issuing a GET. (The GET clause retrieves data forward from the record pointer. This means that if you want to issue a series of GETs that all start at the top of the file, you can execute the CLOSE clause between GETs to reset the record pointer.)

EXAMPLE
```
RUNTIME;
ACTIONS
    MENU the_name,all,empdata,name
    FIND the_name
            ! This example knowledge base
            ! will find and display the date hired
            ! for a selected employee.
    GET the_name=name,empdata,date_hired
    DISPLAY "{the_name} was hired in
{date_hired}."
    RESET the_name
            ! CLOSE is used to reset the record
```

```
                        ! pointer so that the next GET clause
                        ! will start at the top of the
                        ! file instead of the position left by the
                        ! last GET.
          CLOSE empdata
          FIND the_name
                        ! This part of the knowledge
                        ! base finds and displays the date
                        ! hired for another selected
                        ! employee.
          GET the_name=name,empdata,date_hired
          DISPLAY "{the_name} was hired in
          {date hired}.";
*
*

ASK name: "For which employee would you
like to find out the hire date?";
*
*
```

Note that the ! character is used in this example to add comment lines to the knowledge base. Any line of text preceded by an exclamation point is ignored during knowledge base execution. For more information, see the discussion of ! Comment Lines at the end of this chapter.

NOTES & CAUTIONS:

■ The CLOSE clause can close only one file at a time. Naming more than one database filename, or no filename, results in a syntax error. Using CLOSE with the name of an unopened file has no effect and creates no error condition.

■ Do not confuse this clause with the *VP-Info* and dBASE CLOSE command, which closes and makes unavailable all open files. This command has no equivalent in *VP-Expert*.

■ *VP-Expert* allows a maximum of six open database files. When six files are already open and you want to access an additional file, use CLOSE to close one of the currently open files.

■ There is no OPEN clause in *VP-Expert*. The GET clause is, in effect, *VP-Expert's* OPEN clause.

MORE INFORMATION:

See examples in Chapter 5 and the GET clause in this chapter.

CLS

INSTRUCTION TYPE:
Clause

USAGE:
CLS

PARAMETERS:
None required or permitted.

DESCRIPTION:
The CLS clause clears the consultation window. In a non-runtime (three-window) consultation, the two bottom windows are not affected.

EXAMPLE:
```
ACTIONS
     DISPLAY "The following consultation will help
you to determine the best computer system for
your home or business needs.

A series of questions will be asked. Each
question is accompanied by a menu of options.
To make a menu selection, move the lightbar
to the option you want and press the ENTER
key. If you do not know the answer to a
question, type a question mark (?).

(Press any key to continue).~"

     CLS

     DISPLAY " .......
     *
     *
```

The CLS clause in this example clears the screen of the text generated by the first DISPLAY clause so that the text generated by the next DISPLAY clause will begin on a blank screen.

COLOR

See "Notes & Cautions" for information about how this clause affects text on monochrome monitors.

INSTRUCTION TYPE:
Clause

USAGE:
COLOR=<*integer*>

PARAMETERS:
The integer supplied to COLOR must be from 0 to 31.

DESCRIPTION:
The COLOR clause is used to change text color on color monitors. It can also be used to display blinking text.

Since COLOR is a clause (and not a statement like BKCOLOR), it can be used to change text characteristics as often as you like during a consultation. Whenever a COLOR clause is executed in a rule or ACTIONS block, it causes subsequent text to appear as specified until another COLOR clause is executed.

The numbers 0-15 indicate the 16 available colors (see table below). The numbers 16-31 cause corresponding colored text to blink on and off. The color associated with each blinking number is determined by subtracting 16 from the blinking value.

Color	Normal	Blinking
Black	0	16
Blue	1	17
Green	2	18
Cyan	3	19
Red	4	20
Magenta	5	21
Brown	6	22
White	7	23
Gray	8	24
Light Blue	9	25
Light Green	10	26
Light Cyan	11	27
Light Red	12	28
Light Magenta	13	29
Yellow	14	30
Bright White	15	31

EXAMPLE:

```
RUNTIME;
ACTIONS
   COLOR = 3
   DISPLAY "The following consultation will
help you to determine the best computer
system for your home or business needs.

A series of questions will be asked. Each
question is accompanied by a menu of
options. To choose an option in response to
a question, move the lightbar to the option
and press the ENTER key. If you do not know
the answer to a question, type a question
mark (?).

Press ENTER to begin the consultation.~"

   COLOR = 4
   FIND need
   *
   *
   *
```

The first COLOR clause in this example causes the DISPLAY text to appear in cyan. After the DISPLAY clause is executed, another COLOR clause switches the text color to red. Subsequent text appears in red until another COLOR clause is executed.

NOTES & CAUTIONS:

- The numbers for blinking text are toggles. This means that when text is set to blink, it continues to blink until another "blinking code" is encountered. To cause one line to blink in red and the next line to display non-blinking black text, you would use a combination like this:

```
*
*
COLOR = 20
DISPLAY "This line blinks in red."
COLOR = 16
DISPLAY "This line is in non-blinking black."
*
*
```

  If COLOR = 0 were substituted for the second COLOR clause, the color of subsequent text would change, but the text would continue to blink. To turn off (toggle) blinking, you must give another "blinking code."

- On monochrome monitors, values 0 through 7 display regular text; 8 through 15 produce bright text. (1 and 9 are exceptions; they produce underlined text—in regular and bright, respectively.) Values 16 through 31 toggle blinking for text with characteristics derived by subtracting 16 from the blinking value.

- When changing background and foreground colors, choose combinations that create readable displays. (The background color is determined by the BKCOLOR statement.)

- Text generated by the MENU clause or CHOICES statement is not affected by the COLOR clause.

- Supplying a number to this clause outside the 0-31 range results in the error message, "The color must be from 0 to 31."

MORE INFORMATION:
See the BKCOLOR statement and the DISPLAY clause for related information.

COLUMN

See "Row, Column, or Named Range Access" under PWKS and WKS.

DISPLAY

INSTRUCTION TYPE:
Clause

USAGE:
DISPLAY "*<text>*"

DISPLAY text can be a maximum of 1,000 characters, including spaces.

PARAMETERS:
The text supplied with the DISPLAY clause must be enclosed within double quotation marks. (Double quotes are the only characters on the keyboard that cannot be used as text.)

DESCRIPTION:
The DISPLAY clause provides the *VP-Expert* system designer with a means of displaying messages to the user. When the clause is executed during a consultation, the text within the double quotes is displayed in the consultation window. This clause is important for the "conclusion messages" that inform the user of consultation results.

DISPLAY Clause Options

The tilde is helpful for stopping lengthy DISPLAY text from scrolling off screen before the user has a chance to finish reading it.

The Tilde (~)
If the tilde character (~) is included in DISPLAY text, the message pauses (at the point of the tilde) until the user presses any key. If no tildes are present, the consultation automatically continues after the message is presented.

Any number of tildes can be used in a DISPLAY clause.

Curly Brackets ({ })

When DISPLAY text is presented during a consultation, variable names enclosed in curly brackets are replaced by their corresponding values. For example:

```
DISPLAY "The best cheese for the course is a
{The_Cheese}."
```

If *The_Cheese* was assigned the value *Brie* during the consultation, this clause would display the message "The best cheese for the course is a Brie."

> *Note: If the variable shown in curly brackets has no known value when the DISPLAY clause is executed, the value will simply be omitted; e.g., "The best cheese for the meal is a ."*

The Number Sign (#)

Preceding a variable name inside curly brackets with a number sign (#) displays the confidence factor as well as the value of the variable. For example:

```
DISPLAY "The best cheese for the course is a
{#The_Cheese}."
```

If *Brie* was assigned to *The_Cheese* with a confidence factor of 100, the message would be:

```
The best cheese for the course is a Brie CNF 100.
```

Right Variable Alignment

If you precede a variable name in curly brackets with an integer (*n*), the displayed value will be right aligned in an *n* space area. (If the number of characters in the variable's value exceeds the specified number, the value will be cut off on the right.) The following clause would right align the value of *The_Cheese* in a 15-space area.

```
DISPLAY "The best cheese for the course is a
{15The_Cheese}."
```

The result would be:

```
The best cheese for the course is a           Brie.
```

Note: If you want to display a confidence factor with right-aligned text, place the # sign before the alignment number; e.g., {#15The_Cheese}. But make sure the space indicated is sufficient to include the confidence factor; otherwise, the display will be truncated on the right. (At least 7 characters should be allotted for the confidence factor (CNF 100)).

EXAMPLE:

```
RUNTIME;
ACTIONS
  DISPLAY "Welcome to the charming world of cheese!.
Press any key to begin the consultation.~"
  FIND The_Cheese
  DISPLAY " The best cheese for this course is a
{#The_Cheese}.";


RULE 1
IF      Course = Appetizer
THEN    Consistency = Soft
        BECAUSE "The consistency of the cheese is
determined by the course.";
  *

  *

  *
```

This knowledge base uses a DISPLAY clause first to welcome the user to the consultation, and then to display a conclusion message at the end of the consultation. Note the use of symbols ~, #, and { }. Note also that the ! "comment line" character is used in the first DISPLAY text. When contained within the double quotes in DISPLAY, ASK, or BECAUSE text, the exclamation point does not have its normal effect. (See the end of this chapter for information about comment lines.)

For lengthy messages the RECEIVE clause can be used to read text in from a text file. See the RECEIVE clause for more information.

NOTES & CAUTIONS:

■ If a PRINTON clause has been executed, DISPLAY messages will be sent to the printer as well as to the screen. The printer must be properly connected or an error will occur. Use the PRINTOFF clause to turn off output to the printer. PRINTON will stay in effect until a PRINTOFF is encountered.

■ When a DISPLAY clause contains a large amount of text, use the tilde (~) to prevent the first part of the message from scrolling off screen before the user has a chance to read it.

■ The usual restriction on ''reserved words'' does not apply to DISPLAY text. Any *VP-Expert* keyword can be included in DISPLAY text as long as it appears between the double quotes.

■ If the DISPLAY clause is the last clause of a rule or ACTIONS block, do not forget to add the semicolon required at the end of the rule or block. Omitting the semicolon will cause a syntax error.

MORE INFORMATION:

See Chapter 4 for more information about the DISPLAY clause. See PRINTON and PRINTOFF for information on sending messages to the printer. See also ASK and BECAUSE for information about other ways of generating text during a consultation.

EJECT

INSTRUCTION TYPE:
Clause

USAGE:
EJECT

PARAMETERS:
None required or permitted.

DESCRIPTION:
This clause causes your printer to eject the remainder of the current page and go to the top of the next page. This clause is typically used with the PDISPLAY clause (or with DISPLAY if PRINTON is used).

EXAMPLE:

```
ACTIONS
    *
    *
    FIND The_Cheese
    SORT The_Cheese
    PDISPLAY "The most appropriate cheese for the
course is {#The_Cheese}."
    EJECT
    *
    *
    *
PLURAL: The_Cheese;
*
*
```

After the PDISPLAY clause in this example finishes printing a sorted list of cheeses, the EJECT clause will eject the current page and place the printer head at the top of the next page.

NOTES & CAUTIONS:

■ This clause is only useful with continuous form paper.

■ If the printer is not connected to the system or turned on, or if it's not "on line," the system may appear to "hang" when an EJECT clause is encountered. The printer should always be checked before starting a consultation in which an EJECT clause will be used.

MORE INFORMATION:
See PDISPLAY, DISPLAY, and PRINTON in this chapter.

ELSE

See RULE.

END

INSTRUCTION TYPE:
Clause

USAGE:
*

*

WHILEKNOWN
*

*

END
*

*

PARAMETERS:
The END clause must be preceded in the knowledge base by the WHILEKNOWN clause.

DESCRIPTION:
The END clause is used in a knowledge base to signal the end of a WHILEKNOWN-END loop. See the WHILEKNOWN clause for more information.

EXAMPLE:
See the WHILEKNOWN clause.

NOTES & CAUTIONS:
■ If a knowledge base contains a WHILEKNOWN clause without a corresponding END clause, no error will be reported. However, the desired loop will not be achieved.

MORE INFORMATION:
See the WHILEKNOWN and RESET clauses in this chapter. See also Chapter 5 for examples of the WHILEKNOWN-END loop.

ENDOFF

INSTRUCTION TYPE:
Statement

USAGE:
ENDOFF;

PARAMETERS:
None required or permitted.

DESCRIPTION:
Placing this one-word statement anywhere in the knowledge base eliminates the need to press *END* to finalize a MENU or CHOICES menu selection for a single-valued variable. (Menus for plural variables are not affected.) To make a menu choice, the user simply needs to move the lightbar to an option and press *ENTER*.

EXAMPLE:
```
ENDOFF;
ACTIONS
   FIND plant
   DISPLAY "A {plant} is an excellent
choice for you.";
*
*
*
```

NOTES & CAUTIONS:
- While this statement can be placed anywhere in the knowledge base, it is most conveniently located at or towards the top of the file.

- The ENDOFF statement only affects menus for single-valued variables.

- When ENDOFF is present, the DEL key cannot be used to change menu choices.

EXECUTE

INSTRUCTION TYPE:
Statement

USAGE:
EXECUTE;

PARAMETERS:
None required or permitted.

DESCRIPTION:
This statement causes a consultation to begin automatically upon execution of the Main Menu Consult command. When this statement is not present in a knowledge base, the user is required to give an additional command (Go) to start a consultation.

EXAMPLE:

```
RUNTIME;
EXECUTE;
ACTIONS
  DISPLAY "Welcome to the charming world of cheese!
Press any key to begin the consultation.~"
  FIND The_Cheese
  DISPLAY "The best cheese for this course is a
{#The_Cheese}.";

RULE 1
IF      Course = Appetizer
THEN    Consistency = Soft
BECAUSE "The consistency of the cheese is determined
by the course.";
*
*
*
```

The EXECUTE statement in this sample knowledge base starts the consultation as soon as the user gives the Consult command from the *VP-Expert* Main Menu.

NOTES & CAUTIONS:

■ If this statement is included in a knowledge base, the user cannot access other commands offered on the Consult menu prior to running a consultation. (These include Help, Variable, Rule, Set, and Set's associated Trace, Fast, and Slow commands). However, since these commands are primarily used for development purposes, this is not a problem for runtime consultations.

■ When chaining knowledge bases, placing the EXECUTE statement in the second knowledge base smoothes the transition.

MORE INFORMATION:
See Chapter 8 for information about *VP-Expert* menu commands.

FIND

INSTRUCTION TYPE:
Clause

USAGE:
FIND <*variable*>

PARAMETERS:
The only FIND clause parameter is a variable name.

The method the inference uses to search for values is called "backward chaining." See Chapter 2 for a description of how backward chaining works.

DESCRIPTION:
The FIND clause is used in a *VP-Expert* knowledge base to identify variables whose values are needed to successfully complete the consultation. Whenever a FIND clause is executed, the *VP-Expert* inference engine attempts to find a value (or, if the named variable is a plural variable, *values*) for the given variable.

When a FIND clause is contained in the ACTIONS block of a knowledge base, the variable named in the clause is called a "goal variable."

There is usually at least one FIND clause in the ACTIONS block of a knowledge base, because the FIND clause identifies the major "goals" of the consultation. The FIND clause can also be useful in rules. By adding the clause to a rule, you can instruct the *VP-Expert* inference engine to find a particular variable in the event that the rule passes. For example, if the following rule passed, the FIND clause would cause the ASK statement to execute.

```
*
*
RULE 14
IF    preference = tropical AND
      budget = low_med AND
      tim_year = fall
THEN  area = Yucatan
      FIND Yucatan;
*
*

ASK Yucatan: "Would you consider the Yucatan
Peninsula in Mexico?";

CHOICES Yucatan: Yes, No;
*
*
```

Using a sequence of FIND clauses to influence the inference engine's path through the knowledge base accomplishes a form of "forward chaining." Thus, we say that VP-Expert uses both forward and backward chaining to solve problems during a consultation. See the GET and MENU clauses for other examples of forward chaining in VP-Expert.

If multiple FIND clauses occur in a single ACTIONS block or rule, *VP-Expert* attempts to find a value for each of the variables in the order they appear. In other words, the inference engine only moves to the next clause after it has found a value or values for the variable named in the previous FIND clause, or after it determines that no value can be found for that variable.

If a plural variable is named in a FIND clause, the inference engine will attempt to find as many values for it as possible.

EXAMPLE:

```
RUNTIME;
ACTIONS
  DISPLAY "Welcome to the charming world of cheese!
Press any key to begin the consultation.~"
  FIND The_Cheese
  DISPLAY "The best cheese for this course is a
{#The_Cheese}.";

RULE 1
IF      Course = Appetizer
THEN    Consistency = Soft
        FIND Complement;

RULE 2
IF      Course = Salad OR
        Course = Dessert
THEN    Consistency = Firm
        FIND Complement;
*

*
```

This sample knowledge base shows three FIND clauses. The first, contained in the ACTIONS block, sends the inference engine looking for a value for the goal variable, *The_Cheese*. When that value is found, the consultation will be complete. Two other FIND clauses appear in RULES 1 and 2. If either of these rules pass during the consultation, the inference engine is instructed to find a value for the variable *Complement*.

NOTES & CAUTIONS:

■ If a FIND clause names a variable for which there is no passing rule or ASK statement, the AUTOQUERY statement, if present in the knowledge base, generates the question, "What is the value of ___?" The user's response to the question will be assigned as the value of the variable. If AUTOQUERY is absent, the variable's value remains UNKNOWN. See UNKNOWN in this chapter for more information.

MORE INFORMATION:

See the ASK, AUTOQUERY, and PLURAL statements.

FORMAT

INSTRUCTION TYPE:
Clause

USAGE:
FORMAT <*variable, integer1. integer2*>

PARAMETERS:
The first parameter is a name of a variable which has a numeric value.

The second parameter, *integer1*, specifies the total number of places, including the decimal point, in the format of the value of *variable*.

The last parameter, *integer2*, specifies the number of decimal places (behind the decimal point) in the format of the value of *variable*.

DESCRIPTION:
The FORMAT clause is used with a DISPLAY or PDISPLAY clause to provide a format for displaying a floating point number.

EXAMPLE:
```
*
ACTIONS
    FIND radius
    FORMAT radius, 8.4
    DISPLAY "The radius = {radius}.";
*
*
```

The FORMAT and DISPLAY clauses in this example display a message in which the value of the variable *radius* is displayed with a total of 8 places—including the decimal point—with 4 decimal places after the decimal point.

GET

The term "database rule" is used to emphasize a similarity to conventional VP-Expert rules. IF the conditions stated in the database rule are met by a record, THEN a value is assigned to at least one variable.

A GET clause can only retrieve one or all fields from a database file. To retrieve more than one field (but less than all), use multiple GET clauses.

INSTRUCTION TYPE:
Clause

USAGE:
GET *<ALL/database_rule,[path]DBF_filename,ALL/fieldname>*

PARAMETERS:
The first parameter in a GET clause is either the keyword ALL (for all records) or a "database rule" specifying one or more conditions by which a record will be selected from the database file. See "The Database Rule" on the next page for more information.

The second parameter, *DBF_filename* (with a path optionally specified), must be an existing database file with a DBF extension. However, the extension must not be explicitly provided, or a syntax error will result.

The third parameter is either the keyword ALL (indicating all fields) or the name of a single field in the database file designated in the GET clause.

DESCRIPTION:
The GET clause is used to retrieve values from a database file created in *VP-Info*, dBASE II, dBASE III, or dBASE III+.

More precisely, the GET clause opens, if necessary, a given database file and retrieves one or all fields from either the next record of the file (starting from the record pointer), or from the next record that matches the conditions stated in the *database rule*. Retrieved values are assigned to non-plural variables with the same name as the database fields from which they were taken. (For example, if "hot" is retrieved from a database field whose field name is "temperature," *hot* would be assigned to the *VP-Expert* variable *temperature*.) Such variables can subsequently be manipulated like any other in *VP-Expert*.

Using a GET clause to retrieve values from database records is an example of "forward chaining" in VP-Expert, since the database rule applies to a prescribed sequence of records.

Note that the GET clause searches forward from the record pointer. This means that at the start of a consultation and following the execution of a CLOSE clause, the search begins at the top of the database file. If another GET is subsequently issued, the GET searches forward from the last retrieved record. (After a GET, the record pointer remains on the last record from which data was retrieved.) In order to issue a sequence of GETs that all begin at the top of the file, use the CLOSE clause between GETs to reset the record pointer. (See the CLOSE clause.)

The GET clause is frequently used within a WHILEKNOWN-END loop to successively retrieve field values from a database file. See "Notes & Cautions" for more information.

The Database Rule

In a "database rule," conditions are stated using the following format:

variable   relational operator   fieldname

Here, *variable* is the name of a knowledge base variable; *relational operator* is one of the operators shown in the table below; *fieldname* is the name of a field in the database file.

Relational Operators

=	equal to	>	greater than
<	less than	>=	greater than or equal to
<=	less than or equal to	<>	not equal to

The logical operators AND and OR can be used to combine up to ten conditions in a database rule. For example:

```
GET the_wine=wine AND the_price <= price,wines,price
```

See "Using Logical Operators" in Chapter 4 for more information about using logical operators.

EXAMPLES:

```
GET ALL,wines,ALL
```

Moving forward from the record pointer, this clause retrieves all fields from the next record in a file called WINES.DBF. Note that the first ALL of the clause (i.e., GET ALL...) indicates, not that all records should be retrieved at once, but rather that the next record should be selected from among *all* the records in the file (in other words, the selected record need not match any special condition.)

```
GET the_wine = wine,wines,price
```

This retrieves the PRICE field from the next record (starting from the record pointer) in the file WINES.DBF whose WINE field value matches the current value of the *VP-Expert* variable *the_wine*.

```
GET the_wine = wine AND the_price <= price,wines,price
```

This GET clause retrieves the PRICE field from the first record in the file for which the current value of the *VP-Expert* variable, *the_wine*, matches the contents of the WINE field AND the current contents of the *VP-Expert* variable, *the_price*, is less than or equal to the PRICE field.

```
GET the_wine = wine OR the_price < price,wines,price
```

This retrieves the PRICE field from the next record in the file for which the current value of the *VP-Expert* variable, *the_wine*, matches the contents of the WINE field OR the current value of the *VP-Expert* variable, *the_price*, is less than the contents of the PRICE field.

NOTES & CAUTIONS:
- A single GET clause can be used in a WHILEKNOWN-END loop to successively retrieve selected fields from ALL records in a file, or every record matching the condition or conditions stated in the database rule. For example, look at this knowledge base:

```
ACTIONS
    WHILEKNOWN go
        RESET name
        MENU name,ALL,empdata,lname
        FIND name
        MRESET name
        GET name=lname,empdata,hire_date
        CLOSE empdata
        DISPLAY "{name} was hired in {hire_date}.
```

```
Press any key to continue.~"
    CLS
    RESET go
    FIND go
  END;

RULE 1
IF name <> UNKNOWN
THEN go = yes;

ASK name: "What is the last name of the
employee for whom you want the hire date.
(Type a question mark if, instead, you want
to end the consultation).";
```

During a consultation, this knowledge base repeatedly asks the user to select an employee whose hire date they would like to see. When the user finally types a question mark to indicate that they want to quit the consultation (see the ASK clause in the sample), the variables *name* and subsequently *go*, become UNKNOWN, and the loop executes one final time.

Note the use of RESET, MRESET, CLOSE, and CLS in this example. The RESET clauses ensure that the FIND clauses will be executed with each iteration of the loop; MRESET erases from memory the menu created by each execution of the MENU clause; CLOSE causes each GET to begin its search from the top of the EMPDATA file; and CLS clears the screen after each DISPLAY message is presented. For more information about these clauses, see RESET, CLOSE, and CLS.

- A variable named in a database rule should not have the same name as any field in any open database file. Such a case can generate unexpected results—especially if the GET clause is contained inside a WHILEKNOWN-END loop.

- Field values retrieved by GET need not conform to the normal 20-character limit on values. GET can retrieve values of up to 256 characters.

- Note that the GET clause opens the named database file if it is not already open. (GET is, in effect, *VP-Expert*'s "OPEN" clause.)

■ *VP-Expert* allows only six open data files. If six data files are already open and a GET is issued for a seventh file, an error message is reported. In a case where you want to open a seventh database file, use CLOSE to close one of the open files before issuing the GET.

■ Whenever the GET clause brings in data from a database, it first automatically RESETs all knowledge base variables whose names are identical to the field names of the retrieved fields. In other words, any previous values assigned to these variables are erased. Note that these values will be reset even if the GET is unsuccessful in finding a record that fits the database rule. In the event that this occurs, all variables with names matching the database field names will be set to UNKNOWN. This can be useful in a WHILEKNOWN-END loop for stopping the loop when the end of the file has been reached. For example:

```
ACTIONS
    WHILEKNOWN name
        GET all,empdata,all
        DISPLAY "{name}"
    END;
```

This loop would continue to display the last name in the file forever if the GET clause did not eventually RESET the variable *name* to UNKNOWN.

Note: A WHILEKNOWN-END loop always executes one time if the value named in the WHILEKNOWN clause is UNKNOWN. This is why, in the preceding example, the clauses in the loop initially execute without a known value for name.

MORE INFORMATION:

See Chapter 5 for more examples of the GET clause. See also CLOSE, PUT, WHILEKNOWN, and UNKNOWN in this chapter.

IF

See RULE.

INDEX

INSTRUCTION TYPE:
Clause

USAGE:
INDEX <[*path*]*index_filename,field_name*>

PARAMETERS:
The first parameter of the INDEX clause is the name of an existing *VP-Info* or dBASE II index file with an NDX extension. However, the extension must not be explicitly provided, or a syntax error will result. If necessary, a path can also be specified.

The second parameter is the name of the database field that the index file was "indexed on." (This is called the "key field" or "index key" of the index file.)

Note that although *VP-Info* and dBASE II allow database files to be indexed on multiple fields, this clause only works for index files indexed on a single field.

DESCRIPTION:
This clause makes use of *VP-Info* or dBASE II index files to fetch records in less time.

VP-Info and dBASE II index files, in effect, reorder the records of a database (DBF) file, based alphabetically on a character field named in the index command. (A name and address data file, for example, could be indexed on the LAST_NAME field. The resulting index file would reorder the records alphabetically by last name.)

In *VP-Expert*, the INDEX clause is used, prior to a GET clause, to speed up the access of selected records.

EXAMPLE:

```
*
ACTIONS
   FIND lname
   FIND yrs_emp
   INDEX lstname,last_name
   GET lname = last_name,employee,address
   *
   *
   *
```

The GET clause in this example would retrieve the contents of the *address* field from the next record *in the indexed order* whose *last_name* field matches the contents of the variable, *lname*.

NOTES & CAUTIONS:

- The index file named in the INDEX clause must be a *VP-Info* or dBASE II index file. *VP-Expert* does not recognize dBASE III index files.

- The INDEX clause only works with index files indexed on a single field. Index files created using multiple field concatenation cannot be used.

- The "database rule" in a GET clause is somewhat restricted when the INDEX clause is used prior to a GET. Expressions containing the key field can only use the = sign (e.g., the_wine = wine); other relational operators cannot be used. Note, however, that expressions naming database fields other than the key field are not similarly restricted. In the following example, the compound expression in the GET clause is legal since the second expression names a non-key field:

```
   *
   *
   INDEX winelist,wine
   GET the_wine = wine AND the_price <= price,wines,ALL
   *
   *
```

- If a GET clause expression compares a *VP-Expert* plural variable with the index key, only the first value assigned to the plural variable will be used.

- If one-third or more of the records in a file are to be selected, then using an INDEX clause will not speed up the retrieval process. When very few records are likely to be selected, INDEXed file access makes a major difference in speed.

MORE INFORMATION:

Refer to your *VP-Info* or dBASE II documentation for information about creating index files. See also the GET clause.

LOADFACTS

INSTRUCTION TYPE:

Clause

USAGE:

LOADFACTS <*[path]text_filename*>

PARAMETERS:

A path can optionally be specified using the same format as that used by DOS (e.g.,\files\data). This tells *VP-Expert* where to find the named file. The default is the current directory.

The required parameter used with the LOADFACTS clause is the name of a text file previously created with a SAVEFACTS clause. No extension is needed. Supplying an extension will result in an error.

DESCRIPTION:

LOADFACTS is the third and final clause used in the process of "chaining" two knowledge base files together.

Chaining knowledge base files permits the use of knowledge bases that would otherwise be too large to be contained in memory. Using this technique, two or more knowledge bases are "chained" together for use in a single consultation.

The three clauses used to chain files are SAVEFACTS, CHAIN, and LOADFACTS.

Here are the basic steps required in knowledge base chaining.

- Use SAVEFACTS to save the known values (facts) from the current consultation.
- Issue a CHAIN clause naming a new knowledge base file. (The old knowledge base file will be closed, and this file will take its place in the current consultation.)
- Use LOADFACTS to load the values saved by SAVEFACTS into the new knowledge base.

SAVEFACTS and CHAIN should occur in the first knowledge base file. LOADFACTS must be contained in the new knowledge base file.

See the SAVEFACTS and CHAIN clauses for more information.

EXAMPLE:
See the CHAIN clause.

NOTES & CAUTIONS:
- LOADFACTS reads from an ASCII text file which contains variables and their values. The following is the format of this file:

  variable1 = value1 CNF n
  variable2 = value2 CNF n

  Data from the execution of external programs can be stored in this format and then retrieved by the knowledge base using LOADFACTS.

- It is not possible to selectively retrieve values from a file created by the SAVEFACTS clause.
- In order to achieve a smooth transition when chaining from one knowledge base file to another, place the EXECUTE statement in the file containing the LOADFACTS clause.

MORE INFORMATION:
See CHAIN and SAVEFACTS.

MENU

INSTRUCTION TYPE:
Clause

USAGE:
MENU <*variable,ALL/database_rule,[path]DBF_filename, fieldname*>

PARAMETERS:
The first parameter is the name of a *VP-Expert* variable.

The second parameter is either the *VP-Expert* keyword ALL, or a *database rule* specifying one or more conditions by which records in the database file will be selected. For instructions on specifying conditions in a database rule, see the GET clause.

The third parameter, *DBF_filename*, is the name of an existing database file with a DBF extension. However, the extension must not be explicitly provided, or a syntax error will result. If necessary, a path can also be specified.

The fourth parameter, *fieldname*, tells *VP-Expert* which field's contents to use as menu choices. This fieldname must correspond to a fieldname in the database file specified in the clause.

DESCRIPTION:
The MENU clause generates a menu of options to accompany a question displayed by a corresponding ASK statement, or by AUTOQUERY. This clause is similar to the CHOICES statement, but, unlike CHOICES, it takes its options from the field values of a given database file.

The use of database rules in the MENU and GET clauses is an example of forward chaining in VP-Expert.

The keyword ALL or a database rule determines which records in the file will contribute field values. If ALL records are specified, values will be taken from the given field of ALL records in the database file. If a database rule is used, only those records matching the given condition or conditions will contribute values. In either case, only unique values appear in the resulting menu.

One notable difference between MENU and CHOICES is that unlike the CHOICES statement, the MENU clause cannot be placed anywhere in the knowledge base. The MENU clause must be placed where it will be executed *before* the corresponding ASK or AUTOQUERY statement is executed. (Though it need not be *immediately* before.)

EXAMPLE:

Consider a small file called BOOK.DBF which contains authors' names, book titles, and book types. The database looks like this:

AUTHOR	TITLE	TYPE
Hemingway	Old Man and Sea	Novel
Ludlum	Bourne Identity	Novel
Shafer	AI Programming	Tech
Moose	Berkeley USA	Interviews
Trupin	Dakota Diaspora	Memoirs

The MENU clause and ASK statement in the sample knowledge base below would create this prompt:

```
What type of book do you want to read?
Novel                Tech                Interviews
Memoirs
```

```
RUNTIME;
ACTIONS
  MENU book_type,ALL,book,type
  FIND book_type
  *
  *
  *
ASK book_type:"What type of book do you want to read?";
*
*
*
```

NOTES & CAUTIONS:

- Any text retrieved as a menu choice must fit within *VP-Expert's* 20-character limit for variable names and values.

- It is possible to determine the number of menu items returned in the menu by testing the value of a system variable called MENU_SIZE. This can be useful for creating rule conditions like the following, which execute a clause only if MENU_SIZE meets a given condition.

```
RULE 13
IF    MENU_SIZE > 3
THEN  show = yes
      FIND location;
```

- If a CHOICES statement and a MENU clause name the same variable, the CHOICES statement will be ignored if the MENU clause has been executed.

- If a plural variable is named in a condition of a database rule, all values of that variable are used.

- Large menus created with the MENU clause can occupy big blocks of memory. If there are a number of large menus, you may encounter an out-of-memory condition. To prevent this, use the MRESET clause to release the memory allocated to a menu after the menu has been displayed. See MRESET for more information.

MORE INFORMATION:

See Chapter 5 for more information about the MENU clause and its associated system variable MENU_SIZE. For information about related *VP-Expert* commands, see also the GET and MRESET clauses and the CHOICES statement.

MENU_SIZE

INSTRUCTION TYPE:

System variable

USAGE:

Used for checking the size of a menu generated by a MENU clause.

PARAMETERS:

None required or permitted.

DESCRIPTION:

The system variable MENU_SIZE contains the number of options in a menu generated by the last MENU clause. This variable can be used in rules like any other variable.

EXAMPLE:

```
   *
   *
   MENU type, ALL, book, genre
   DISPLAY "You may select from these
{MENU_SIZE} types of books."
   FIND type
   *
   *
ASK type: "Make your selection.";
*
*
```

In this example, the MENU clause assigns MENU_SIZE the number of options that will appear in the menu to accompany the ASK statement. The DISPLAY clause informs the user exactly how many options there are when it displays the value of MENU_SIZE.

NOTES & CAUTIONS:
- It is possible to change the value of MENU_SIZE by simply assigning it a new value, e.g., MENU_SIZE = 10; however, such an assignment will not affect the menu.

MORE INFORMATION:
See MENU for more information.

MRESET

INSTRUCTION TYPE:
Clause

USAGE:
MRESET *<variable>*

PARAMETERS:
The only parameter is the name of a *VP-Expert* variable which was specified in a previously executed MENU clause.

DESCRIPTION:
The MRESET clause releases memory allocated to the last menu created with the MENU clause naming the same *VP-Expert* variable.

EXAMPLE:

```
ACTIONS
    MENU the_name,ALL,empdata,name
    FIND the_name
    MRESET the_name
    GET the_name = name,empdata,date_hired
    DISPLAY "{the_name} was hired in {date_hired}."
    *
    *
ASK name: "For which employee would you
like to find out the hire date?";
*
*
```

The MRESET clause in this example releases the memory allocated to the menu created by the preceding MENU clause. The placement of MRESET is such that it will execute only after the menu has been displayed.

NOTES & CAUTIONS:

- Creating a large menu with the MENU clause takes a lot of memory. If many large menus are used during a single consultation, an out-of-memory condition can arise. In general, it is good practice to use MRESET as you finish using each menu.

- Make sure to place the MRESET clause where it will execute after the menu has been displayed.

MORE INFORMATION:

See the MENU clause in this chapter.

NAMED

See "Row, Column, or Named Range Access" under PWKS and WKS.

OR

See the RULE keyword for a listing of the relational operators.

INSTRUCTION TYPE:

Logical operator

USAGE:

<condition1> OR *<condition2>*

PARAMETERS:

The OR logical operator always occurs between two *conditions*. A condition is an expression that compared a variable to a value using one of the relational operators, e.g., *temp > 350*.

DESCRIPTION:

The keyword OR is used to combine conditions in rule premises, and in database rules in GET and MENU clauses. In order for a rule containing the OR operator to pass, one or both of the conditions connected by the OR must be true. If OR is used in a database rule in a GET or MENU clause, records must satisfy one or both conditions connected by the OR in order to be selected by the clause.

EXAMPLE:

```
*
*
RULE select1
IF     listing_price <= 175000 AND
       neighborhood = zone_A OR
       neighborhood = zone_G OR
       bedrooms >= 3
THEN   selection[i] = okay;
*
*
*
```

See the AND keyword for information about the AND logical operator.

Notice that the rule in the above example contains both the AND and the OR logical operators. In such cases, OR takes precedence over AND. The easiest way to understand what this means is to imagine a set of parentheses surrounding the expressions separated by OR—e.g., (A = B OR C = D). If more than one OR operator is used sequentially in a rule (or database rule), as in our example, the parentheses should be imagined on either side of the outermost expressions connected by the ORs. For example, the rule above would be interpreted like this:

```
IF    listing_price <= 175000 AND
      (neighborhood = zone_A OR
      neighborhood = zone_G OR
      bedrooms >= 3)
THEN  selection[i] = okay;
```

In order for the rule to pass, the first condition (*listing_price <=175000*) must be true, AND one or more of the following conditions must be true.

NOTES & CAUTIONS

- Using the AND and OR logical operators, you can combine up to ten conditions in a rule premise or database rule. However, you should make sure you understand how complex conditions will be interpreted by *VP-Expert* when the rule is tested.

MORE INFORMATION:

See "Using Logical Operators" in Chapter 4 for more information about using AND and OR to create complex rule conditions. See GET in Chapter 9 for information about database rules.

PDISPLAY

INSTRUCTION TYPE:
Clause

USAGE:
PDISPLAY "*<text>*"

PARAMETERS:

The parameter supplied to the PDISPLAY clause must be a string of text typed between double quotation marks. (Any keyboard character except double quotes can be used as text.)

DESCRIPTION:

This clause operates identically to DISPLAY, except that it causes the printer to print the message.

See the DISPLAY clause for more detailed information.

EXAMPLE:

```
*
*
RULE 3
IF   this_rule = pass
THEN this_message = print
     PDISPLAY "This message will be printed by the
printer.";
*
*
```

If this example rule were to pass during a consultation, the PDISPLAY clause would cause a properly connected printer to print the message.

NOTES & CAUTIONS:

■ In order for this clause to work correctly, your printer must be attached to the current output port, turned on, and "on line."

■ For sending messages to the screen as well as to the printer, use the PRINTON clause in conjunction with the DISPLAY clause.

■ For information about special display characters that can be used in PDISPLAY text, see the DISPLAY clause.

MORE INFORMATION:

See the DISPLAY, PRINTON, and PRINTOFF clauses in this chapter.

PLURAL

INSTRUCTION TYPE:
Statement

USAGE:
PLURAL: <*variable1*[,*variable2*...]>;

PARAMETERS:
A maximum of ten variables can be named in each PLURAL statement. (These can include elements of dimensioned variables, but subscripts cannot be variables; digits must be used, e.g., sales[1].) Multiple variables must be separated by commas; spaces are optional.

DESCRIPTION:
The PLURAL statement identifies "plural variables," or variables that can be assigned multiple values during a consultation. When the *VP-Expert* inference engine sets out to find values for such variables, it assigns to them as many values as it possibly can before ending the search. (If a variable is not plural, the inference engine stops looking for values after a single value is found.)

EXAMPLE:
```
ACTIONS
    DISPLAY "Welcome to the charming world of cheese!
Press any key to begin the consultation.~"
    FIND The_Cheese
    DISPLAY "The best cheese for this course is
a {#The_Cheese}.";

RULE 1
IF      Course = Appetizer
THEN    Consistency = Soft
    BECAUSE "The consistency of the cheese is determined
by the course.";
*
ASK Course: "
With what course will you be serving cheese?";

CHOICES Course: Appetizer,Salad,Dessert;
*
PLURAL: Course;
*
*
```

The PLURAL statement is used in this sample knowledge base to allow the user to choose more than one course item when the ASK and CHOICES statements display the following prompt during a consultation:

```
With what course will you be serving cheese?
Appetizer             Salad             Dessert
```

NOTES & CAUTIONS:

■ When a question with a menu of choices is presented to a user, more than one value can be chosen if the variable taking the values is a plural variable. If the variable is not plural, only one choice is allowed.

■ If the user is presented with a question that is *not* accompanied by a menu of choices, only one "value" can be typed in response. This is true even if the variable taking its value from the prompt is a plural variable.

■ The ENDOFF statement has no effect on a menu of choices presented for a PLURAL variable. It is still necessary to press *ENTER* after each choice, and to press *END* to finalize all choices.

MORE INFORMATION:

For a description of how the inference engine's path is affected by plural variables, see Chapter 2.

POP

INSTRUCTION TYPE:
Clause

USAGE:
POP *<variable1,variable2>*

PARAMETERS:
The first parameter of the POP clause is the name of a *VP-Expert* plural variable.

The second parameter is the name of a non-plural variable.

DESCRIPTION:
The POP clause is used to manipulate the separate values of a plural variable individually.

Think of a plural variable as a ''stack'' of values—the last assigned value being at the top of the stack. When the POP clause is executed, the plural variable's ''top value'' is taken from the stack and assigned to the single-valued variable named in the clause. The next value in the plural variable ''stack'' then moves to the top of the stack. Since each invocation of the POP clause removes the top variable from the plural variable stack, a WHILEKNOWN-END loop can be used to extract each value from the stack one at a time.

EXAMPLE:
Look at this very simple knowledge base:

```
ACTIONS
    FIND favorite
    WHILEKNOWN favorite1
        RESET favorite1
        POP favorite, favorite1
        DISPLAY "{favorite1} is one of my favorite
foods."
    END;

ASK favorite: "Choose 5 of your favorite
kinds of food from the menu displayed below.";
```

```
CHOICES favorite: fruit,vegetables,
cheese_dishes,baked_sweets,meat_&_potatoes,
fried_food,chicken,pasta,Chinese_food,
Japanese_food,Mexican_food,junk_food;
```

```
PLURAL:favorite;
```

During execution of this knowledge base, the user is asked to select five kinds of food from a menu of food types. Each selection is assigned as a separate value of the plural variable *favorite*. After the user presses *END* to complete the selection process, the POP and DISPLAY clauses in the WHILEKNOWN-END loop display a message for each of the selected food types, starting with the last selection chosen. Note the RESET clause. It is used here to reset *favorite1* to UNKNOWN when all of the values of the plural variable have been used. Without it, the last value in the stack would be repeatedly displayed in an endless loop.

NOTES & CAUTIONS:

■ If the first variable named in a POP clause is not named in a PLURAL statement, or has no value assigned to it, the POP clause is ignored. No error condition results.

■ Note that with each repeated execution of the POP clause, the value previously assigned to the single-valued variable is overwritten with the new value.

MORE INFORMATION:

See the WHILEKNOWN clause for information about creating WHILEKNOWN-END loops. For information about plural variables, see the PLURAL statement.

PRINTOFF

INSTRUCTION TYPE:
Clause

USAGE:
PRINTOFF

PARAMETERS:
None required or permitted.

DESCRIPTION:
When executed, this disables PRINTON's effect on the DISPLAY clause. Subsequent DISPLAY clauses return to displaying information on the screen only.

EXAMPLE:
```
ACTIONS
    *
    *
   PRINTON
   DISPLAY "This line of text will be sent to the screen
and the printer."
   PRINTOFF
   DISPLAY "This line of text will appear only on the
screen."
    *
    *
```

NOTES & CAUTIONS:
■ Use the PDISPLAY clause to send information to the printer only.

MORE INFORMATION:
See DISPLAY, PDISPLAY, and PRINTON in this chapter.

PRINTON

INSTRUCTION TYPE:
Clause

USAGE:
PRINTON

PARAMETERS:
None required or permitted.

DESCRIPTION:
When executed, PRINTON causes all subsequent DISPLAY clauses to display information to *both* the screen and the printer.

EXAMPLE:
```
ACTIONS
    *
    *
    PRINTON
    DISPLAY "This line of text will be sent to the screen
and the printer."
    PRINTOFF
    DISPLAY "This line of text will appear only on the
screen."
    *
    *
```

NOTES & CAUTIONS:
■ Make sure your printer is on when starting knowledge bases that use the printer.

■ Use the PDISPLAY clause to send information to the printer only.

MORE INFORMATION:
See DISPLAY, PDISPLAY, and PRINTOFF in this chapter.

PUT

INSTRUCTION TYPE:
Clause

USAGE:
PUT <[*path*]*DBF_filename*>

PARAMETERS:
The *DBF_filename* supplied to the PUT clause must be an existing file with a DBF extension. However, the extension must not be explicitly provided, or a syntax error will result. If necessary, a path can also be specified.

DESCRIPTION:
The PUT clause is one of the two clauses that can be used to write information to a database file from within *VP-Expert*. (The other is the APPEND clause.) Whereas APPEND adds a completely new record to the end of a database file, PUT is used to edit an existing record.

When *VP-Expert* executes a PUT clause, it writes the values of pre-assigned variables to fields in the current record of the database file named in the PUT clause. The current record will be the record accessed by the last GET clause. Each ''pre-assigned variable'' must have the same name as the field to which its value will be written.

In order to change the field contents of a particular database record:

1. GET the appropriate record (if the record pointer is not already on the appropriate record).

2. Assign values to knowledge base variables having the same names as the fields you want to change.

3. Issue a PUT clause to transfer the new values to the current record.

Note: Step 2 can be accomplished in two ways. The FIND clause can be used; or, following the GET clause, values can be assigned using direct value assignment (e.g., lname = Johnson). In either case, the values to be added to the record must be assigned after the GET is issued; otherwise, the current values in the record accessed by GET will overwrite the assigned values.

EXAMPLE:

```
RUNTIME;
ACTIONS
   old_name = Owens
   GET old_name = lname,empdata,ALL
   lname = Johnson
   PUT empdata
   DISPLAY "Jane {lname} is now married. Previously
her last name was Owens.~ "
   *
   *
```

The PUT clause in this example assigns the value *Johnson* to the *lname* field in the record accessed by the GET clause.

NOTES & CAUTIONS:

■ Only fields that you want to modify need to be assigned values before a PUT. Additional fields in the current record will be unaffected by the PUT clause.

■ Sequence of operations is important when issuing a PUT. If the replacement values are assigned to variables before issuing a GET, those values will be overwritten by the field values of the record accessed by the GET.

■ Values sent to data files with the PUT clause can exceed the normal 20 character limit if the values were assigned by a GET clause. When assigned by a GET, values can be up to 256 characters in length.

MORE INFORMATION:

See GET and APPEND in this chapter.

PWKS

INSTRUCTION TYPE:
Clause

USAGE:
PWKS <*variable,location,[path]WKS_filename*>

PARAMETERS:

The first parameter in the PWKS clause is the name of a *VP-Expert* variable.

The second parameter, *location*, is a spreadsheet cell, row, column, or range.

The final parameter, *WKS_filename,* must be an existing *VP-Planner* (or 1-2-3) worksheet file with a WKS extension. However, the extension must not be explicitly provided, or a syntax error will result. If necessary, a path can also be specified.

See the WKS clause for a discussion of dimensioned variables.

DESCRIPTION:

The PWKS clause is the opposite of the WKS clause, which transfers information from a *VP-Planner* (or 1-2-3) worksheet file into *VP-Expert* variables. PWKS transfers values *from VP-Expert* variables *into* a *VP-Planner* (or 1-2-3) worksheet.

If the variable named in the PWKS clause is a dimensioned variable, values are transferred row-wise into the spreadsheet file at the location specified in the second parameter of the PWKS clause.

Single Cell Access

count = 10

Single Cell Access

If the value of a variable is to be stored in the contents of a single cell of a worksheet file, the *location* parameter will be a single cell address. For example:

```
PWKS count, C8, pricefil
```

This loads the single value of the variable *count* into cell C8 of the worksheet PRICEFIL.WKS.

Range Access

count

10	20	30	40	50	60

count [1] count [2] count [3] count [4] count [5] count [6]

Range Access

To write a range of cells to a worksheet file, the range can be
identified by its top left- and bottom right-hand corner cell addresses
separated by two periods (and no spaces). For example:

```
PWKS count,D2..E4,pricefil
```

This clause causes the elements of the dimensioned variable *count*,
starting at *count[1]*, to be loaded into the contents of worksheet cells
D2 through E4 (from worksheet file PRICEFIL.WKS).

When a range of cells is accessed, they are written from left to right,
row by row. Thus, in this example, the elements of the dimensioned
variable *count* are assigned to the contents of worksheet cells in the
order shown above.

Row, Column, or Named Range Access

A single row or column can also be written to a worksheet file. *VP-Expert* recognizes explicit or indirect addressing to indicate the location in the worksheet. Row location is identified using the format:

ROW = *<row_heading>* or ROW = (*<variable>*)

Column location is identified using the format:

COLUMN = *<column_heading>* or COLUMN = (*<variable>*)

Named ranges can also be identified using these formats. For example:

NAMED = *<range_name>* or NAMED = (*<variable>*)

The parameter in these examples can be an explicit worksheet row heading, column heading, or range name contained in the worksheet. Alternatively, the parameter can be a *VP-Expert* variable that has been assigned a value corresponding to a worksheet row heading, column heading, or range name—in which case the variable must be enclosed in parentheses.

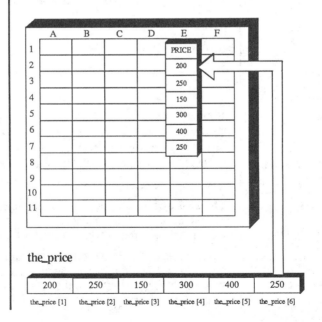

To illustrate, the following PWKS clause (corresponding to the previous illustration) sends values to a column of cells with the heading PRICE (in the PRICEFIL.WKS worksheet). Note that the value *price* is assigned to the variable *pricevar* before the PWKS clause is executed.

```
*
pricevar = price
PWKS the_price,COLUMN = (pricevar),pricefil
*
```

A similar PWKS clause, writing to a row instead of a column, might look like this:

```
*
pricevar = price
PWKS the_price,ROW = (pricevar),pricefil
*
```

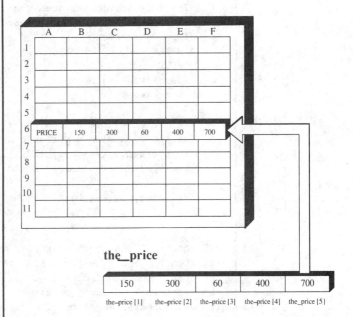

the_price

150	300	60	400	700
the_price [1]	the_price [2]	the_price [3]	the_price [4]	the_price [5]

The value assigned to the variable named in the row, column, or range specification need not be assigned in the ACTIONS block, as shown above. It can also be assigned in a rule or by the user at an ASK prompt. However, this must occur prior to the execution of the PWKS clause, or the PWKS clause will not work.

And keep in mind that if the parentheses around the variable name are omitted, *VP-Expert* treats the variable name as a literal range name, row heading, or column heading. For example:

```
PWKS the_price,COLUMN = pricevar,pricefil
```

Here it looks for a column named "pricevar."

EXAMPLE:

```
RUNTIME;
ACTIONS
    *
    week=1
    ! The loop below allows the user to fill
    ! up the dimensioned variable sales
    ! with the income for week 1,2,3 and 4.
    ! The loop terminates when the user
    ! enters UNKNOWN (?) for 'income'.
    WHILEKNOWN income
        RESET income
        FIND income
        sales[week]=(income)
        week=(week+1)
    END
    ! This PWKS clause writes the elements
    ! of the dimensioned variable sales
    ! to the range from cells E3 to E6 in
    ! the VPP/1-2-3 worksheet named "Sheet."

    PWKS sales,E3..E6,sheet
    *
    *

ASK income: "This question should be
repeated 5 times. The first time it
appears, enter the income figures from
the first week of last month; when
it next appears, enter the income
from the next week of last month, and so
on. When this question appears a fifth
time, type a question mark (?).";
```

Note that the ! character adds "comment lines" to the sample knowledge base. For more information, see the end of this chapter.

NOTES & CAUTIONS:

- *VP-Planner* and *VP-Expert* are not case sensitive when indicating row headings, column headings, or range names.

- *VP-Expert* only transfers data into worksheet cells that already contain data.

- Data being transferred into the worksheet must be the same data type as the data already stored in corresponding worksheet cells. In addition, the length of the new text data cannot be longer than the data which was previously stored in that cell. If it is, it will be cut off in the cell. (Note that *length* here refers to the actual length of the contents of the cell, not the column width of the cell.)

MORE INFORMATION:

See the WKS clause in this chapter for more information. See also Chapter 6.

RECEIVE

INSTRUCTION TYPE:
Clause

USAGE:
RECEIVE <[*path*]*filename,variable*>

PARAMETERS:
The first parameter is the name of an ASCII text file with specification of a path optional and no file extension.

The second parameter must be a valid *VP-Expert* variable name.

DESCRIPTION:
The RECEIVE clause imports the current line of the named text file into a *VP-Expert* consultation. The contents of this line are stored in the variable named in the RECEIVE clause. Note that values imported by RECEIVE are not subject to the normal 20-character length restriction. They may be up to 80 characters in length.

When you first execute the RECEIVE clause, the current line is the first line of the file. Subsequent executions extract the next line, then the next line, and so on. By placing this clause and the DISPLAY clause inside a WHILEKNOWN-END loop, the entire contents of a text file can be displayed to the user during a consultation.

EXAMPLE:

Consider a text file named SAMPLE that looks like this:

```
Using the RECEIVE clause, single lines of
text files, or complete text files, can be read
into a VP-Expert consultation.
```

The RECEIVE and DISPLAY clauses in the following WHILEKNOWN/-END loop would cause the complete text of the file to be displayed to the user.

```
RUNTIME;
ACTIONS
    WHILEKNOWN samplevar
        RECEIVE sample, samplevar
        DISPLAY "{samplevar}"
    END;
*
*
*
```

NOTES & CAUTIONS:

■ Note that in a WHILEKNOWN-END loop, each execution of the RECEIVE clause (as shown above) overwrites the previous contents of the variable "receiving" the text.

■ The usual 20-character limit on a value assigned to a knowledge base variable does not apply to the variable receiving data from the RECEIVE clause. Lines up to 80 characters long can be received.

■ Used within a WHILEKNOWN-END loop, this clause is convenient for replacing lengthy DISPLAY text that would otherwise clutter up the knowledge base.

■ The RECEIVE clause has an opposite, SHIP, which sends (ships) variable values to a text file. See SHIP for more information.

MORE INFORMATION:

See the SHIP and SHOWTEXT clauses in this chapter.

RECORD_NUM

INSTRUCTION TYPE:
System variable

USAGE:
Used for checking the location of the record pointer in a database file.

PARAMETERS:
None required or permitted.

DESCRIPTION:
The system variable RECORD_NUM contains the number of the last database record accessed by a GET clause. This variable can be used in rules like any other variable in the knowledge base.

EXAMPLE:
```
*
RULE 5
IF   RECORD_NUM = 13
THEN found = true
     DISPLAY "The current record number is {RECORD_NUM}";
*
*
```

This example shows the RECORD_NUM system variable used twice: once in the condition of a rule, and once in a DISPLAY clause. See DISPLAY for information about using curly brackets to display the value of a given variable.

NOTES & CAUTIONS:

■ It is possible to change the value of RECORD_NUM by simply assigning it a new value, e.g., RECORD_NUM = 23; however, such an assignment will *not* affect the position of the record pointer.

■ RECORD_NUM cannot be used in a GET database rule to search for a specific record.

MORE INFORMATION:
See the GET clause.

RESET

INSTRUCTION TYPE:
Clause

USAGE:
RESET *<variable>*

PARAMETERS:
The *variable* parameter is a *VP-Expert* variable name.

DESCRIPTION:
The RESET clause removes any values assigned to the named variable and returns it to UNKNOWN.

The most frequent use of the RESET clause is in a WHILEKNOWN-END loop where a variable's value is being repeatedly sought, but where the value must be returned to UNKNOWN before each iteration of the FIND clause.

EXAMPLE:

```
ACTIONS
    FIND favorite
    SORT favorite
    WHILEKNOWN favorite1
        RESET favorite1
        POP favorite, favorite1
        DISPLAY "{favorite1} is one of my favorite foods."
    END;

ASK favorite: "Choose 5 of your favorite
kinds of food from the menu displayed below";

CHOICES favorite: fruit,vegetables,
cheese_dishes,baked_sweets,meat_&_potatoes,
fried_food,chicken,pasta,Chinese_food,
Japanese_food,Mexican_food,junk_food;

PLURAL:favorite;
```

The RESET clause in this example prevents an endless loop from occurring when the final value is read in by the POP clause and displayed.

For additional examples of the RESET clause, see PWKS, WHILEKNOWN, and ''Notes & Cautions'' for the GET clause.

NOTES & CAUTIONS:

■ When used in a WHILEKNOWN-END loop, the RESET clause does not have to name the same variable named in the WHILEKNOWN clause.

MORE INFORMATION:

See the WHILEKNOWN clause for information about constructing *VP-Expert* WHILEKNOWN-END loops.

ROW

See "Row, Column, or Named Range Access" under PWKS and WKS.

RULE

INSTRUCTION TYPE:
Statement

USAGE:
RULE *<rule_label>*

IF   *<condition1>* [AND/OR]
                    [*condition2* [AND/OR]]
                    [etc.]

THEN   *<conclusion1>* [CNF N]
                    [*conclusion2* [CNF N]]
                    [etc.]
                    [clause1...]
                    [clause2...]

[ELSE   *<conclusion3>* [CNF N]
                    [*conclusion4* [CNF N]]
                    [etc.]

                    [clause1]
                    [clause2]
                    [etc.]]

[BECAUSE   *<text>*]
;

PARAMETERS:
The representation above shows the basic construction and optional elements of a knowledge base rule.

The Rule Name
The first rule parameter is a legal rule name consisting of the characters RULE (in upper or lower case), a space, and a *rule_label* consisting of 1 to 20 characters. Available label characters include numbers, letters, and the special characters: _ % $ ^ |. Use the underscore (_) to separate words in a rule label (spaces are not allowed).

The Rule Premise

The next rule parameter, referred to as the rule *premise*, is the keyword IF followed by one or more *conditions*. These conditions are written in the form:

variable   *relational operator*   *value*

For example: **IF the_color <> red**

The relational operators are:

=	(equals)
>	(greater than)
<	(less than)
>=	(greater than or equal to)
<=	(less than or equal to)
<>	(not equal to)

For complete information about using the logical operators to combine rule conditions, see ''Using Logical Operators'' in Chapter 4, and AND and OR in this chapter.

The logical operators AND and OR can optionally be used to combine multiple expressions to form complex rule conditions. For example:

```
IF   the_color = red AND
     flavor = sweet OR
     sauce = hot
```

There is a ten-condition limit on the rule premise.

The Rule Conclusion

The next parameter, the rule *conclusion*, consists of the keyword THEN followed by a list of one or more expressions written in the form:

variable = value

Note that the equal sign is the only operator allowed in a conclusion expression.

Confidence factors of the form *CNF n* can optionally be included following the value specified in the conclusion. See Chapter 7 for complete information about *VP-Expert* confidence factors.

The ELSE Option

Following the rule conclusion, the ELSE keyword and alternate conclusions can optionally be added to a rule. See ''The ELSE Keyword'' following the RULE ''Description.''

Optional Clauses

Clauses can optionally be appended to the THEN or ELSE part of the rule. These will execute in the order they appear if the rule passes during a consultation.

The BECAUSE Keyword

The optional BECAUSE keyword and associated text provide explanatory text for display in response to the Why? and How? menu commands. If present, BECAUSE must come at the end of a rule. See BECAUSE in this chapter for more information.

The Semicolon

Every rule must end with a semicolon (;). This can be placed at the end of the last line in the rule, or below the rule on a line of its own.

DESCRIPTION:

The *VP-Expert* rule is where the "expertise" of the expert system is contained.

For example, look at this simple rule:

```
RULE 1
IF     married = no AND
       children = no
THEN   exemptions = none;
```

This rule says, in effect, "IF, during a consultation, the value of the variable *married* is found to be *no* AND the value of the variable *children* is found to be *no*, THEN the variable *exemptions* should be assigned the value *none*."

If, during a consultation, the premise of this rule is found to be true, the variable named in the conclusion is assigned the value *none*, and the rule will be said to have "passed."

Rule construction is flexible. The same rule could be written:

```
rule 1
if married = no
and
children = no
then exemptions = none;
```

Or like this:

```
RULE 1 IF married = no AND children = no
THEN exemptions = none;
```

In regard to formatting and letter case, there are many ways to write a rule. The crucial points to remember are:

■ A rule must have a legal rule name.

■ A rule must contain the keyword IF followed by a space and at least one valid condition.

■ A rule must contain the keyword THEN followed by a space and at least one valid conclusion.

■ A rule must end with a semicolon (;).

■ All other possible rule elements are optional.

The ELSE Keyword

An "ELSE conclusion" can optionally be added after the conclusion of any rule. When present in a rule it says, in effect, "If the premise stated in the rule is known NOT to be true, do this."

Consider this rule:

```
RULE 35
IF      the_color = red
THEN    the_fruit = apple
ELSE    the_fruit = orange;
```

This rule says, "If *the_color* is *red*, then *the_fruit* is *apple*. If *the_color* is anything other than *red*, *the_fruit* is *orange*."

> *Note: In order for an ELSE to provide a value to a variable, the inference engine must establish that the premise of the rule is not true. Remember that unless the rule containing the ELSE is visited by the inference engine, the ELSE has no effect.*

Consider the following knowledge base:

```
ACTIONS
  FIND city
   *
   *
RULE 1
IF    day = Tuesday
THEN  city = Belgium;

RULE 2
IF    day = Wednesday
THEN  city = Brussels;

RULE 3
IF    day = Friday
THEN  city = London
ELSE  city = Fresno;

RULE 4
IF    day = Thursday
THEN  city = Paris;
 *
 *
 *
ASK day: "What day of the week is it?"

CHOICES day: Sunday,Monday,Tuesday,Wednesday,Thursday,
Friday,Saturday;
```

For complete information about how the VP-Expert inference engine finds its path through the rules of the knowledge base, see Chapter 2.

When this knowledge base is executed during a consultation, the inference engine will start at the FIND clause in the ACTIONS block and begin seeking a value for the variable *city*. Since *city* is contained in the conclusion of the first rule in the knowledge base, the inference engine looks at RULE 1 first. Looking at the premise of RULE 1, the inference engine sees it needs a value for the variable *day*, thus causing a display of this question and menu:

```
What day of the week is it?
Sunday               Monday               Tuesday

Wednesday            Thursday             Friday

Saturday
```

If the user chooses *Sunday* or *Monday*, RULE 1 and RULE 2 will both be tried and fail, causing the inference engine to move to RULE 3. RULE 3 will pass, assigning *Fresno* as the value of *city*.

If the user chooses *Tuesday*, RULE 1 will pass.

If the user chooses *Wednesday*, RULE 1 will fail and RULE 2 will, therefore, be tried and pass.

If the user chooses *Thursday*, RULEs 1 and 2 will fail, and RULE 3 will pass, assigning *Fresno* as the *city* of the day.

RULE 4, which specifically names *Thursday*, will not be tried. This case is important to note. If an ELSE is added to a rule, be sure its execution won't preclude the execution of another more precise rule.

If the user chooses *Friday*, then the *city* is *London*.

If *Saturday* is chosen, RULE 3, again, will pass.

Adding Clauses to a Rule

Any *VP-Expert* clause can be added to a rule following the rule conclusion.

A clause, when present in a rule, is executed if and when a rule passes during a consultation. For example, a DISPLAY clause in a rule displays text to the user only if the rule passes, and at the time the rule passes. Similarly, a FIND clause sends the inference engine to find a value for a given variable only if the rule in which it is contained passes. Clauses following an ELSE in a rule will only be executed if the premise of the rule is found to be false.

Any number of clauses can be added to the end of the rule, and they are executed in the order in which they appear.

EXAMPLE:
```
*
*
RULE 1
IF     temperature > 101
THEN   fever = yes;
*
*
```

This is the simplest form of a *VP-Expert* rule, consisting of a rule name, a single condition, and a single conclusion. If the value of the variable *temperature* is known when this rule is tested, its value will be compared with the numeric value *101*. (If the value of the variable is not known, the inference engine will set out to find a value for the variable. See Chapter 2 for a complete discussion of how the inference engine uses rules during a consultation.) IF the value of *temperature* exceeds *101*, THEN the rule passes and the variable *fever* is set to *yes*. If the value is less than or equal to 101, the rule fails.

```
*
*
RULE 2
IF     temperature > 101 AND
       resting = yes
THEN   fever = yes
       FIND symptoms
ELSE   fever = no;
*
*
*
```

This rule is more complicated. If the value of the variable *temperature* is known to be greater than *101*, and if the value of *resting* is *yes*, then *fever* is set to *yes,* and the FIND clause sends the inference engine out to find a value for the variable *symptoms*. If only one or neither of these conditions is met, the ELSE sets the variable to *no*.

NOTES & CAUTIONS:

■ Rule names need not be unique; however, you *should* give a different name to each rule. If you do not, the Trace and Rule commands will be ineffective, and the knowledge base, in general, will be much less manageable during development.

■ See the TRUTHTHRESH clause for important information regarding confidence factors.

MORE INFORMATION:

See Chapter 2 for a discussion of exactly how rules are interpreted and used by the *VP-Expert* inference engine during a consultation. See Chapter 7 for an explanation of confidence factors. See also the TRUTHTHRESH clause; understanding this clause is critical for knowing how rules work when they contain confidence factors.

RUNTIME

INSTRUCTION TYPE:
Statement

USAGE:
RUNTIME;

PARAMETERS:
None required or permitted.

DESCRIPTION:
Placing this one-word statement anywhere in the knowledge base eliminates the two bottom windows during a *VP-Expert* consultation. This statement should be added to a knowledge base when development is finished and the knowledge base is ready for end user or "runtime" consultations.

EXAMPLE:

```
RUNTIME;
ACTIONS
    FIND The_Cheese
    DISPLAY "The best cheese for the course is a
{#The_Cheese};
*
*
*
```

NOTES & CAUTIONS:

■ The RUNTIME statement should only be added to a knowledge base after the testing and debugging phases of the expert system development are complete. When the RUNTIME statement is present in the knowledge base, *VP-Expert* does not display the system's actions as it processes the consultation.

MORE INFORMATION:

See Chapter 1 for an example of a runtime consultation.

SAVEFACTS

INSTRUCTION TYPE:

Clause

USAGE:

SAVEFACTS <[*path*]*text_filename*>

PARAMETERS:

A path can optionally be specified using the same format as that used by DOS (e.g., \files\data). This tells *VP-Expert* where to find the named file. The default is the current directory.

The *text_filename* parameter used with the SAVEFACTS clause must be a valid DOS filename with no extension. If an extension is supplied, an error condition will result.

DESCRIPTION:

When the SAVEFACTS clause is executed during a consultation, the names and values of all variables whose values are presently known in the consultation will be stored in a text file created by the SAVEFACTS clause. The data stored has the following format:

variable = value CNF n

SAVEFACTS is the first step in the process of chaining knowledge base files. See the CHAIN clause in this chapter for more information.

EXAMPLE:

See the CHAIN clause.

NOTES & CAUTIONS:

■ SAVEFACTS saves *all* assigned values to a text file. SAVEFACTS cannot be used to save selected values.

■ If the text file named in the SAVEFACTS clause already exists, it will be overwritten when the SAVEFACTS clause is executed.

MORE INFORMATION:

See the LOADFACTS and CHAIN clauses.

SHIP

INSTRUCTION TYPE:

Clause

USAGE:

SHIP <[*path*]*text_filename,variable*>

PARAMETERS:

The first parameter of the SHIP clause is the name of a text file with no extension. If necessary, a path can be specified. The default is the current directory.

The second parameter is a single-valued *VP-Expert* variable.

DESCRIPTION:

SHIP stores the contents of the named variable as the last item in the text file named in the SHIP clause.

EXAMPLE:

```
ACTIONS
    count = 1
    WHILEKNOWN send
      RESET send
      FIND send
      SHIP tryit,count
      DISPLAY "{count}"
      count=(count+1)
    END;


RULE 1
IF count < 16
THEN send = yes;
```

The SHIP clause shown in this sample knowledge base places the numbers 1 through 16 in a file named TRYIT. The DISPLAY clause displays the numbers during execution.

NOTES & CAUTIONS:

■ If the file named in the SHIP clause does not exist, SHIP creates the file and places the variable's value as the first element in the file.

MORE INFORMATION:

See the RECEIVE clause for information about transferring data *from* a text file *to* a knowledge base variable. See also the WHILEKNOWN clause.

SHOWTEXT

INSTRUCTION TYPE:
Clause

USAGE:
SHOWTEXT<[*path*]*TXT_filename,variable*>

PARAMETERS:
The first parameter is the name of an ASCII text file with a TXT extension. (The extension should not be specified, however, or an error will result.) If necessary, a path can be specified.

The second parameter must be a valid *VP-Expert* variable.

DESCRIPTION:
Recommended for advanced users only, this clause displays the page in the given text file whose heading is the value of the specified variable. For SHOWTEXT to work, the text file must begin with an index table of headings and their positions within the file. The position indicated for each heading represents the number of characters (bytes) from the end of the index table to the first character of the heading. (Spaces and the invisible carriage returns and linefeeds that occur at the end of each line are counted as characters.) A BASIC program named INDEXER.BAS has been included on the *VP-Expert* program disk. Use this to add the index table to the beginning of the text file. (Consult your BASIC manual for information on executing BASIC programs.)

EXAMPLE:
To see an example of a text file used with SHOWTEXT, open the *VP-Expert* Help System file, VPXHELP.TXT.

NOTES & CAUTIONS:
- Following the heading index, every "page" in the text file must be preceded by the *.pa* page break command.
- Every page in the text file must have a unique heading.
- Headings are subject to the same restrictions as most other *VP-Expert* values. They can be up to 20 characters, can contain no spaces, etc.

SORT

INSTRUCTION TYPE:
Clause

USAGE:
SORT *<variable>*

PARAMETERS:
The variable supplied to the SORT clause must be a *VP-Expert* plural variable (i.e., it must be named in a PLURAL statement).

DESCRIPTION:
This clause is used to sort the various values of a plural variable into descending order of confidence factor.

EXAMPLE:
```
ACTIONS
        FIND The_Cheese
        SORT The_Cheese
        DISPLAY "A number of cheeses are suitable though
some are preferred over others. The following display
begins with the cheese most recommended, and lists
subsequent cheeses in descending order of suitability.
The number which follows each cheese in the list is the
confidence factor, indicating the degree of confidence we
have that the cheese is an appropriate one for the
occasion.
{#The_Cheese}";
*
*
*
PLURAL The_Cheese;
*
*
```

Note in this example that the variable named in curly brackets in the DISPLAY clause need only occur once. Since it is a plural variable, *VP-Expert* automatically displays all values associated with it.

NOTES & CAUTIONS:

■ If you attempt to use SORT for a single-valued variable, no error will result; the SORT clause will simply be ignored when the knowledge base is executed.

MORE INFORMATION:

See Chapter 7 for information about confidence factors. See also the PLURAL statement and the POP clause. A full discussion of the use of plural variables appears in Chapter 4.

THEN

See RULE.

TRUTHTHRESH

INSTRUCTION TYPE:
Clause

USAGE:
TRUTHTHRESH=<*integer*>

PARAMETERS:
The parameter in the TRUTHTHRESH clause must be an integer between 0 and 100.

DESCRIPTION:
The integer supplied in the TRUTHTHRESH clause determines the minimum confidence factor required for a value in a rule condition in order for the condition to be considered true. In other words, if the value in a condition has a confidence factor that is less than the number named in the TRUTHTHRESH clause, the condition will be considered false.

VP-Expert has a default "truth threshold" of 50. This means that unless you use the TRUTHTHRESH clause to make a change, rule conditions containing values that have been assigned confidence factors of less than 50 will be considered "false." For example, in the following rule, if the value *Appetizer* was assigned to the variable *Course* with a confidence factor of 40, and the value *Soft* was assigned to the variable *Consistency* with a confidence factor of 100, the rule would fail.

```
RULE 3
IF   Course = Appetizer AND
     Consistency = Soft
THEN Complement = Bread;
```

For the rule to pass, the variables *Course* and *Consistency* must be assigned the values *Appetizer* and *Soft* with confidence factors of 50 or greater.

Since TRUTHTHRESH is a clause, it can be used in both rules and the ACTIONS block. If a TRUTHTHRESH clause is contained in a rule, it comes into effect only after the rule passes. (Therefore, it does not affect the rule in which it is contained.) The TRUTHTHRESH value remains as set in that rule until another TRUTHTHRESH clause is executed, or the consultation ends.

EXAMPLE:

```
ACTIONS
     TRUTHTHRESH=40
     FIND area
     *
     *
RULE 14
IF   climate = tropical AND
     budget = low_med AND
     season = fall
THEN area = Yucatan
     TRUTHTHRESH=60;
*
*
```

If the confidence factor of any value named in the premise of this rule is less than 40 (the confidence factor set in the ACTIONS block), the rule will fail.

If the rule passes, the TRUTHTHRESH clause contained in the rule is executed and a new "truth threshold" value of 60 is set for the consultation. This value will only change if a new TRUTHTHRESH clause is executed in another rule or later in the ACTIONS block.

NOTES & CAUTIONS:

■ Remember that confidence factors relate only to rule *conditions* and not rule conclusions.

■ The number set by the TRUTHTHRESH clause represents a *minimum* value. In other words, a condition will be considered true if its value has a confidence factor greater than or equal to the number indicated in the TRUTHTHRESH clause.

MORE INFORMATION:
See Chapter 7 for more information on confidence factors.

UNKNOWN

INSTRUCTION TYPE:
System value

USAGE:
Used to identify variables whose values are not known.

PARAMETERS:
None required or permitted.

DESCRIPTION:

The UNKNOWN keyword is used by *VP-Expert* to identify variables whose values are not known. During a consultation, variables which have not been assigned values are automatically UNKNOWN. If the user types a question mark (?) in response to an ASK or AUTOQUERY prompt, the variable remains UNKNOWN, and the consultation continues.

Having a keyword UNKNOWN to account for variables with no assigned values allows the person designing the knowledge base to write rules like the following:

```
RULE 3
IF    course = UNKNOWN
THEN  question = yes;
```

UNKNOWN variables are not variables that have the value of the character string "UNKNOWN." They are variables whose values are not known.

EXAMPLE

```
*
*
ASK allergy: "Is the patient allergic to any
medicines?";

CHOICES allergy: YES, NO;
*
*
```

If these statements were executed during a consultation and the user typed a question mark in response to the resulting question prompt, the variable *allergy* would remain UNKNOWN, and the consultation would continue. The person designing the knowledge base could write a rule accounting for an UNKNOWN value.

For example:

```
RULE 6
IF    allergy = UNKNOWN
THEN  question = yes
      FIND history;
```

NOTES & CAUTIONS

■ Unless the person who creates the knowledge base writes rules to explicitly deal with UNKNOWN values, typing a question mark at one or more question prompts may result in an inconclusive consultation.

■ UNKNOWN values can only be specified in rule conditions, and by typing a question mark at a question accompanied by a menu. If the user types "unknown" at a question prompt with no accompanying menu, the variable will be assigned the value of the text string *unknown*. The result is the same if an expression like *variable = unknown* appears in the ACTIONS block or in a rule conclusion.

WHILEKNOWN

INSTRUCTION TYPE:
Clause

USAGE:
*
*
WHILEKNOWN <*variable*>
    *
     *
      *
END
*
*
*

PARAMETERS:
The variable parameter in the WHILEKNOWN clause can be any *VP-Expert* variable.

The END clause must always be used with WHILEKNOWN. It signals the end of a WHILEKNOWN-END loop. Remember to place a semicolon after END if it appears at the end of a rule or ACTIONS block.

DESCRIPTION:

Clauses appearing between the WHILEKNOWN keyword and the END keyword are repeatedly executed in a loop fashion so long as the value of the variable named in the WHILEKNOWN clause has a known value. Once the value of the variable becomes UNKNOWN, the clauses contained in the WHILEKNOWN-END construct are executed one final time. (The loop stops executing when END is encountered and the variable named in the WHILEKNOWN clause is UNKNOWN.)

This command is frequently used with the GET clause to access records in a database file. See "Notes & Cautions" for the GET clause for more information.

EXAMPLES:

```
ACTIONS
  WHILEKNOWN go
    RESET name
    MENU name,ALL,empdata,lname
    FIND name
    MRESET name
    GET name=lname,empdata,hire_date
    CLOSE empdata
    DISPLAY "{name} was hired in {hire_date}.
Press any key to continue.~"
    CLS
    RESET go
    FIND go
  END;


  RULE 1
  IF name <> UNKNOWN
  THEN go = yes;

ASK name: "What is the last name of the
employee for whom you want the hire date?
(Type a question mark if, instead, you want
to end the consultation).";
```

During a consultation, this knowledge base repeatedly asks the user to select an employee whose hire date they would like to see. Once the user types a question mark to indicate a desire to quit the consultation (see the ASK clause in the sample), the variables *name* and, subsequently, *go*, become UNKNOWN, and the loop executes one final time.

Note the use of RESET, MRESET, CLOSE, and CLS in this example. The RESET clauses ensure that the FIND clauses will be executed with each iteration of the loop; MRESET erases from memory the menu created by each execution of the MENU clause; CLOSE causes each GET to begin its search from the top of the EMPDATA file; and CLS clears the screen after each DISPLAY message is presented. For more information about these clauses, see RESET, CLOSE, and CLS.

NOTES & CAUTIONS:

■ If the variable named in the WHILEKNOWN clause is UNKNOWN when the loop initially executes, it is all right. Anytime the variable in a WHILEKNOWN clause is UNKNOWN, the loops executes one time automatically.

■ If an index file is to be accessed from inside a WHILEKNOWN-END loop, the INDEX clause should *not* appear inside the loop. If it does, each time the loop is executed, the first record of the indexed order will be retrieved. Thus, the loop will re-retrieve the same record again and again.

■ *VP-Expert* does not recognize nested WHILEKNOWN-END loops.

MORE INFORMATION:

See Chapters 5 and 6 for information on transferring data to and from external files. See also INDEX, RESET, and GET.

WKS

INSTRUCTION TYPE:
Clause

USAGE:
WKS <*variable,location,[path]WKS_filename*>

PARAMETERS:
The first parameter of the WKS clause is the name of the variable into which data from a *VP-Planner* or 1-2-3 worksheet is to be read.

The second parameter is the worksheet cell, column, row, or range from which data will be read.

The final parameter is the name of a *VP-Planner* or Lotus 1-2-3 WKS file. The filename must be an existing file with a WKS extension. However, the extension must not be explicitly provided, or a syntax error will result. If necessary, a path can also be specified. The default is the current directory.

DESCRIPTION:
The WKS clause reads data from a *VP-Planner* or 1-2-3 worksheet into elements of a *VP-Expert* dimensioned variable.

A *VP-Expert* dimensioned variable stores multiple values as a one-dimensional array of *elements*, each element representing the value of a single worksheet cell. Elements of the dimensioned variable are assigned (and subsequently identified by) a unique bracketed number, or subscript, corresponding to its placement in the column, row, or range from which it was copied. For example, the variable names price[1], price[2], and so on, would be assigned to the elements of the dimensioned variable *price*.

If the data in only one cell is read into a variable by the WKS clause, the variable created will be single-valued, not dimensioned.

price

10	20	30	40
price [1]	price [2]	price [3]	price [4]

Single Cell Access

If the contents of a single cell are to be written to a variable, the *location* parameter will be a single cell address. For example:

```
WKS count,C8,pricefil
```

This loads the contents of cell C8 from worksheet PRICEFIL.WKS into the single-valued variable *count*.

Single Cell Access

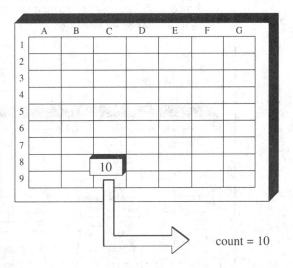

Range Access

To transfer values from a range of cells in a worksheet file, the range can be identified by its top left and bottom right-hand corner cell addresses separated by two periods (and no spaces). For example:

```
WKS count,C5..D7,pricefil
```

This clause causes the contents of the worksheet cells C5 through D7 (from the worksheet file PRICEFIL.WKS) to be loaded into the elements of the dimensioned variable *count*.

When a range of cells is accessed, they are read from left to right, row by row. Thus, in the following illustration, the contents of the worksheet cells are assigned to elements of the dimensioned variable *count* in the following order:

Range Access

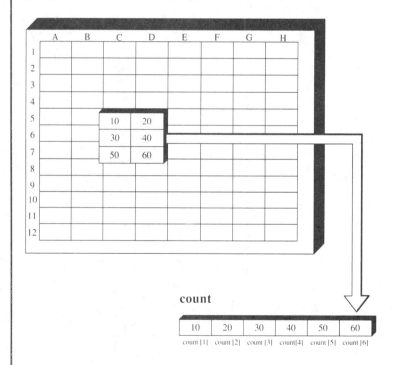

Row, Column, or Named Range Access

A row, column, or named range can also be accessed from a worksheet file. *VP-Expert* recognizes explicit or indirect addressing to indicate the location in the worksheet. Row location is identified using the format:

ROW = <*row_heading*> or ROW = (<*variable*>)

Column location is identified using the format:

COLUMN = <*column_heading*> or COLUMN = (<*variable*>)

Named ranges from the worksheet can also be identified using this format. For example:

NAMED = <*range_name*> or NAMED = (<*variable*>)

The parameter in these examples can be an explicit worksheet row heading, column heading, or range name occurring in the worksheet. Or, the parameter can be a *VP-Expert* variable that has been assigned the value of a worksheet row heading, column heading, or range name, in which case the variable must be enclosed in parentheses. In this case, to retrieve a column of cells with the heading *price*, the user would need to assign the value *price* to a variable—for example, *pricevar*—and name that variable in the WKS clause. For example:

```
*
pricevar = price
WKS the_price,COLUMN = (pricevar),pricefil
*
```

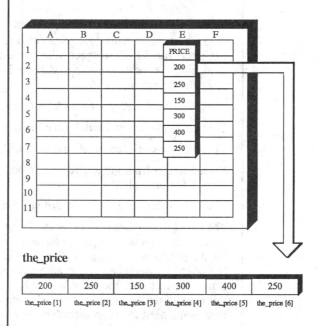

the_price

200	250	150	300	400	250
the_price [1]	the_price [2]	the_price [3]	the_price [4]	the_price [5]	the_price [6]

Note that the WKS clause only retrieves the cells *below* the heading; the heading itself is not retrieved.

A similar WKS clause, retrieving a row instead of a column, might look like this:

```
*
pricevar = price
WKS the_price,ROW = (pricevar),pricefil
*
```

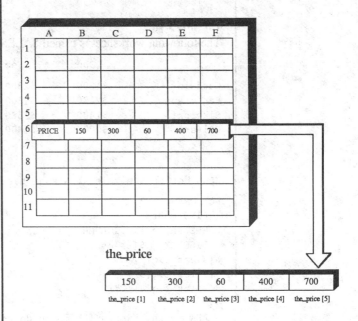

the_price

150	300	60	400	700
the_price [1]	the_price [2]	the_price [3]	the_price [4]	the_price [5]

In this example, *VP-Expert* seeks a cell containing the value *price*. It then assigns the cell values to the right of that cell to the elements of the dimensioned variable *the_price*.

The value assigned to the variable named in the row, column, or range specification need not be assigned in the ACTIONS block, as shown. It can also be assigned in a rule or by the user at an ASK prompt. However, this must occur prior to the execution of the WKS clause, or the WKS clause will not work.

If the parentheses around the variable name are omitted, *VP-Expert* treats the variable name as a literal range name, row heading, or column heading. For example:

```
*
*
WKS the_price,COLUMN = Apr,price
*
```

Here *VP-Expert* looks for a column named "Apr."

EXAMPLE:

The following worksheet is named SALES.WKS.

```
                    Jan        Feb        Mar        Apr
Goodwin           $1200      $2300       $900      $1100
Patterson         $2100      $1600       $750      $1300
Sikorski          $1400      $1500      $1200      $1000
Culver            $2000      $1400      $1100       $900
```

```
Consider this simple knowledge base:

ACTIONS
  FIND month
  WKS sales_fig,COLUMN = (month),sales
  DISPLAY " ${sales_fig[1]}
${sales_fig[2]}
${sales_fig[3]}
${sales_fig[4]}.";

  ASK month: "For which month do you want to
retrieve sales figures?";

  CHOICES month: Jan,Feb,Mar,Apr;
```

During a consultation, this knowledge base displays a prompt and a menu that requires the user to choose a month for retrieving sales figures. When the user chooses, that month is assigned as the value of the variable *month*. The WKS clause then retrieves the column with the heading that matches the chosen value and assigns each cell in that column as one element of the dimensioned variable *sales_fig*.

If the user were to choose the value *Jan*, the retrieved values would be assigned as follows:

sales_fig[1] = 1200
sales_fig[2] = 2100
sales_fig[3] = 1400
sales_fig[4] = 2000

NOTES & CAUTIONS:

- *VP-Planner* and *VP-Expert* are not case sensitive when comparing row headings, column headings, or range names.

- Empty cells in a worksheet column, row, or range named in a WKS clause are treated as though they do not exist. Naming a single empty cell in a WKS clause has no effect.

- Do not get dimensioned variables confused with plural variables. A plural variable is a variable that can have more than one value assigned to it during a consultation. A dimensioned variable is an array of variables, each of which is independently accessible and addressable by *VP-Expert*. (Elements of dimensioned variables can be declared plural, which effectively creates two-dimensioned variables.)

MORE INFORMATION:

See the PWKS clause for information about writing data to a worksheet. See Chapter 6 for more examples of the WKS clause in action.

WORKON

INSTRUCTION TYPE:
Clause

USAGE:
WORKON <*path,[path]WKS_filename*>

PARAMETERS:
The first parameter, a path or drive designation, tells *VP-Expert* where to find the *VP-Planner* program file (VP.COM). If the file is in the root directory, simply give a drive designation; e.g., C:.

The second parameter is the name of a valid *VP-Planner* worksheet file. The WKS extension should not be provided, or a syntax error will result. A path can be specified, if necessary. If no path is indicated, the previously specified path or directory is assumed.

DESCRIPTION:

When the *VP-Expert* inference engine encounters the WORKON clause during a consultation, the user is taken directly to the named *VP-Planner* worksheet where normal worksheet operations can be performed. Upon exiting the worksheet, the user is returned to *VP-Expert* to resume the consultation where it left off.

EXAMPLE

```
*
*
RULE 10
IF      avg_sales >= 10000 AND
        year_hired >= 85
THEN    bonus = yes

        DISPLAY "Press a key to go to a worksheet and
enter bonus information:~"

        WORKON  \vpp,slsbonus;
*
*
```

This example shows a rule with a DISPLAY clause and a WORKON clause attached. If this rule were to pass during a consultation, the DISPLAY clause would display the message, ''Press a key to go to a worksheet and enter bonus information.'' (The tilde (~) character in the DISPLAY clause causes the program to pause until any key is pressed.) When the user presses a key, the WORKON clause is executed, causing the SLSBONUS.WKS worksheet file to appear on screen.

NOTES & CAUTIONS:

- If the *VP-Planner* worksheet file named in the WORKON clause does not exist, the error message ''File Not Found'' is displayed. If the user presses the ENTER key, an empty *VP-Planner* worksheet will appear. When saved, this worksheet will default to the name supplied by the WORKON clause.

- Remember this clause only works with *VP-Planner*. To call Lotus 1-2-3, use the CCALL clause.

MORE INFORMATION:

See the WKS and PWKS clauses in this chapter.

! (Comment Line)

INSTRUCTION TYPE:
Special symbol

USAGE:
!*<text>*

PARAMETERS:
The parameter following the ! symbol is a single line of text consisting of any keyboard characters.

DESCRIPTION:
The exclamation point character (!) is used to create lines in a knowledge base that will be ignored during a consultation. This is useful for adding comment lines, or for "turning off" elements of the knowledge base. (You may sometimes want to place an ! before a clause or statement rather than remove it from the knowledge base.)

The ! character can occur anywhere in the knowledge base and need not be on the left margin. If it occurs on the same line but *after* a clause or statement, the clause or statement will still be executable. For example:

```
*

PLURAL:price;   !This comment will have no
!affect whatsoever on the PLURAL statement
!preceding it.

*
```

EXAMPLES:

```
*
!This line in the knowledge base will be
!ignored. Note that additional comment lines
!require additional exclamation points.
*
*
DISPLAY " The ! in this text will not 'turn
off' subsequent text because it's contained
within the double quotes surrounding this
display text."
*
*
!RUNTIME;
! The exclamation point on the line above
!turns off the RUNTIME statement.
*
*
```

NOTES & CAUTIONS:

- If the ! character occurs inside the double quotes in ASK, DISPLAY, PDISPLAY, or BECAUSE text, it will be treated like any other character.

- Remember that multiple comment lines require multiple exclamation points; there is no ''carry over'' from one line to another.

CHAPTER TEN

Math Function Reference

In addition to the four basic arithmetic operations—addition, subtraction, multiplication, and division—ten mathematical functions can also be used in a *VP-Expert* knowledge base. These include four arithmetic and six basic trigonometric functions.

This section details each of these special functions. In addition, general information about using math in a knowledge base is provided.

Specifying Mathematical Operations

Mathematical operations can be used in a knowledge base to specify values in rule conditions, or to specify values in expressions that assign a value to a variable. For example, take a look at the following rule:

```
RULE 1

IF   price <= (4 * cost)
THEN profit_margin = low;
```

This rule translates "If the value of *profit* is less than or equal to 4 times the value of the variable *cost*, then *profit_margin* is *low*.

This next rule uses a mathematical operation to assign a value to the variable *price*.

```
RULE 2
IF    product = book
THEN  price = (cost * 5);
```

If this rule passes, 4 times the value of the variable *cost* is assigned to the variable *price*.

Math operations can be used anywhere you can legally name a value in a knowledge base expression.

Arithmetic Operations

VP-Expert uses the following standard symbols to represent the four arithmetic operations:

+	Addition
-	Subtraction
*	Multiplication
/	Division

General Rules

When using mathematical operations to specify values in a knowledge base, follow these simple rules:

■ Always enclose math operations in parentheses. For example:

```
circumference = (3.1416 * diameter)
```

■ With the exception of the four basic operations (+ - * /), you must precede all math functions with the @ ''at'' sign, and you must always enclose the ''argument'' of the function in parentheses. For example:

```
variable = (@SQRT(X))
```

■ Operations can be nested using parentheses, but careful attention should be paid when ''pairing'' the parentheses. Missing or misplaced parens can cause mathematical errors.

■ All trigonometric functions require an argument supplied in radians, not degrees. An angle expressed in degrees can be converted to radians using either of the following formulas:

radians = (angle * 3.1416/180)
radians = (.0175 * degrees)

Special Mathematical Functions

The following special functions can be used in a *VP-Expert* knowledge base:

@ABS(X)
Returns the absolute value of X.

@ACOS(X)
Returns the arccosine of the angle X expressed in radians.

@ASIN(X)
Returns the arcsine of angle X expressed in radians.

@ATAN(X)
Returns the arctangent of angle X expressed in radians.

@COS(X)
Returns the cosine of angle X expressed in radians.

@EXP(X)
Returns the value of the exponential function, e^x.

@LOG(X)
Returns the natural logarithm of X.

@SIN(X)
Returns the sine of the angle X expressed in radians.

@SQRT(X)
Returns the square root of X.

@TAN(X)
Returns the tangent of the angle X expressed in radians.

APPENDIX A

The VP-Expert Editor

For information about using your own word processor as the VP-Expert Editor, see the EDIT command in Chapter 8.

While developing a knowledge base, you'll continually be switching between editing the knowledge base and running practice consultations. *VP-Expert's* built-in word processor—referred to as the "Editor"—makes switching and editing easy.

Read this section to find out how to use the *VP-Expert* Editor. Information includes how to:

- Create and save files.
- Move the cursor.
- Delete text.
- Reformat paragraphs.
- Manipulate blocks of text.
- Give search and replace commands.
- Print files.

The EDIT Command

1Help	2Induce	3Edit	4Consult	5Tree	6FileName	7Path	8Quit

The Edit command on the *VP-Expert* Main Menu takes you into the *VP-Expert* Editor.

If you give the Edit command immediately after starting the program, you're presented with a menu of KBS files and asked to choose one. If instead you type a new filename, you're taken to a blank editing screen. (If you don't type a file extension, a KBS extension is assumed.)

If you run a consultation before giving the Edit command, the knowledge base file you were using is automatically loaded. To edit another file instead, give the Main Menu FileName command before giving the Edit command. FileName lets you choose another file to work with.

Special Keys

Inside the *VP-Expert* Editor, these keys perform the following functions:

In the Editor, function key command assignments are indicated at the bottom of the screen. Press ALT, CTRL, or SHIFT to see how these assignments change when combined with these keys.

ALT	Combines with the function keys to perform file commands. See "File Saving, Listing, and Reformatting" in this appendix for more information.
BACKSPACE	Deletes the character to the left of the cursor.
DEL	Deletes the character at the cursor position. See "Delete Commands" in this appendix.
CTRL	Typed simultaneously with *ENTER*, creates a blank line. Also combines with the function keys to perform block commands. See "Manipulating Blocks of Text" for more information.
ESC	Cancels incomplete operations, e.g., Start Block (*CTRL-F3*), Save (*ALT-F6*), etc.

END   Moves cursor to the end of the line. Starts printing when the print menu is on screen. See "Printing a File" for more information.

ENTER   At the end of a line, creates a hard carriage return. Also combines with *CTRL* to create a blank line, or change a soft carriage return to a hard one. See "Hard and Soft Carriage Returns" for more information.

INS   Toggles Insert mode. With Insert ON, inserted text pushes existing text to the right. With Insert OFF, inserted text overwrites existing text. When you enter the Editor, Insert is ON.

PRTSC   Prints the contents of the screen when pressed with the *SHIFT* key.

SHIFT   Used for capitalization. Also combines with the function keys to perform search and replace operations. See "Search and Replace" for more information.

TAB   Advances the cursor to the next tab stop. Tabs are set every 5 spaces.

Default Settings

When you enter the *VP-Expert* Editor, the following default settings are in force:

Insert: ON

To turn Insert OFF, use the INS key.

Document Mode: OFF

Press *F9* to switch Document Mode ON. See about *F9* under "On-Screen Formatting" for information about how the Document Mode setting affects certain commands.

Current settings are indicated at the bottom of the screen.

Moving the Cursor

The following commands (and equivalent CTRL commands) move the cursor in the *VP-Expert* Editor:

The "equivalent commands" shown on the right of this table are the same as those used in WordStar.

Command	Action	Equivalent
UP ARROW	Moves cursor one line up.	CTRL-e
DOWN ARROW	Moves cursor one line down.	CTRL-x
LEFT ARROW	Moves cursor left one character.	CTRL-s
RIGHT ARROW	Moves cursor right one character.	CTRL-d
CTRL-LEFT ARROW	Moves cursor left one word.	CTRL-a
CTRL-RIGHT ARROW	Moves cursor right one word.	CTRL-f
PGUP	Moves cursor to previous screen.	CTRL-r
PGDN	Moves cursor to next screen.	CTRL-c
CTRL-PGUP	Moves cursor to top of file.	
CTRL-PGDN	Moves cursor to bottom of file.	
HOME	Moves cursor to the beginning of the line.	

END	Moves cursor to the end of the line.
TAB	Moves cursor forward one tab stop.
SHIFT-TAB	Moves cursor back one tab stop.

With Document Mode ON (OFF is the default), the VP-Expert Editor has a wordwrap function that automatically breaks lines when they reach the right margin. This creates soft carriage returns.

Hard and Soft Carriage Returns

While editing a file, you'll notice that one of two highlighted symbols appears at the end of each line. The ◄ symbol appears wherever you've typed *ENTER* to end the line. This is referred to as a *hard return*. The • symbol appears at the end of lines where you have not pressed *ENTER*. This is called a *soft return*. Soft carriage returns occur only with Document Mode ON.

You may sometimes need to replace a soft return with a hard return. For example, each line in a *VP-Expert* induction table must end with a hard return. To make the replacement, place the cursor on the soft return symbol and press *CTRL-ENTER*.

Delete Commands

The following commands delete text in the *VP-Expert* Editor.

Command	Action
DEL (CTRL-g)	Deletes character at cursor.
BACKSPACE (CTRL-h)	Deletes character left of cursor.
CTRL-t	Deletes from cursor to end of word.
CTRL-y	Deletes entire line.

Inserting and Combining Lines

To insert a blank line in the *VP-Expert* Editor, position the cursor at the left margin where you want the line to appear and press *CTRL-ENTER*. Repeat the command to add additional lines.

To combine two adjacent lines of text, place the cursor on the hard or soft return symbol of the top line and type *CTRL-t*. The line below will move up to the cursor position. (If there are any blank lines between the two lines, repeat the command until the blanks disappear and the two lines come together.)

Using the Function Keys

The function keys perform numerous functions in the *VP-Expert* Editor. Function keys can be typed alone, or in combination with the *ALT*, *CTRL*, and *SHIFT* keys.

- Typed alone, function keys are used for on-screen formatting, such as boldface and underline.

- Combined with the *ALT* key, function keys perform file and disk operations.

- Combined with the *CTRL* key, function keys are used for block operations.

- Combined with *SHIFT*, function keys perform search and replace commands.

    Note: When using the Editor, the function key commands are listed along the bottom of the screen. Pressing ALT, CTRL, or SHIFT changes the command listing to show how function key assignments change when combined with each of these keys.

The following pages show how the function keys work—alone, and used with *ALT*, *CTRL*, and *SHIFT*.

On-Screen Formatting: The Function Key Commands

The following commands are issued when the function keys are typed alone.

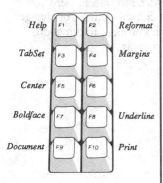

Help F1
TabSet F3
Center F5
Boldface F7
Document F9
F2 Reformat
F4 Margins
F6
F8 Underline
F10 Print

F1   **On-screen Help.** While editing a file, pressing *F1* displays on-screen information on *VP-Expert* statements, clauses, and keywords.

F2   **Reformat a paragraph.** This command readjusts a paragraph to margin settings after editing has altered line lengths. To use, place the cursor on the first line to be reformatted and press *F2* (or *CTRL-b*). To reformat an entire document, use *ALT-F2*, Global Reformat. (To use this command, Document Mode must be ON. See *F9* for more information.)

F3   **Tab Set.** Pressing *F3* places a tab setting or removes an existing tab setting in the column of the cursor's current position.

F4   **Margins and Justify.** Pressing *F4* displays a screen where you can change left and right margin settings and turn Justify ON or OFF. The default settings are left margin, 0, right margin, 65, and Justify OFF. (Justify is disabled when Document Mode is OFF. See *F9* for more information.) Press *END* to exit this screen after you have made your modifications.

F5   **Center.** Pressing *F5* centers the line the cursor is in. (This only works with Document Mode ON. See *F9* for more information.)

F7   **Boldface ON/OFF.** Pressing *F7* turns boldfacing ON and OFF. The current status is displayed at the bottom right of the screen.

F8   **Underline ON/OFF.** Pressing *F8* turns underlining ON and OFF. (On color monitors underlined text appears in blue, underlined boldfaced text in light blue.) Spaces are not underlined. To underline spaces, replace the spaces with the underline character.

F9   **Document Mode ON/OFF.** *F9* turns Document Mode ON
     and OFF. OFF is the default setting. The status is displayed at
     the bottom left. With Document Mode OFF, wordwrap, justify,
     centering, and reformatting are disabled.

F10 **Print.** Pressing *F10* calls the Print Menu to screen. Here you
     can press *END* to print the file with current settings, or change
     settings and then press *END* to print. For more information,
     see ''Printing a File'' later in this appendix.

File Saving, Listing, and Reformatting: The ALT Function Key Commands

You can give these commands by combining the following function keys with the ALT key:

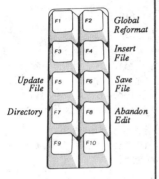

ALT-F2   **Global Reformat.** Pressing *ALT-F2* reformats the entire document from the cursor position forward. The cursor remains in its original position. (To use this command, Document Mode must be ON.)

ALT-F4   **Insert File.** Use *ALT-F4* to insert an existing file at the location of the cursor.

ALT-F5   **Update File.** *ALT-F5* saves your document without leaving the Editor. The cursor remains in position, and the previously saved version of the file becomes a backup (BAK) file.

ALT-F6   **Save File.** This command saves the file to disk and leaves the Editor. The previously saved version becomes a backup (BAK) file.

ALT-F7   **Disk Directory.** Pressing *ALT-F7* lets you list files on the current drive or a specified drive. DOS wildcard characters * and ? can be used to specify groups of files.

ALT-F8   **Abandon Edit.** This command quits the Editor without saving changes made since the last save.

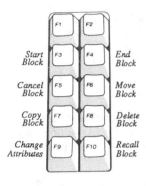

Start Block — F3
Cancel Block — F5
Copy Block — F7
Change Attributes — F9
End Block — F4
Move Block — F6
Delete Block — F8
Recall Block — F10

Manipulating Blocks of Text:
The CTRL Function Key Commands

Pressing the CTRL key and the following function keys perform these block commands:

CTRL-F3   **Start Block.** Pressing *CTRL-F3* marks the cursor position as the start of a block.

CTRL-F4   **End Block.** Pressing *CTRL-F4* marks the cursor position as the end of a block. Text between the start and end of the block will appear highlighted on screen. If you attempt to end a block before marking the start, this message will appear: *No file exists, press ESC*.

CTRL-F5   **Cancel Block.** Once a block has been marked, pressing *CTRL-F5* cancels it (turning the highlighting off). Moving a block also cancels it.

CTRL-F6   **Move Block.** Pressing *CTRL-F6* moves a marked block to the cursor position. Don't confuse this with copying a block. This command causes the block to disappear from its original location.

CTRL-F7   **Copy Block.** This command copies a marked block to the cursor position. The original block remains highlighted in its original location. Use *CTRL-F5* to cancel when copying is complete.

CTRL-F8   **Delete Block.** Pressing *CTRL-F8* deletes a marked block. As a safety precaution, the cursor must be inside the block to be deleted. If you accidentally delete a block, immediately press *CTRL-F10* to recover it. (If you move the cursor before recovering the block, the block will be returned to the new cursor position.) See *CTRL-F10* for more information.

CTRL-F9   **Change Attributes.** When a block has been marked, pressing *CTRL-F9* offers a list of "attributes" to choose from: *normal, underline, boldface,* or *combined* (underline and boldface). Typing the initial letter of any of these choices changes the text in the block to the chosen attribute.

CTRL-F10   **Recall Block.** *CTRL-F10* recalls the most recently deleted word, line, or block to the cursor position. (This command will not retrieve anything deleted before a Save, Abandon, or Reformat.)

SHIFT

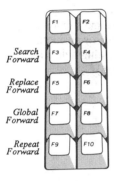

*Search
Forward*

*Replace
Forward*

*Global
Forward*

*Repeat
Forward*

Search and Replace:
The SHIFT Function Key Commands

The SHIFT key and these function keys perform the following search and replace commands:

SHIFT-F3   **Search Forward.** This command moves the cursor forward to the first instance of a given text string. (The text string may include spaces and any keyboard character.) If no match is found, the message *Not found* is displayed.

SHIFT-F5   **Replace Forward.** This command replaces the next instance of a given text string with another text string. If no match for the first string is found, *Not found* is displayed.

SHIFT-F7   **Global Replace Forward.** This command replaces every instance of a given text string with a new string, starting from the cursor position. After giving the command, you'll be asked if you want to approve each change. Answer by typing **Y** or **N**. To stop a global replacement, press *ESC*.

SHIFT-F9   **Repeat Previous Search.** Pressing *SHIFT-F9* repeats the most recent Search, Search and Replace, or Global Replace command.

Printing A File

To print a document from the *VP-Expert* Editor, press *F10* to display the Print Menu:

```
    Top Margin          6           Bottom Margin       6


    Line Spacing        1           Page Offset         10


    Lines on Page       66          Continuous Forms?    y


    Page Width          65          Number Pages?        y



          Next Position:      ENTER or Tab
          Previous Position:  Back Tab
          When All Values Are Set, Press End
```

This menu displays default print settings. To use these settings, press *END* and the printer will begin printing the file.

To change the settings, simply type in new ones. *ENTER* and *TAB* move the cursor forward to the next setting. *SHIFT-TAB* (Back Tab) moves the cursor back to the previous setting. Press *END* when you're ready to start printing.

Pressing ESC at the Print Menu abandons any changes you may have made to the print settings and returns to the document.

If you change these settings, the new settings will become the defaults (for all files, not just the current file) when you save the file. If you abandon the file after printing (*ALT-F8*), the previous settings will be restored.

Print Menu Options

- On the Print Menu, the numbers next to *Top Margin* and *Bottom Margin* represent the number of lines between the text and the top and bottom of the page. At 6 lines per inch, this gives a one-inch top and bottom margin, and 54 lines of text on an 11-inch page.

- *Line Spacing* is set to 1 for single spacing. Changing the number to 2 results in double spacing, 3, triple spacing, and so on.

- *Page Offset* on the Print Menu refers to the distance between the left edge of the paper and the zero left margin setting. Changing the page offset value shifts the left margin to the left or right, but doesn't affect line length as determined by the left and right margins. (*F4* is used to set margins.)

- *Lines on Page* tells the printer how long the paper is. The setting of 66 assumes an 11-inch page with 6 lines per inch. Change this value if you're using a different size page.

- If you aren't using continuous form paper, and must change paper after each page, change the *Continuous Form* setting to **N**.

- The *Page Width* setting is used to center page numbers in the bottom margin. Don't confuse this with text width, which is determined by *F4* margin settings.

- If you don't want page numbers centered at the bottom of each page, change the *Number Pages?* setting to **N**.

APPENDIX B

VP-Expert Keywords

@ABS	CLOSE	POP
@ACOS	CLS	PRINTOFF
@ASIN	COLOR	PRINTON
@ATAN	COLUMN	PUT
@COS	DISPLAY	PWKS
@EXP	EJECT	RECEIVE
@LOG	ELSE	RECORD_NUM
@SIN	END	RESET
@SQRT	ENDOFF	ROW
@TAN	EXECUTE	RULE
ACTIONS	FIND	RUNTIME
ALL	FORMAT	SAVEFACTS
AND	GET	SHIP
APPEND	IF	SHOWTEXT
ASK	INDEX	SORT
AUTOQUERY	LOADFACTS	THEN
BCALL	MENU	TRUTHTHRESH
BECAUSE	MENU_SIZE	UNKNOWN
BKCOLOR	MRESET	WHILEKNOWN
CALL	NAMED	WKS
CCALL	OR	WORKON
CHAIN	PDISPLAY	
CHOICES	PLURAL	

VP-Expert Statements

ACTIONS	ENDOFF
ASK	EXECUTE
AUTOQUERY	PLURAL
BKCOLOR	RULE
CHOICES	RUNTIME

VP-Expert Clauses

APPEND	RESET
BCALL	PDISPLAY
CALL	POP
CCALL	PRINTOFF
CHAIN	PRINTON
CLOSE	PUT
CLS	PWKS
COLOR	RECEIVE
DISPLAY	RESET
EJECT	SAVEFACTS
END	SHIP
FIND	SHOWTEXT
FORMAT	SORT
GET	TRUTHTHRESH
INDEX	WHILEKNOWN
LOADFACTS	WKS
MENU	WORKON

APPENDIX C

VP-EXPERT MENU COMMAND TREE

Set Menu

| 1 Help | 2 Trace | 3 Slow | 4 Fast | 5 Quit |

Induce Menu

| 1 Help | 2 Create | 3 Database | 4 Text | 5 Worksht | 6 Quit |

Go Menu

| 1 Help | 2 How? | 3 Why? | 4 Slow | 5 Fast | 6 Quit |

Consult Menu

| 1 Help | 2 Go | 3 WhatIf | 4 Variable | 5 Rule | 6 Set | 7 Quit |

Tree Menu

| 1 Help | 2 Text | 3 Graphics | 4 Quit |

Main Menu

| 1 Help | 2 Induce | 3 Edit | 4 Consult | 5 Tree | 6 Filename | 7 Path | 8 Quit |

APPENDIX D

Error Messages

While using *VP-Expert*, error messages are sometimes presented to alert you to errors in the knowledge base. The following list gives a brief explanation of every message that can occur.

Can't find database file

File is not present in specified drive/path. Check for spelling errors in drive/path and filename.

Can't find worksheet file

The file named in a WKS or PWKS clause does not exist. Check for spelling errors in your filename and path.

Error in END clause

An END clause must occur for each WHILEKNOWN clause in the knowledge base.

Error in math expression

Check for missing parentheses, numbers, or illogical formulas.

Field does not exist in index file

Check for spelling errors in your INDEX clause.

Illegal cell name

Cell names must begin with one or two letters followed by an integer from 1 to 9999.

Illegal color

Color values can range from 0 to 16.

Illegal confidence factor

Confidence factors can range from 0 to 100.

Illegal statement

An invalid statement has been encountered. Check keyword spelling and statement syntax.

Illegal truth threshold

A truth threshold value can range from 0 to 100.

Index file not found

The file referred to in an INDEX clause is not present in the specified drive/path. Check for spelling errors.

Math expression too long

A math expression cannot be over 256 characters long. If you have longer formulas, try breaking them into smaller pieces.

Missing comma

Variables in ASK, CHOICES, and PLURAL statements must be separated by commas.

No comparisons are allowed in database rule

In a database rule, only the equal sign can be used in conditions that contain fields of a database file named in an INDEX clause.

Out of memory error

Memory limit has been exceeded. Try partitioning your knowledge base into smaller units and using the CHAIN clause.

Premature end of file

Make sure that the last character in the knowledge base is a semicolon (;).

Recursion too deep

Backward chaining is limited to 10 levels of recursion.

Syntax error

A syntax error in a clause or statement is preventing execution of the knowledge base.

Text string too long

ASK, BECAUSE, and DISPLAY text is limited to 1,000 characters.

Too many columns

A maximum of 11 columns can be contained in an induction table.

Too many examples

A maximum of 150 rows can be contained in an induction table.

Too many fields

Databases containing more than 256 fields cannot be used with *VP-Expert*.

Too many files open

Up to 6 database files can be open at once. Use the CLOSE clause to close database files which are no longer needed.

Trace file not present

In order to use the Text or Graphics options on the Tree Menu, a consultation using the active knowledge base must have been executed in Trace mode.

Trace file too big

Trace files longer than 500 lines cannot be examined using a Graphics tree.

Word too long

Rule names and most variables and values cannot exceed 20 characters. (Exceptions are the values of variables created by the GET or RECEIVE clause.)

APPENDIX E

Bibliography

Here is a brief list of published works on the subject of "artificial intelligence" and expert systems. Be sure to browse the shelves of your favorite technical bookstore for more recent material.

Barr, Avron, and Feigenbaum, E. A., eds. *Handbook of Artificial Intelligence*, 3 vols. Los Altos, CA: William Kaufmann, Inc., 1981.

Boden, Margaret. *Artificial Intelligence and Natural Man*. New York: Basic Books, Inc., 1977.

Brownston, Lee; Farrell, Robert; Kant, Elaine; and Martin, Nancy. *Programming Expert Systems in OPS5*. Reading, MA: Addison-Wesley, 1985.

Feigenbaum, Edward, and McCorduck, Pamela. *The Fifth Generation*. London: Michael Joseph, 1984.

Harmon, Paul, and King, David. *Expert Systems: Artificial Intelligence in Business*. New York: John Wiley & Sons, 1985.

Hayes-Roth, Frederick; Waterman, Donald A.; and Lenat, Douglas B., eds. *Building Expert Systems*. Reading, MA: Addison-Wesley, 1983.

Hunt, Morton. *The Universe Within: A New Science Explores the Human Mind*. New York: Simon & Schuster, 1982.

Michie, Donald. *Introductory Readings in Expert Systems*. New York: Gordon & Breach, 1982.

Newell, A., and Simon, Herbert A. *Human Problem Solving*. Englewood Cliffs, NJ: Prentice-Hall, 1974.

Nilsson, Nils J. *Principles of Artificial Intelligence*. Palo Alto, CA: Tioga Publishing Co., 1980.

Schank, Roger. *The Cognitive Computer*. Reading, MA: Addison-Wesley, 1984.

Shafer, Dan. *Silicon Visions*. New York: Brady Books, Prentice-Hall, 1986.

Van Horn, Mike. *Understanding Expert Systems*. New York: Bantam, 1986.

Weiss, S. M., and Kulikowski, C. A. *A Practical Guide to Designing Expert Systems*. Totowa, NJ: Rowman & Allanheld, 1984.

INDEX

CUSTOMER
INFORMATION

PAPERBACK SOFTWARE INTERNATIONAL

List of Compatible Computers

VP-Expert runs on the IBM PC, PC-AT, PC-XT, and most work-alikes with 256K or more RAM memory (384K on Tandy 1000), one disk drive (two recommended) and DOS version 2.0 or higher. A printer is required for printed output. We have successfully run *VP-Expert* on the following systems:

AT&T PC Model 6300	NCR Personal Computer Model 6
Compaq (all models)	Sharp PC 7000
IBM PC	Talbott Comet (all models)
IBM PC-AT	Tandy 1000, 1200HD, 3000
IBM PC-XT	TeleVideo TS1605 Series
ITT XTRA	Xerox 6065

In order to view a graphic trace of a *VP-Expert* consultation, an IBM CGA or EGA, a Hercules Monochrome graphics adapter, or a compatible video adapter is required.

VP-Expert may not run with certain co-resident programs. *VP-Expert* may require more RAM memory if co-resident programs or DOS version 3.xx are being used.

The *VP-Expert* disk is copy-protected. A non-copy-protected disk is available for a nominal charge. See the *Software Registration Form* included in the DiskPack for more information.

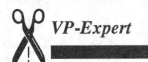

PAPERBACK SOFTWARE INTERNATIONAL

Software Order Form

☐ **VP-Planner**. Advanced 1-2-3-compatible spreadsheet program that accesses dBASE and Multidimensional databases. Requires one disk drive (two recommended) and 256K memory** (320K to use multidimensional database). Color/Graphics adapter optional for using graphics.*
☐ 5¼" IBM disk format   ☐ 3½" IBM disk format   _____ copies @ $99.95 = _____

☐ **VP-Info** is a powerful, high-speed database management program. It is datafile-compatible with both dBASE II and dBASE III, so you can use both types of files together, without conversion. A built-in one-step compiler speeds your programs without making development more complicated. Its extended command language offers more power, control, and flexibility. Requires one disk drive (two recommended) and 256K memory.
☐ 5¼" IBM disk format   ☐ 3½" IBM disk format   _____ copies @ $99.95 = _____

☐ **VP-Expert** is a rule-based expert system development tool designed to allow experts in any field to capture their knowledge so it may be easily accessible to others. *VP-Expert* does not require special programming knowledge or equipment, so anyone can harness the potential of artificial intelligence to teach, advise, or diagnose. Features include an inductive front-end, plain English rules, a built-in text editor, interface with database, spreadsheet and ASCII files, text and graphic rule traces, optional windows, confidence factors, backward and forward chaining, floating-point math, scientific functions, and the ability to run external programs. Requires one disk drive and 256K memory. Graphics card optional to display graphic trace.
☐ 5¼" IBM disk format   ☐ 3½" IBM disk format   _____ copies @ $99.95 = _____

☐ **Executive Writer** is a powerful, full-featured word processor that makes writing, editing, and printing documents quick and easy. Special features include keyboard macros, numbered footnotes, indexing, and advanced page formatting and printing commands. Requires one disk drive (two recommended), 128K memory.** Color/Graphics adapter optional for using graphics.*
_____ copies @ $69.95 = _____

☐ **Executive Filer** is an electronic filing system which manages text and graphics. *File Cards,* holding up to 1500 words each, are useful for cross-indexing, outlining, and instant retrieval of information. File cards are stored and retrieved using keywords you select. Keep letters, notes, outlines, spreadsheets—information of any kind—organized and available at a keystroke. A complete program by itself, *Executive Filer* also combines with *Executive Writer* to become The Idea Processor.™ Requires one disk drive (two recommended), 192K memory.** Color/Graphics adapter optional for using graphics.*
_____ copies @ $49.95 = _____

Note: 5¼" disk format will be provided unless otherwise indicated where applicable. 3½" disk format not available where not listed.

VP-Expert

☐ **Anthony Dias Blue Wines on Disk** is an expert system—a computer program that uses artificial intelligence techniques coupled with Mr. Blue's internationally reknowned wine expertise—that helps you choose from over 600 top-rated American wines for any meal or occasion. *Wines on Disk* recommends both popular wines and those harder to find but worth looking for. Each entry is fully annotated with vineyard information, prices, ratings, and Mr. Blue's tasting impressions, so you can be sure to find a vintage suited to your palate—and your budget. Requires one disk drive and 256K memory.

_____ copies @ $39.95 = _____

☐ **Draw-It** graphics program makes your computer a full-color drawing board. Terrific for illustrations, charts, business graphs, games, and entertainment. *Draw-It* graphics can be integrated into *Executive Writer* documents. And *Draw-It's* special SAVESCRN function lets you capture and edit images from almost any program. Requires one disk drive, 192K memory,** Color/Graphics adapter.*

_____ copies @ $29.95 = _____

☐ **My ABC's** includes 6 educational games for young children. Combining music and delightful color graphics, games teach letter and number recognition, counting, and concentration skills. Requires one disk drive, 128K memory (including Tandy 1000), Color/Graphics adapter.

_____ copies @ $19.95 = _____

You can order direct from:

Paperback Software International
2830 Ninth St., Berkeley, CA 94710

California residents ONLY add 7% tax = _____

Shipping and Handling = _____ $ 5.00 _____

Orders outside of U.S.A. add $15.00 per copy ordered = _____

TOTAL _____

* IBM/Epson or compatible graphics printer required to print graphics.

** Tandy 1000 require 384K memory minimum to run *VP-Info* or *VP-Planner*, and require 256K to run all other programs except *My ABC's*.

All products work on the IBM PC, PC/XT, PC/AT and most compatible computers and require DOS version 2.00 or higher.

PAPERBACK SOFTWARE ®

Indicate quantities and total for each item. Allow 2-3 weeks for delivery. Checks accepted from U.S. banks ONLY. VISA/MasterCard must be valid for U.S. Dollar purchases made in U.S.A.

☐ Check   ☐ VISA   ☐ MasterCard

☐ Card number _____ Expiration date _____

Ship to _____

Address _____

City _____ State/Province _____ Zip _____

Country _____

Signature as it appears on your card: _____

A GREAT DEAL more.

Now available at better computer stores, software stores and bookshops everywhere.

PAPERBACK SOFTWARE INTERNATIONAL

Telephone Consulting Service

If you have questions or problems with your software, PSI has trained technicians available to assist you. To use the PSI Consulting Service, call 415-644-8249 weekdays between 9 a.m. and 5 p.m., Pacific Time. You will be charged for this service. The current rate is $5 for the first five minutes and $1 for each additional minute, payable by either VISA or MasterCard. To use the service efficiently, follow the guidelines listed below.

1. Before calling, check the instruction book to see if it contains the information you need. Review areas such as installation CAREFULLY to make sure you have prepared the program properly and that you have not misread or skipped an instruction.

2. If applicable, be prepared to discuss the exact sequence of keystrokes that led to your problem.

3. Tell the PSI technician if you have used the service before so that he or she will not have to explain procedures.

4. Have pencil and paper available for taking notes.

If the problem cannot be solved immediately, the PSI technician will call you back when the solution has been worked out. You will be charged only for the time the technician actually worked on the problem. All questions will be answered as quickly as possible. In some instances, the technician may not be able to solve your specific problem (for example, a hardware malfunction); however, you will be charged for this time.

If all support lines are busy, you will receive a busy signal. If the phone rings, the next available technician will answer as soon as possible.

PAPERBACK SOFTWARE INTERNATIONAL

VP-Expert Runtime System

If you develop *VP-Expert* applications for sale or distribution to other people you may be interested in the *VP-Expert* Runtime System.

Application programs created with *VP-Expert* cannot be run unless *VP-Expert* is present. Without the *VP-Expert* Runtime System, anyone who wishes to use an application program you create must also own a copy of *VP-Expert*. In most cases this is acceptable, such as in an office where a copy of *VP-Expert* has been purchased for each computer.

In some situations, however, you may wish to provide everything needed to use your application program. Remember, you must not give anyone a copy of *VP-Expert*; to do so would be in direct violation of the Federal Copyright Act and the *VP-Expert* Software License Agreement.

The *VP-Expert* Runtime System is the portion of *VP-Expert* necessary to run *VP-Expert* applications. You may obtain a license from Paperback Software International (PSI) which allows you to copy and redistribute the *VP-Expert* Runtime System. After you complete and sign the Redistribution Agreement and submit it to PSI with a check or money order for the fee specified, PSI will agree to such copying and redistribution by returning a signed copy of the Redistribution Agreement to you with a disk containing the *VP-Expert* Runtime System.

You may not redistribute the *VP-Expert* Runtime System without an application program, nor may you copy and/or redistribute the *VP-Expert* documentation.

For more information or to obtain this license, contact PSI and request a copy of the ''VP-Expert Runtime System Redistribution Agreement.''

Paperback Software International
2830 Ninth Street
Berkeley, CA 94710

PAPERBACK SOFTWARE INTERNATIONAL

Limited Warranty

All Paperback Software International disks are warranted to the registered owner to be free of defects for 90 days from date of purchase. Should a disk prove defective *within* the warranty period, mail the disk and a copy of the sales receipt to the address below. A replacement disk will be shipped without charge.

Should a disk become defective *after* the 90-day warranty period, the registered owner may purchase a replacement disk for $5.00. Mail the defective disk and a check, money order, or your VISA or MasterCard number (include the MasterCard bank code) with the expiration date and your authorized signature to:

Paperback Software International
Warranty Replacement Department
2830 Ninth Street
Berkeley, CA 94710

NOTICE

Paperback Software program disks are copy-protected.

Non-copy-protected program disks are available at a nominal charge to registered owners who sign the Single User License Agreement which is on the back of the registation form included in the DiskPack.

PAPERBACK SOFTWARE INTERNATIONAL

Software License Agreement

Before opening this package, read the following terms and conditions carefully.

Opening this package means that you accept these terms and conditions. If you do not agree to them, return the unopened package to your dealer for a refund of the purchase price.

The Software in this package is offered only on the condition that you (the purchaser) agree to the following terms and conditions:

1. The Software remains the property of Paperback Software International (PSI), but PSI grants you a nonexclusive license to use the software subject to this Agreement. The Software and this book are copyrighted.

2. You agree not to copy, disassemble, change or modify the Software, or any copy or modification of this instruction book without authorization from PSI.

3. This license is not a sale of the original Software or any copy.

4. PSI designed this Software for use with the computer system(s) listed in this book. With proper application, the Software will perform substantially as described in this book. However, PSI does not warrant that the functions contained in the Software will meet your particular requirements or that the operation of the Software will be uninterrupted or error-free. The diskettes delivered to you on which the Software is recorded are free from defects in materials and faulty workmanship under normal use. The representations above do not cover items damaged, modified or misused after delivery to you.

   If a diskette should prove defective or if the Software does not perform as described in this book, you shall immediately return any defective diskette or non-conforming Software to PSI and, as your sole remedy, PSI shall either replace the diskette or software or refund the purchase price at PSI's election.

   THE FOREGOING WARRANTIES ARE LIMITED IN DURATION TO THE PERIOD OF 90 DAYS FROM THE DATE OF ORIGINAL DELIVERY TO YOU. THE FOREGOING WARRANTIES ARE IN LIEU OF ALL OTHER WARRANTIES, EXPRESS OR IMPLIED, INCLUDING, BUT NOT LIMITED TO, THE IMPLIED WARRANTIES OF MERCHANTABILITY AND FITNESS FOR A PARTICULAR PURPOSE ON THE DISKETTES

   AND THE SOFTWARE. PSI SHALL IN NO EVENT BE LIABLE FOR ANY INDIRECT, INCIDENTAL OR CONSEQUENTIAL DAMAGES, WHETHER RESULTING FROM DEFECTS IN THE DISKETTES OR FROM ANY DEFECT IN THE SOFTWARE ITSELF OR DOCUMENTATION THEREOF. IN NO EVENT SHALL THE LIABILITY OF PSI FOR DAMAGES ARISING OUT OF OR IN CONNECTION WITH USE OR PERFORMANCE OF THE SOFTWARE OR DISKETTES EXCEED THE LICENSE FEE ACTUALLY PAID BY YOU.

   Any implied warranties which are found to exist are hereby limited in duration to the 90-day life of the express warranties on the diskettes given above. Some states do not allow the exclusion or limitation on how long implied warranties last, so these exclusions or limitations may not apply to you. Warranties give you specific legal rights and you may also have other rights which vary from state to state.

5. You will not transfer the Software to someone else unless that person consents to the terms of this Agreement. If you do transfer the Software to someone else, you must include all copies of the Software and related material you may have.

6. If you violate any of the terms in this Agreement, PSI may terminate this Agreement and the license granted and shall be entitled to all rights and remedies available in law or equity, including, without termination, specific performance. Upon termination of this Agreement for any reason, you agree to return your copy of the Software to PSI at your expense.

7. This Agreement is construed in accordance with, and governed by, the laws of the State of California. Should any part of this Agreement be declared invalid or unenforceable, the validity and enforceability of the remainder of the Agreement shall not be affected thereby. This Agreement can only be modified by a written agreement signed by you and PSI.